Modernist Literature

Edinburgh Critical Guides to Literature
Series Editors: Martin Halliwell, University of Leicester and
Andy Mousley, De Montfort University

Published Titles:
Gothic Literature, Andrew Smith
Canadian Literature, Faye Hammill
Women's Poetry, Jo Gill
Contemporary American Drama, Annette J. Saddik
Shakespeare, Gabriel Egan
Asian American Literature, Bella Adams
Children's Literature, M. O. Grenby
Contemporary British Fiction, Nick Bentley
Renaissance Literature, Siobhan Keenan
Scottish Literature, Gerard Carruthers
Contemporary American Fiction, David Brauner
Contemporary British Drama, David Lane
Medieval Literature 1300–1500, Pamela King
Contemporary Poetry, Nerys Williams
Victorian Literature, David Amigoni
Modernist Literature, Rachel Potter
Modern American Literature, Catherine Morley

Forthcoming Titles in the Series:
Restoration and Eighteenth-Century Literature, Hamish Mathison
Romantic Literature, Serena Baiesi
African American Literature, Jennifer Terry
Postcolonial Literature, Dave Gunning

Modernist Literature

Rachel Potter

EDINBURGH
University Press

© Rachel Potter, 2012

Edinburgh University Press Ltd
22 George Square, Edinburgh

www.euppublishing.com

Typeset in 11.5/13 Ehrhardt
by Servis Filmsetting Ltd, Stockport, Cheshire, and
printed and bound in the United States of America

A CIP record for this book is available from the British Library

ISBN 978 0 7486 3431 6 (hardback)
ISBN 978 0 7486 3432 3 (paperback)
ISBN 978 0 7486 3433 0 (webready PDF)
ISBN 978 0 7486 5529 8 (epub)
ISBN 978 0 7486 5528 1 (Amazon ebook)

The right of Rachel Potter
to be identified as author of this work
has been asserted in accordance with
the Copyright, Designs and Patents Act 1988.

Contents

Series Preface   vii
Acknowledgements   viii
Chronology   .   ix

Introduction   1
  When was Modernism?   1
  What was Modernism?   7
  Modernist Poetry: T. S. Eliot's 'The Love Song of
    J. Alfred Prufrock'   15
  Modernist Prose: James Joyce's *Ulysses*   22

Chapter 1 Modernist Networks, 1914–28: Futurists,
           Imagists, Vorticists, Dadaists   37
  London, 1914   39
  New York, 1917   49
  Paris, 1922   54
  1928   66

Chapter 2 Modernism and Geography   80
  Modernism and Realism   84
  Dublin   94
  Exiled Writing   102

Chapter 3 Sex, Obscenity, Censorship   113

Law and Literature   114
Modernism and Feminism   124
Sexuality   135

Chapter 4 Modernism and Mass Culture   146
Modernist Authority   148
Cinema   152
Popular Fiction and Journalism   167

Chapter 5 Modernism and Politics   177
Revolution and Economics   181
War   198

Conclusion   211

Student Resources   218
Electronic Resources   218
Glossary   219
Questions for Discussion   225
Guide to Further Reading   227

Index   237

Series Preface

The study of English literature in the early twenty first century is host to an exhilarating range of critical approaches, theories and historical perspectives. 'English' ranges from traditional modes of study such as Shakespeare and Romanticism to popular interest in national and area literatures such as the United States, Ireland and the Caribbean. The subject also spans a diverse array of genres from tragedy to cyberpunk, incorporates such hybrid fields of study as Asian American literature, Black British literature, creative writing and literary adaptations, and remains eclectic in its methodology.

Such diversity is cause for both celebration and consternation. English is varied enough to promise enrichment and enjoyment for all kinds of readers and to challenge preconceptions about what the study of literature might involve. But how are readers to navigate their way through such literary and cultural diversity? And how are students to make sense of the various literary categories and periodisations, such as modernism and the Renaissance, or the proliferating theories of literature, from feminism and Marxism to queer theory and eco–criticism? The Edinburgh Critical Guides to Literature series reflects the challenges and pluralities of English today, but at the same time it offers readers clear and accessible routes through the texts, contexts, genres, historical periods and debates within the subject.

Martin Halliwell and Andy Mousley

Acknowledgements

Firstly I would like to thank the editors of this series, Martin Halliwell and Andy Mousley, for their initial interest and support for this book. In the final stages of the project, their close editorial recommendations were both insightful and invaluable. Thanks also to Jackie Jones and the staff at Edinburgh University Press for their help with the project. I have been teaching courses on modernism and modernist writers for many years, first at Queen Mary, University of London, and more recently in the School of English, Drama and Creative Writing at the University of East Anglia. This book is the result of these experiences. Thank you to the wonderful colleagues and students I have worked with over this time. More specifically, I would like to thank Jeremy Noel-Tod, Lyndsey Stonebridge, Jo Poppleton, Lydia Fellgett and Karen Schaller, all of whom read parts of this manuscript and gave detailed and perceptive advice. Finally, thanks to Henry, Thomas and Stella for the good times.

Chronology

Date	Historical and Cultural Events	Publications
1900	Labour Party formed with Ramsay Macdonald as its secretary	Joseph Conrad, *Lord Jim*; Sigmund Freud, *The Interpretation of Dreams*
1901	Queen Victoria dies; Coronation of Edward VII	Rudyard Kipling, *Kim*
1902	Anglo–Boer War ends; Tally's Electric theatre opens in Los Angeles	Joseph Conrad, *Heart of Darkness*
1903	Foundation of Women's Social and Political Union by the Pankhursts; Wright brothers' first successful flight	Samuel Butler, *The Way of All Flesh*; Henry James, *The Ambassadors*; Georg Simmel, *The Metropolis and Mental Life*; W.B. Yeats, *In the Seven Woods*
1904	Abbey Theatre opens in Dublin	Joseph Conrad, *Nostromo*; Henry James, *The Golden Bowl*

Date	Historical and Cultural Events	Publications
1905	Albert Einstein proposes theory of relativity; Henri Matisse shows *Woman With a Hat* at the Fauvist exhibition in Paris	Ford Madox Ford, *The Soul of London*
1906	Liberal Party elected to government in Britain	John Galsworthy, *The Man of Property*
1907	Cubist exhibition in Paris; *Votes for Women* newspaper founded in London	Henri Bergson, *Creative Evolution*
1908	Henry Ford produces his first Model T automobile; Ford Madox Ford begins *The English Review*	
1909	Filippo Marinetti issues 'The Founding and Manifesto of Futurism'	Ezra Pound, *Personae*; Gertrude Stein, *Three Lives*; H.G. Wells, *Ann Veronica*
1910	First Post-Impressionism exhibition in London; Edward VII dies and is succeeded by George V; Asquith government in crisis due to miners' strike, campaign for Irish Home Rule and Suffragette agitation; Henri Matisse paints *The Dance*	Ford Madox Ford, *A Call*; E.M. Forster, *Howards End*; W.B. Yeats, *The Green Helmet and Other Poems*

Date	Historical and Cultural Events	Publications
1911	First publication of *Rhythm*; 'Der Blau Reiter' group founded in Munich; Marie Curie receives a second Nobel Prize for the discovery of radium; the first complete English translation of Frederic Nietzsche published	D.H. Lawrence, *The White Peacock*; Katherine Mansfield, *In a German Pension*; Ezra Pound, *Canzoni*
1912	Second Post-Impressionism exhibition in London; Futurist exhibition in Paris; sinking of *Titanic*; Suffragettes begin their window-breaking campaign; Ezra Pound writes 'In a Station of the Metro' for *Poetry* magazine	Ezra Pound, *Ripostes*; Karl Jung, *Psychology of the Unconscious*
1913	Filippo Marinetti issues 'Manifesto of Futurism'; Einstein's 'General Theory of Relativity' released; the Russian Futurist Manifesto published	D.H. Lawrence, *Sons and Lovers*; Ezra Pound, *Personae*; Marcel Proust, *Swann's Way*
1914	Outbreak of the First World War; the first issues of *Blast, Egoist* and *The Little Review* are published	James Joyce, *Dubliners*; Mina Loy, 'Aphorisms on Futurism' and 'Feminist Manifesto'; Ezra Pound (ed.), *Des Imagistes*; Gertrude Stein, *Tender Buttons*; W.B. Yeats, *Responsibilities*

Date	Historical and Cultural Events	Publications
1915	Obscenity trial of *The Rainbow* in London	Ford Madox Ford, *The Good Soldier*; D.H. Lawrence, *The Rainbow*; Mina Loy, *Love Songs 1–4*; Ezra Pound, *Cathay*; Dorothy Richardson, *Pointed Roofs*; Virginia Woolf, *The Voyage Out*
1916	Easter Rising in Dublin; first Dada performances in Zurich	H.D., *Sea Garden*; James Joyce, *A Portrait of the Artist as a Young Man*; Ezra Pound, *Lustra* and *Gaudier-Brzeska*; Dorothy Richardson, *Backwater*; W.B. Yeats, *Reveries Over Childhood*
1917	The USA enters to war on the Western Front; Russian Bolshevik Revolution; Balfour Declaration; Hogarth Press founded by Leonard and Virginia Woolf	T.S. Eliot, *Prufrock and Other Observations*; Mina Loy, *Songs to Joannes*; Ezra Pound, *Three Cantos*; Dorothy Richardson, *Honeycomb*; W.B. Yeats, *The Wild Swans at Coole*
1918	Influenza pandemic in Britain; Representation of the People Act enfranchises women over thirty; Tristan Tzara issues 'Dada Manifesto, 1918'	James Joyce, *Exiles*; Wyndham Lewis, *Tarr*; Katherine Mansfield, *Prelude*
1919	'Manifesto of the Bauhaus' published; signing of the Treaty of Versailles marks the end of the Great War; Armistice Day	T.S. Eliot, *Poems*; Mina Loy, *Psycho-Democracy*; Ezra Pound, *Quia Pauper Armavi*; Dorothy Richardson, *Interim* and *The Tunnel*; Virginia Woolf, *Night and Day*

Date	Historical and Cultural Events	Publications
1919 (cont.)	celebrations; Weimar Republic established; League of Nations created at the Paris Peace Conference	
1920	Burial of the Unknown Warrior; Dada festival in Paris; first issue of *Contact*	T.S. Eliot, *The Sacred Wood*; Sigmund Freud, *Beyond the Pleasure Principle*; D.H. Lawrence, *Women in Love*; Ezra Pound, *Hugh Selwyn Mauberley*; Dorothy Richardson, *Deadlock*; W.B. Yeats, *Michael Robartes and the Dance*
1921	*The Little Review* is prosecuted in New York for obscenity over its publication of *Ulysses*; creation of Irish Free State	Marianne Moore, *Poems*
1922	Mussolini becomes Italian Prime Minister; War Office Enquiry into 'shell-shock'; creation of the BBC	T.S. Eliot, *The Waste Land*; James Joyce, *Ulysses*; Mina Loy, *Brancusi's Golden Bird;* Virginia Woolf, *Jacob's Room*
1923	Le Corbusier writes *Towards a New Architecture*; onset of hyperinflation in Germany	Djuna Barnes, *A Book*; Mary Butts, *Speed the Plough*; Sigmund Freud, *Ego and Id*; Mina Loy, *Lunar Baedecker* [sic] and *Anglo–Mongrels and the Rose* [first three sections]; Dorothy Richardson, *Revolving Lights*

Date	Historical and Cultural Events	Publications
1924	First Labour government in Britain; British Empire exhibition in London; first Surrealist Manifesto issued; Lenin dies in Russia	T.S. Eliot, *Homage to John Dryden*; Ford Madox Ford, *Some Do Not* (first volume of *Parade's End*)
1925	Adolf Hitler publishes *Mein Kampf*; the Locarno Treaties are signed in Switzerland	Mary Butts, *Ashe of Rings*; Mina Loy, *Anglo-Mongrels and the Rose* [final sections]; Virginia Woolf, *Mrs Dalloway* and *The Common Reader*; W.B. Yeats, *A Vision*
1926	General Strike in Britain	H.D., *Palimpsest*; D.H. Lawrence, *The Plumed Serpent*
1927	*The Jazz Singer* is the first 'talkie' to achieve box-office success; first issue of film journal *Close Up*	T.S. Eliot, *Journey of the Magi*; Martin Heidegger, *Being and Time*; James Joyce, *Pomes Penyeach*; Wyndham Lewis, *Time and Western Man*; Dorothy Richardson, *Oberland*; Laura Riding and Robert Graves, *A Survey of Modernist Poetry*; Jean Rhys, *The Left Bank and other stories*; Virginia Woolf, *To the Lighthouse*
1928	Alexander Fleming discovers penicillin; Sergei Eisenstein releases his film *Oktober*; voting age for British women is lowered to 21; *The Well of Loneliness* obscenity trial in London	Djuna Barnes, *Ryder* and *Ladies' Almanack*; Mary Butts, *Armed with Madness*; James Joyce, *Anna Livia Plurabelle*; Radclyffe Hall, *The Well of Loneliness*; D.H. Lawrence, *Lady Chatterley's Lover*; Virginia Woolf, *Orlando*; W.B. Yeats, *The Tower*

Date	Historical and Cultural Events	Publications
1929	Wall Street Crash on October 29, 'Black Tuesday'; Second Surrealist Manifesto; Bunuel and Dali release *Un Chien Andalou*	Robert Graves, *Goodbye to All That*; Virginia Woolf, *A Room of One's Own*; W.B. Yeats, *A Packet for Ezra Pound*
1930	Mahatma Ghandi leads the Salt March in India	T.S. Eliot, *Ash Wednesday*; Wyndham Lewis, *The Apes of God*
1931	Oswald Moseley founds British Union of Fascists; Gold Standard abandoned	Samuel Beckett, *Proust*; H.D., *Red Roses for Bronze*; Dorothy Richardson, *Dawn's Left Hand*; Jean Rhys, *After Leaving Mr MacKenzie*; Virginia Woolf, *The Waves* and *The Second Common Reader*
1932	The atom is split at Cambridge University	Mary Butts, *The Death of Felicity Taverner*
1933	Hitler becomes Chancellor of Germany	T.S. Eliot, *The Use of Poetry and the Use of Criticism*; W.B. Yeats, *The Winding Stair*
1934	Hitler becomes Führer of Germany; Nuremburg Rally; Soviet Union joins League of Nations; the house 'Fallingwater' is designed by Frank Lloyd Wright	Wyndham Lewis, *Men Without Art*; Ezra Pound, *The A.B.C. of Reading*; Jean Rhys, *Voyage in the Dark*
1935	Nuremburg Laws passed in Germany; Baldwin Government begins its policy of appeasement	H.D., *Nights*; T.S. Eliot, *Four Quartets* (1935–42); Dorothy Richardson, *Clear Horizon*

Date	Historical and Cultural Events	Publications
1936	International Surrealist Exhibition held in London; Spanish Civil War (1936–9) begins; Charlie Chaplin's *Modern Times* released; abdication crisis in Britain	Djuna Barnes, *Nightwood*; Walter Benjamin, *The Work of Art in the Age of Mechanical Reproduction*; John Maynard Keynes, *The General Theory of Employment, Interest and Money*; Stevie Smith, *Novel on Yellow Paper*
1937	Mass Observation launched in Britain	Mary Butts, *The Crystal Cabinet*; Wyndham Lewis, *The Revenge for Love* and *Blasting and Bombardiering: Autobiography (1914–1926)*; Virginia Woolf, *The Years*
1938	'Crystal night' in Germany	Samuel Beckett, *Murphy*; Mary Butts, *Last Stories*; Laura Riding, *Collected Poems*; Virginia Woolf, *Three Guineas*
1939	Second World War (1939–45) begins	James Joyce, *Finnegans Wake*; Jean Rhys, *Good Morning Midnight*
1940	Start of the London Blitz; Churchill forms Coalition Government; Paris falls to German occupation	T.S. Eliot, *East Coker*
1941	Trotsky assassinated in Mexico; Japan bombs Pearl Harbour, consequentially USA enters the war	Rebecca West, *Black Lamb and Grey Falcon*
1942	RAF begins bombing German cities	Albert Camus, *L'Etranger*; T.S. Eliot, *Little Gidding*
1943	Mainland Italy is invaded by Allied Forces	Jean-Paul Sartre, *Being and Nothingness*

Date	Historical and Cultural Events	Publications
1944	Warsaw Uprising; Lawrence Olivier's *Henry V* opens in London	H.D., *The Walls Do Not Fall* and *What Do I Love?*; Mina Loy, *Les Lauriers Sont Coupés*; Marianne Moore, *Nevertheless*
1945	Dresden bombing; the Allies liberate Auschwitz; America drops atom bombs on Hiroshima and Nagasaki; end of World War II; Nuremberg Trials (1945–6) begin	H.D., *Tribute to the Angels*; Ezra Pound, *Pisan Cantos*

Introduction

WHEN WAS MODERNISM?

> To clear the drifts of spring
> Of our forebear's excrements
> Mina Loy, 'O Hell' (1920)[1]

Different dates have been assigned to the beginnings and endings of an English-language literary modernism, 'clear', as Mina Loy puts it, of its 'forebear's excrements'. Its European origins have been found in the ironic gestures of Charles Baudelaire's 1850s poems about Paris prostitutes, in Henrik Ibsen's plays about liberated women of the 1880s and 1890s, or in the violent avant-garde leap into the future of F. T. Marinetti's 'Founding and Manifesto of Futurism' (1909).[2] Its Anglo-American beginnings have been discovered in Joseph Conrad's evocation of interiority in *The Nigger of the 'Narcissus'* (1897), in Gertrude Stein's incantatory sentences in *Three Lives* (1909), or in a particular historical moment: as Virginia Woolf's retrospectively stated 'on or about December 1910 human character changed'.[3]

Its endings have been located in the Second World War, or have been seen to lie in the last significant poems or stories of individual writers; modernism, on this view, dies with James Joyce's *Finnegans Wake* (1939), Virginia Woolf's *Between the Acts* (1941), T. S. Eliot's *Four Quartets* (1936–42), H. D.'s *Helen in Egypt* (1961) or

Ezra Pound's last section of *The Cantos* (1972). For some, modernism is not something in the past, but a style of writing which is still being produced. Marjorie Perloff argues that contemporary poets such as J. H. Prynne and Susan Howe are twenty-first-century modernists. Rod Mengham and John Kinsella, in their 2004 edited collection of poems *Vanishing Points: New Modernist Poems*, use the term 'late modernist' to group a number of contemporary poets who have 'stayed in touch with the agendas of modernism'.[4] Peter Middleton and Nicky Marsh, in their edited collection of essays *Teaching Modernist Poetry* (2010), also use the term 'late modernist poetics' to refer to contemporary poetry which has 'continuities' with the 'moments of high modernism'.[5]

These different dates and points of focus reveal the multiple faces of modernism. The word was applied only retrospectively to the Anglo-American literary texts produced at the end of the nineteenth century and the beginning of the twentieth century; and that retrospective naming has worked to define an ever-shifting field of cultural activity. Originally a word that related to the modernising tendencies in the Christian Church, it was sporadically adopted by writers and artists before the Second World War. The first book to use the word 'modernist' with regard to writing was *A Survey of Modernist Poetry* (1927) by poets Robert Graves and Laura Riding, who identified and defended the 'difficulty' of modernist as opposed to 'traditional' poetry and discussed the fact that modernist writing was necessarily distanced from the 'plain' or 'ordinary' reader.[6] The question of difficulty was paramount in other essays about poetry at this time. T. S. Eliot, in *The Use of Poetry and the Use of Criticism* (1933), explained that poets sometimes needed to be 'difficult', either because they were unable to express themselves 'in any but an obscure way', or because complexity was the result of their experiments with form.[7] While I. A. Richards in *The Principles of Literary Criticism* (1924), F. R. Leavis in *New Bearings in English Poetry* (1932) and Helen Gardner in her more focused study of T. S. Eliot in *The Art of T. S. Eliot* (1949) also analysed the complexity and 'difficulty' of modern poems, they did not use the word 'modernist' to describe these innovations.[8]

Graves, Riding, Richards, Leavis and Gardner all focused close critical attention on poems as semi-autonomous entities. A different critical tradition interpreted a select number of English-language poems and novels as part of the politicised aesthetic of the European avant-garde. The Hegelian–Marxist critics of the Frankfurt School in the late 1930s and 1940s positioned the texts of James Joyce, T. S. Eliot and Samuel Beckett in relation to German Expressionism, works by Franz Kafka, Thomas Mann, Marcel Proust and others. Debates between Georg Lukács, Bertolt Brecht, Theodor Adorno and Ernst Bloch, among the most provocative in the history of twentieth-century criticism, focused on the social and political purpose of *Ulysses* or *The Waste Land*. Lukács criticised the modernist techniques of interior monologue and poetic fragmentation, arguing that their experimentalism and difficulty constituted a literary retreat from political and historical involvement. His critical adversary Adorno, in contrast, claimed that these same techniques involved a profound engagement with the logic of cultural commodification in a system of advanced capitalism.[9] The political significance of modernist techniques have continued to divide opinion.

After the Second World War, Anglo-American critics were keen to identify a canon of pre-war literary texts defined by a set of shared themes and formal properties, but failed to create an over-arching label. There was a broad consensus, however, about the literary value of a select group of early twentieth-century monumental achievements: W. B. Yeats's *The Tower* (1928), Joyce's *A Portrait of the Artist as a Young Man* (1916) and *Ulysses* (1922), Lawrence's *The Rainbow* (1915) and *Women in Love* (1921), Eliot's *The Waste Land* (1922) and *Four Quartets* (1936–42; published as a series in 1944), Lewis's *Tarr* (1918), and *The Apes of God* (1930), Woolf's *Mrs Dalloway* (1925) and *To the Lighthouse* (1927) and Pound's *The Cantos* (1922–72).

It was not until the late 1960s and early 1970s, when a number of groundbreaking historical studies were published, that the term modernism was adopted and the shared literary features assumed by the term diagnosed. For the American critic Hugh Kenner, writing in 1972, the modernist era was Pound's – he was the instigator, energiser and poetic master who sat at the centre of cultural activity and directed proceedings.[10] Pound's influence extended into Kenner's writing style, which adopted Pound's polyglot registers and fragmented forms. Others looked to Europe to situate the formal experimentation of Anglo-American writers. In the essays collected together in *Modernism: A Guide to European Literature, 1890–1930*, edited by Malcolm Bradbury and James McFarlane, modernism is a 'seismic' shift in literature and the arts, and James Joyce and Gertrude Stein are read alongside Italian and German writers such as Italo Svevo and Thomas Mann.[11]

With the incorporation of Continental theory into the study of literature in the late 1970s and 1980s, there was a change of focus. The study of modernism as a term, and the work of individual writers, started to be significantly informed by post-structuralist, feminist and post-colonial theory. The composition of the modernist canon was itself held up to scrutiny and the texts of a number of previously marginalised writers from the period were reprinted, and their legacy reassessed. Women writers such as Katherine Mansfield, Dorothy Richardson, H. D. (Hilda Doolittle), Gertrude Stein, Djuna Barnes, Marianne Moore, Mina Loy, Nancy Cunard, Laura Riding, Mary Butts, and black modernists Jean Rhys, Nella Larson, Claude McCay and Jean Toomer, among many others, became an important part of the modernist story. As the field of cultural activity mapped by the term modernism expanded, there was a concomitant politicised movement to expose and understand the fascist politics, anti-Semitism, racism and misogyny of Pound, Lewis, Yeats, Eliot, Lawrence and others.[12]

A number of studies in this period traced the intellectual origins of the movement. Michael Levenson's careful history *A Genealogy of Modernism: A Study of English Literary Doctrine, 1908–1922* (1984) extended earlier debates about the politics of modernist writing by revealing that the literary texts and essays of Ford Madox Ford, T. E. Hulme, Wyndham Lewis, Ezra Pound and T. S. Eliot were grounded in their criticisms of liberal democracy. Levenson documented the changes of literary focus during the years 1908–22, seeing Eliot's *The Waste Land* as the culmination of arguments surrounding Imagism and Vorticism. Modernism, in this book, is both authoritarian and lawless, wedded to literary tradition and in thrall to the new. Peter Nicholls's introductory book *Modernisms: A Literary Guide* (1995) followed a different poetic genealogy, locating the origins of Anglo-American modernist poetry in nineteenth-century French writing and re-situating women writers such as Stein, H. D. and Loy at the centre of modernism.

In the last twenty years, the authors and texts included under the modernist umbrella have continued to expand. Not only has the promotion and discussion of the work of previously marginalised writers progressed, but there has been a new kind of attention to the unexamined historical contexts within which modernist writing was produced and disseminated, and to modernism as a global phenomenon. The American journal *Modernism/modernity*, set up in 1994 by Lawrence Rainey and Robert van Hallberg and, since 2001, the official publication of the Modernist Studies Association, specifically encourages the interdisciplinary approach to the study of modernism and cultural history.

The word modernism, and the value judgements that originally worked to define it as a term, have been held up to ever-closer scrutiny and scepticism. The bold definitions of literary modernism briefly mentioned above have all been questioned and dissected: Riding's and Graves's notion of poetic difficulty separated from the 'ordinary' reader, Adorno's claim that some modernist works constitute politicised critiques of capitalist society and its reduction of art works to commodities, Bradbury's and McFarlane's declaration that modernism represents a 'seismic' shift in the arts, and Levenson's argument that *The Waste Land* represents the culmination and high point of modernism.

It has been argued, against these claims, that literary modernism, when seen in the light of the histories of the cinema, popular fiction and the publishing industry, can no longer be seen to occupy a privileged aesthetic or political position outside popular cultural forms or the literary marketplace or as a site of resistance to capitalist society. Who decides that a poem by Eliot is of more value than 'The Ballad of the Harp-Weaver' by Edna St Vincent Millay, which won the Pulitzer Prize for Poetry in 1923 and whose circulation vastly outnumbered *The Waste Land* in the 1920s?

And yet, the word, despite all attempts to destabilise its authority and exclusivity, still carries rhetorical force as a literary term. It continues to fascinate and frustrate. Universities still tend to ask students to read *The Waste Land* rather than 'The Ballad of the Harp-Weaver' on their modernism courses and students and readers still ask: what is modernism? It is an important question, given the seemingly ever-extending appearance of the word in English-language book titles and British and American university courses. While some critical studies use the term as a historical, rather than conceptual, marker, readers continue to pick up the collected poems of Eliot or Pound, or to look through *To the Lighthouse* and *Ulysses*, and to ask: why are these books written in the way that they are? What is it about these collections of words that is exciting and innovative? Is this excitement and innovation modernism?

In this book I will attempt to provide some answers to these questions. My guide through modernism is partial and polemical. It is an argument about why these texts might still be usefully labelled as modernist and why their modernism continues to be significant. There is something inherently contradictory about the idea that texts that were written approximately a hundred years ago might be innovative and modern; and yet, the sense that when one reads Eliot's 'The Love Song of J. Alfred Prufrock' (1915), Joyce's *Ulysses* (1922) or Djuna Barnes's *Nightwood* (1936) one experiences something experimental or revolutionary persists. For this reason, my argument starts, provisionally, here, with a consideration of this experience.

Some rather arbitrary boundaries have been imposed on this study. While modernism is a word which relates to developments in the visual arts, music and architecture, this study restricts its focus to writing. It will discuss the work of Anglo-American and Irish writers who lived in London and Paris and other isolated locations in Europe, and will analyse cultural activity in New York in 1917, when writers relocated there because of the war in Europe. But, otherwise, it will not analyse American writers who stayed in the United States, mainly to distinguish this volume from Catherine Morley's *Modern American Literature* (2012) in this same series. This book also limits its focus to the work of English-language writers, a limitation which artificially separates the Paris-based activities of American-born writers such as Gertrude Stein from those of French-born writers such as André Breton.

The modernism of my guide is situated firmly in the early to mid twentieth century, roughly 1914–45. It starts with the formation of artistic groups in London, and ends with a number of isolated literary responses to the Second World War. It involves the expanded group of writers that has featured in discussions of modernism in the past two decades. It includes works by James Joyce, Djuna Barnes, Mina Loy, T. S. Eliot, Ezra Pound, Dorothy Richardson, H. D., Virginia Woolf, Jean Rhys, D. H. Lawrence, Gertrude Stein, Mary Butts, Wyndham Lewis and Laura Riding. Their shared modernism is distinct, I will suggest, from previous incarnations.

WHAT WAS MODERNISM?

The writers listed above would have been surprised – even horrified – to have been lumped together under a single umbrella. Lewis spent his life attacking Bloomsbury values, and Woolf's writing in particular. She, in turn, both feared and despised his caustic judgements and politics. Lawrence and Joyce intensely disliked each other's work: Lawrence claimed that Joyce's writing was disgusting and obscene; while Joyce judged Lawrence's novels to be faintly ridiculous. Riding attacked H. D.'s poetry as vapid and vacuous. A number of fellow writers were simply bemused at what had happened to 'old Ezra' after he started broadcasting on behalf of the Italian fascists in 1941.

The modernism of this guide, then, involves a number of aggressively individualistic writers who expressed different views on writing, technique, politics, philosophy and form. In addition to the pronounced individualism of these writers, a glance at their literary statements reveals a series of aesthetic contradictions. Modernism is both fuelled by innovation, to 'make it new' as Pound famously declared, and should be mindful of literary tradition, as Eliot put it in 'Tradition and the Individual Talent'.[13] While Mina Loy, as we saw in the opening to this book, seeks to 'clear the drifts of spring / Of our forebear's excrements', Pound wanted to make the 'luminous details' of past poetry live again in the present.[14] Modernism is both obscene – *Ulysses*, Lawrence declared, was the most obscene thing ever written – and seen as the last bastion of humane and enlightened values in an industrialised and commodified society.[15] While for Eliot poetry should be 'difficult', Mina Loy thought writing should be democratic.[16] Modernism is both impersonal – poetry must extinguish the 'personality', according to Eliot – and writes the psyche – it creates new forms and techniques to capture what Woolf described as that 'queer conglomeration of incongruous things – the modern mind'.[17] Modernism transgresses – no 'age of literature is so little submissive to authority as ours', declared Virginia Woolf – and imposes order – 'myth' Eliot claimed is a way of ordering the 'anarchy which is contemporary history'.[18] Modernist writing struggles with the dilemmas and contradictions of the modern world and seeks values or patterns of knowledge to order these conflicts. Modernism is seen as progressive and as sceptical of progress. While Woolf states that it is hard not to take it for granted that fiction is 'somehow an improvement upon the old', D. H. Lawrence judges that 'the young need not be so proud of their superiority over the old'.[19]

While these writers express contradictory attitudes to politics, tradition, obscenity, progress and the psyche, they share the desire to experiment with form. Woolf suggests that writers are 'forcing the form they use to contain a meaning which is strange to it'.[20] For Woolf, this formal innovation involves a writing which moves beyond existing genre distinctions. In a diary entry, she states: 'I will invent a new name for my books to supplant "novel". A new — by Virginia Woolf. But what? Elegy?'[21] James Joyce explains that such formal innovations are required to capture the semi-conscious dimensions of lived experience: 'One great part of every human existence is passed in a state which cannot be rendered sensible by the use of wideawake language, cutanddry grammar and goahead prose'.[22] Joyce's joke that the experimental language of *Finnegans Wake* is a more 'sensible' rendering of human existence than conventional prose has a serious point to it. His techniques, he suggests, capture those realms of experience that are simply beyond the range of familiar language and standard grammar.

Despite the glaring differences between the writers discussed in this guide, they are also held together by a shared history. Modernist texts both embrace and recoil from history. In his essay 'The Function of Criticism' (1923), T. S. Eliot argued that between 'the true artists of any time there is, I believe, an unconscious community'.[23] This was a community that lived through a historical period of momentous events: the First World War (1914–18), the Russian revolution (1917), Mussolini's march on Rome (1922), Irish independence (1922), the British general strike (1926), the Wall Street crash (1929), Hitler's rise to power (1933), the Spanish civil war (1936), the outbreak and conclusion of the Second World War (1939–45).

It is also a history of political, legal, philosophical and technological change, a history that puts in place some of the political and intellectual categories that define the contemporary world. The revolutionary ideas of Charles Darwin (1809–82), Karl Marx (1818–83), Friedrich Nietzsche (1844–1900) and Sigmund Freud (1856–1939) shattered understandings of religious faith, politics, class, money, capitalism, subjectivity and the mind, and placed ideas of intellectual revolution at the heart of cultural activity.

While Marx's critique of capitalism and the commodity dominated political accounts of art's role in society, Nietzsche's philosophy of the will and individualism enjoyed a voguish popularity in Britain, particularly in the period before the outbreak of the First World War. Wyndham Lewis pinpoints this popularity in his novel *Tarr*, when he describes how Nietzsche's ideas have made 'aristocrats' of every self-selected artist in Europe.[24] Freud's theories, meanwhile, became particularly significant and widespread after the war. Mary Butts, casting her mind back to the post-war moment, remarked 'I am old enough to remember what it was like when the theories of Freud first escaped from the study and the clinic, and the great game of Hunt-the-Complex began, to the entertainment and alarm of a war-shattered and disillusioned world'.[25]

Alongside the literary engagement with Marx's critique of capitalism, Nietzsche's ideas of individual will and Freud's complexes and accounts of the unconscious, there were other social shifts. Key elements of the modern democratic state were put in place during this period. In Britain, women and working-class men won the right to vote in 1919; the bar preventing women from entering professional jobs such as the civil service and the medical profession was removed; rigid class divisions started to loosen during the

First World War. British imperial power over Ireland and India began to disintegrate, even while Britain became newly powerful in the Middle East.

Other historical changes put in place the technologies and systems which define our world. This is the era in which culture becomes mass culture in the modern sense of the word. We see the development of mass-distribution cinema in the 1910s, particularly during the war, and the creation of two competing centres of film production: Hollywood and Moscow. Writers both embraced and incorporated the new visual language of cinema, and attacked it as a dead mass medium. Virginia Woolf, Dorothy Richardson, Hilda Doolittle and Mary Butts wrote excitedly about the artistic possibilities of the new visual language of cinema. Butts captures the physical imprint of the cinema in her phrase the 'cinematograph of the senses'.[26] Wyndham Lewis and D. H. Lawrence were more anxious about the deadening effects of the new movie culture. Lewis satirised the farcical way in which individuals ape their Hollywood heroes in *The Revenge for Love* (1937). In this book, cinema types infiltrate the very movements of the body. Mina Loy evokes both the excitement and the psychic costs of identifying with cinematic stereotypes such as the 'movie vamp'.[27] In *Lady Chatterley's Lover* (1928), D. H. Lawrence counterposes Connie Chatterley's tenderness to the harshness of the 'celluloid women of today'.[28] Sasha Jensen, in Jean Rhys's novel *Good Morning, Midnight* (1939), warns herself to 'watch out for' the romantic fantasies of 'your filmmind'.[29] These different responses, from celebration to scepticism to anxiety, are illustrative of the more general ambivalence towards new technologies in the period. Rhys's description of Sasha's split mind forms part of a wider interest in the impact of new technology on the psyche.

There were other significant ways in which media became oriented differently at this time. Newspapers become vehicles for the mass distribution of news and entertainment: sales of the *Daily Mail* reached over a million a day in 1902. Books started to be manufactured on a huge scale. In 1916, Albert Boni, Harry Scherman and Maxwell Sackheim started the Little Leather Library Corporation in New York, which made classic novels available to a world audience. They sold a million copies to Woolworths

in the first year. In 1917, Boni and Horace Liveright created the
Modern Library, which reissued European classics. In 1935, the
publisher John Lane established Penguin Books, which deliberately made classics affordable, pricing books at 6d, equivalent at
the time to the cost of ten cigarettes.[30]

Mass cultural forms were the product of rapid industrialisation and technological innovation more generally. The American
manufacturer Henry Ford succeeded in making cars cheaply available by producing his Model T motor car using motorised production lines in 1913. The Italian Futurist writer F. T. Marinetti
celebrates his 'snorting beast' of a car in 'The Founding and
Manifesto of Futurism' in 1909, seeing it as an important element
of technological modernisation and a key symbol of modernity.
Ezra Pound connects being modern with knowing about cars: 'we
no longer think of an automobile as having a door at the back. We
are, that is, modern.'[31] Gertrude Stein remembers fondly how she
drove her Ford motor car, which she nicknamed 'auntie', for the
American Fund for French Wounded during the war. e. e. cummings, in 'she being brand', discovers the connections between
sex and technology. Other writers were worried by the destructive
impact of cars. E. M. Forster, in his pre-war novel *Howards End*
(1910), depicts men screeching around the English countryside in
their cars and thereby ignoring the specificities of locality and difference: 'They were dust, and a stink, and cosmopolitan chatter'.[32]
As well as being a key symbol of technological modernisation, the
car was also seen as altering ideas of space and time. Marcel Proust
excitedly comments on the spatial effects of the car: 'a village which
seemed to be in a different world from some other village becomes
its neighbour in a landscape whose dimensions are altered'.[33]
Wyndham Lewis, in his 1937 novel *The Revenge for Love*, produces
a negative take on Marinetti's 'beast' terminology and Proust's
evocation of the changed dimensions of space: the car is a 'charging beast', a 'muscular machine', a 'time-eating and space-guzzling
automaton'.[34] James Joyce, in *Finnegans Wake*, jokes about the
cultural impact of cars: 'Morris the Man, with the role of a royss'.[35]

An ambivalence towards technological modernisation informs
writing of this period more generally. Mary Butts, in her novel
Death of Felicity Taverner (1932), describes the impact of

technology on the English landscape as like 'the cold arms and legs and abstractions of machinery, an abstract of the cerebral life of towns'.[36] The conflation of mechanisation, urban life, abstraction and a dismembered body creates a nostalgic critique of industrialisation.

Other new technologies were seen to have a profound impact on the relationship between self and world. The first successful telephone transmission in 1876 inaugurated an era of telephonic communication in the early twentieth century. Both Proust and Woolf depict telephones as peculiar conduits for desire. Proust excitedly captures the freedoms of someone listening to an invisible telephonic voice: 'there would come spontaneously to the lips of the listener a smile that is all the more genuine because it is conscious of being unobserved'.[37] Freud, in his insistence that patients face away from the analyst in psychoanalytic consultations, knew something about the truth of Proust's unobserved smile. Virginia Woolf, in her 1927 novel *To the Lighthouse*, focuses on the uncanny effects of hearing the invisible telephone voice of a woman generally identified with her physical beauty: 'He saw her [Mrs Ramsay] at the end of the line, Greek, blue-eyed, straight-nosed. How incongruous it seemed to be telephoning to a woman like that.'[38] Mr Bankes imaginatively fleshes out a Mrs Ramsay as absent as Classical Greece. The telephone changes space and spatial relations in a way that is here connected to temporal or historical dislocations. In a more negative take, Pound complained about modern poets having to shout their 'verses down a speaking tube to the editors of cheap magazines'.[39] In a later, and much darker, meditation, W. H. Auden also pinpoints the way that telephones separate communication from humanity: 'Here war is simple like a monument: / A telephone is speaking to a man'.[40] The telephone in this line is connected to other geographical signifiers of war: flags, maps, plans, and their human signifieds, the 'life' of the penultimate line: 'Where life is evil now: / Nanking; Dachau'. The inventions of the radio, phonograph and the television also changed spatial relationships. In 'The Leaning Tower', Woolf noted the oddity of turning on the wireless, and hearing 'Hitler's voice as we sit at home of an evening'.[41]

There was a remarkable shift in the cultural and social position of women and working-class men in the early twentieth century. It is not just that there was an explosion of avant-garde writing by and about women; it is also that independent women were able to participate in international culture in new kinds of ways. This was a result of basic shifts in their economic, legal and educational position. Many of the important American women writers in the period studied at university, including Gertrude Stein, Marianne Moore, H. D. and Laura Riding. British writers also tended to attend some kind of higher education. We now know that, despite her protestations to the contrary in essays, Virginia Woolf attended university courses in history, Greek, Latin and German at the King's College Ladies Department, University of London, between 1897 and 1901. The London-born writer Mina Loy went to art college in Munich, London and Paris.

Political parties and ideologies changed radically in the early twentieth century. The First World War signalled and propelled the collapse of one kind of world, and facilitated the birth of new kinds of political affiliations. In the chaos of the post-war period communist and socialist upheaval spread across eastern Europe and Britain's imperial and colonial power started to shatter: the Irish Free State was born in 1922, and in India, Britain's biggest and most important colony, people began to agitate for independence. E. M. Forster, in *A Passage To India* (1924), captures the complex nationalism of oppressed countries: 'India a nation! What an apotheosis! Last comer to the drab nineteenth-century sisterhood!'[42]

This scepticism about nationalism was partly a result of the new kinds of nationalisms which sprang up in the Europe after the war. In 1922 Mussolini's Italian fascists marched on Rome and seized power, creating a new kind of mass politics which was heavily dependent on spectacle. Hitler's rise to power in Germany in 1933 was also connected to his manipulation of the mass media to create a politics dependent on images of pan-Germanic national unity. Europe splintered into the ideologically opposed camps of fascism and communism, a politics which radically altered the liberal democracies of France, Britain and America.

These shifts and events had a clear impact on writing. While Wilfred Owen, who went to fight in the First World War, protests against the mutilated bodies of war, which he describes as 'obscene as cancer', other poets create images of a more generalised sense of moral and cultural collapse.[43] Ezra Pound sees civilisation as 'botched' in his post-war poem *Hugh Selwyn Mauberley* (1920).

Two decades later, writers faced another world war. Woolf, mentally exhausted at the prospect, captures the nuances of domestic terror in her posthumously published final novel, *Between the Acts*. Others lived through this second war, and created terrifying synthesised images of domestic and psychic invasion: H. D., for example, writes of the 'falling masonry' of a blitzed London in her poem 'The Walls Do Not Fall' (1944), seeing the shattering of human and moral 'frames' in the destruction of buildings. Where writers of the first war often dwell on the innocence of soldiers in the face of the imperialistic drives of 'old men', poets of the second war struggle to articulate ethical or literary value in the face of barbarism.

These texts are modernist, however, because of something other than their thematic engagement with the conflicted history and new technologies of the early twentieth century. Their modernism resides also in their attempt to register these conflicts at the level of form. In a *Times Literary Supplement* review of 1917, Virginia Woolf suggested that the 'vast events now shaping across the Channel are towering over us too closely and too tremendously to be worked into fiction without a painful jolt in perspective'.[44] Pound, meanwhile, stated that 'War blew up a lot of clichés'.[45] The next two sections will introduce some of the key formal jolts in perspective and form through the close reading of T. S. Eliot's 'The Love Song of J. Alfred Prufrock' and Joyce's use of interior monologue in *Ulysses*. They also highlight Eliot's and Joyce's shared interest in juxtaposing the prosaic elements of everyday life with philosophical and religious reflections about language, perception and meaning. These formal techniques will be discussed in isolation from history and cultural context. They are a starting point for understanding the ways in which modernist writers broke apart the literary conventions and transgressed the rules.

MODERNIST POETRY: T. S. ELIOT'S 'THE LOVE SONG OF J. ALFRED PRUFROCK'

T. S. Eliot's poem 'The Love Song of J. Alfred Prufrock' was completed in 1911, three years before the outbreak of the First World War. Eliot was born in America, but he travelled to Paris in 1910 and then to London in 1914 to study philosophy. His first poems, including 'The Love Song of J. Alfred Prufrock', 'Preludes' and 'Rhapsody on a Windy Night', were written in 1911. He married an English woman, Vivienne Haigh-Wood, in 1915, and then decided to settle in London, where he initially worked in the colonial and foreign department of Lloyds Bank in the City of London. His first volume of poems, *Prufrock and Other Observations*, was published in 1917 and his first collection of critical essays, *The Sacred Wood*, came out in 1920. After suffering a breakdown, he wrote, and in 1922 published, *The Waste Land*, the poem which was to make his name and establish the reputation of the new movement in poetry. This same year he brought out the first edition of *The Criterion*, the important quarterly journal he was to edit until 1939. In 1925 he was employed by Faber and Gwyer (later Faber and Faber) as an editor, a position that he used to sponsor and publish a wide range of experimental poetry and novels through the 1920s and 1930s. In 1927 he was baptised and confirmed into the Church of England and became a British citizen. He continued to write poems and plays, and to publish essays on poetry, writing, religion, education and other cultural matters. *Four Quartets*, his most important later poem, comprises *Burnt Norton* (1936), *East Coker* (1940), *The Dry Salvages* (1941) and *Little Gidding* (1942). Eliot died in 1965. This brief Eliot biography is a helpful starting point for understanding 'The Love Song of J. Alfred Prufrock', which combines his philosophical and poetic interests, and was written at a very early moment in his life as a poet and critic.

'The Love Song of J. Alfred Prufrock' was initially published in the American journal *Poetry* in 1915. It signalled a departure from the poetic conventions of the time through its abandonment of regular metre, a style of poetry which was labelled free verse, after the French term *vers libre*. A scattered number of Anglo-American poets such as William Blake and Walt Whitman, as well as many nineteenth-century French poets, had departed from tight metrical schemes some time previous to the creation of Eliot's poem. However, free verse came to dominate an experimental strand of Anglo-American poetry, of which Eliot was a pivotal figure, in the 1910s, and was to become central to the history of subsequent twentieth-century poetry.

There is something inherently contradictory about the term 'free verse'. How can verse, which implies metrical composition and form, be free? Eliot himself, reacting against the label that had been applied to his poetry, asked precisely this question in 1917: '*Vers libre* does not exist, for there is only good verse, bad verse, and chaos'.[46] While 'The Love Song of J. Alfred Prufrock' does not follow a specific metrical pattern, it does not dispense with rhythm or metre. For Eliot, poetry *is* rhythm. In a comment on Swinburne's complex metres, Eliot makes a telling comment about what he searches for and tries to produce, in poetry: 'the inexplicable line with the music which can never be recaptured in other words'.[47] In a later book, *The Use of Poetry and the Use of Criticism* (1933), he described the auditory imagination as a rhythm of verse which makes the reader 'aware of the deeper, unnamed feelings which form the substratum of our being, to which we rarely penetrate'.[48]

Arresting poetic 'music', for Eliot, requires both oral recognition and innovation. Verse, he argues, involves taking a recognisable form such as 'the iambic pentameter, and constantly withdrawing from it, or taking no form at all, and constantly approximating to a very simple one. It is this contrast between fixity and flux, this unperceived evasion of monotony, which is the very life of verse.'[49] The freedom of Eliot's poetry in 'The Love Song of J. Alfred Prufrock' lies in the negotiation of recognisable metrical patterns such as the iambic pentameter (lines 6 and 7) and the rhythms of other metres.

Many modernist poets were preoccupied with the dangers of poetic monotony, not just prosodically, but also linguistically and thematically. Eliot's description of a balancing act between recognisable forms and novelty helps us to understand other aspects of his poetry. The poem's diction plays on the contrasts between the familiar and the new, particularly through surprising juxtapositions. At moments in 'The Love Song of J. Alfred Prufrock' the language is direct and conversational, while at other points, it is markedly literary or poeticised. This shift is apparent in the very title of the poem: 'The Love Song' seems to announce a romanticised poetic register, which the prosaic 'J. Alfred Prufrock' violates. The poem shifts between prosaic descriptions of Prufrock's bald patch to the charged and portentous registers of lines which echo the Bible. The poem as a whole jumps about rapidly between literary allusion and quotation, with its reference to lines from Hamlet and Dante, to the mundane realities of modern life. The poem's modernism resides partly in these juxtapositions.

The monotonous and repetitive rituals of everyday life are also central to the poem's subject matter. The poem is located, to some extent, in the contemporary moment; it is focused on a financially divided city comprising sordid streets and high-class salons; our central character, J. Alfred Prufrock, is a ridiculously self-conscious figure, who is vainly preoccupied with his bald patch, getting old and the state of his clothes. His love song is humorously off-focus. The lady that he tries to seduce is never fully pictured, and he is acutely aware of his failings as a romantic hero.

It opens with the voice of the poem, presumably the J. Alfred Prufrock of the title, asking a 'you' – a more public part of Prufrock's divided self perhaps, or the reader – to accompany him as he goes on a walk around a city.[50] His journey, however, is not in a straight line; city streets become pampered salons before we leave the city altogether at the end of the poem and encounter a beautiful seascape. There are no clear indications of when or how Prufrock moves from urban streets to domestic interiors; just abrupt juxtapositions of poetic lines in which, for example, rooms with women chatting are placed next to street drains. The poem fails to tell a story; instead, it asks the reader, the 'you' of the opening line, to go somewhere else. It seems as though the reader is being posed a question rather than encouraged to follow a story, to enjoy the connections between dissimilar urban and domestic spaces, images and linguistic registers rather than follow a 'tedious argument'.

Questions abound in this poem. There are overwhelming questions and dropped questions; there are questions about what

Prufrock dares or presumes to do, what he has the strength for and how he might begin. References to mythical stories or literary quotations, some explicit, some glancing, are scattered through the poem, but it is left open what these associations signify. Prufrock imagines himself performing roles in a variety of literary or biblical myths. Such reflections, however, make him realise how ill-suited he is to ape such figures. He is better placed to play the fool rather than a Shakespearean hero. He is prone to visions and revisions in the questions and responses that dominate his mind. In many respects, the poem is a bit like this too. It responds to existing stories, rather than tells one. It asks questions about how to begin and how to act, but fails to say something meaningful.

Many of these connections humorously ridicule Prufrock's timid, self-effacing personality. While Marvell's poet might have felt able to squeeze his strength and sweetness into a ball and ask a telling question, Prufrock seems too inebriated by perfume and tedium to get his ball rolling.[51]

Other links extend beyond the ironic failings of character and are more philosophical. The half-quotation from Marvell creates meaning partly by the disjunction of registers: is 'universe' quite the right word to capture the piecemeal and 'etherised' city through which Prufrock wanders? Would it be possible for anyone to compress this world into a ball, hold it in their hands and see it clearly?

Eliot's poem certainly provides no such synthesis. Its failure to do so is part of the poem's substance. It is not just that the poem is about failure, indecision and loss. It is also that futile efforts to understand reside within a striving after meaning. The poem concludes, for instance, with Prufrock's beautiful vision of 'sea-girls wreathed with seaweed red and brown', a vision, however, which is also a delusion: 'voices wake us, and we drown'.

The staged endeavour to make loss and failure 'mean' something, as Prufrock puts it, structures both this and Eliot's future poems. In 'Gerontion' (1920), *The Waste Land* (1922) and *Four Quartets* the slipperiness of expression and meaning is more generalised and historical, a product of war and revolution.

These struggles, whether they are focused on the self-conscious attempts by Prufrock to say something meaningful, or to a world after war, divided contemporary views on Eliot's poetry. To some, they brought to life both the despair and a new language of despair of a generation. To others, Eliot's fragmented linguistic failures in 'Prufrock', the 'decisions and revisions' simply replaced poetic emotion with a forensic description of unimportant and fragmented body parts and objects.

The positive responses to 'J. Alfred Prufrock' see it as enlivening because it identifies a necessary gap between words and meaning. The diagnosis of failed communication and the struggle to mean was to preoccupy Eliot throughout his life. In *The Waste Land* there is a powerful description of unsuccessful communication: 'I could not / Speak, and my eyes failed, I was neither / Living nor dead, and I knew nothing'.[52] In 'East Coker', the second part of *Four Quartets*, Eliot describes the effort to use words effectively: 'Trying to use words, and every attempt / Is a wholly new start, and a different kind of failure'.[53] In 'The Dry Salvages', the third episode of *Four Quartets*, he describes a disappointment of a different kind: 'We had the experience but missed the meaning'.[54]

New beginnings and missed meanings structure the more personal 'The Love Song of J. Alfred Prufrock', but the gaps are generally ironic and playful, rather than tormented and tragic. In 'The Metaphysical Poets' Eliot identified the difficulty the poet faces when trying to make language communicate, and the necessity for poetic displacements to achieve this: the poet must be 'more allusive, more indirect, in order to force, to dislocate if necessary, language into his meaning'.[55]

The idea that there is a breach between words and meaning or experience is an informing one for much modernist poetry. Many writers argued that language, particularly poetic language, had become clichéd. T. E. Hulme, a poetic critic prominent in the pre-war period, argued that the language and imagery of poetic romanticism had become 'exhausted'.[56] Writers, Hulme argued, needed to regenerate the words at their disposal to capture modern experiences or the modern moment.

In 'The Love Song of J. Alfred Prufrock', the gap between words and meaning is also figured as a feature of clichéd language. The image of the women who come and go talking of Michelangelo conjures up the idea that through repetition, the meaning of the history or art these women discuss will be obscured, almost deleted.

One of the many questions posed by the poem is how its own language might escape this repetitious deletion of meaning. One answer lies in the focus on the word 'time'. We notice different things about the word, depending on whether we have become aware of its repetition. On a first encounter, we perhaps interpret it simply in the sense of its semantic content. After the word has been repeated four times, however, it starts to signify differently. We are encouraged to think less about its semantic content, and instead to notice the material dimensions of the word on the page, or in the ear. In other words, we perhaps begin to think more about the repetition of the word, than about the word itself.

In this sense, it starts to function in a more formal and self-referential way; it becomes a reminder of the temporal dimension of the poem. The word 'time' is being used to signal the pace, the time frame of the poem itself. What has happened is that the word 'time' has started to refer beyond itself. The interesting thing about Eliot's use of this word is that he prompts us to think about the nature of repetition, metre, the time frame of the poem and the relation between the semantic content of a word and its material dimensions on the page or in the ear.

This is clever because these reflections are all reflections, in themselves, about time. The poem prompts us to think about what constitutes time without specifically posing a question. How could we visualise time? Is time repetition, the repetition of the voices of the women in salons, for instance? Or is time repetition in the sense of the established judgements which fix you in a formulated phrase. Or is time a mechanical time of the clock which measures 'out life with coffee spoons'? Or is time the monotony of social relations – the 'tea and cakes and ices' – which distract Prufrock from forcing the moment to its 'crisis'.

Time, figured abstractly, is counterposed to 'the moment', which captures ideas of temporal or historical uniqueness. Prufrock's questions gesture forwards in time to imagine himself in the future when he will be outside of his inebriated present. In order to escape from self-conscious inactivity, he must try to step outside transient, momentary experiences. Getting beyond self-consciousness and saying something meaningful would involve finding some language, or space outside the mechanical and repetitive movement of time. This poem is all about getting beyond, groping towards a moment or form of expression 'after all'.

The ironic portrayal of Prufrock's self-consciousness also creates a particular picture of subjectivity. The poem's opening simile does more than produce a tasteless linguistic register. The lines descend from the sky to a human body whose materiality is brutally apparent: this is a body which is etherised, drugged, helpless, a body which is about to be dissected, or prodded or violated by a scientist or surgeon. Scientific similes run through the poem, and tend to imply that rather than directing his fate, Prufrock is controlled by external factors: he is fixed 'in a formulated phrase', he is 'sprawling on a pin', he is revealed 'as if a magic lantern threw the nerves in patterns on a screen'. These exact and scientific examinations position him as a helpless and numbed individual, as though he were a patient waiting to be dissected.

The materiality of the human body is grounded in this image, and matter threatens to invade and take control of Prufrock's consciousness in the poem as a whole. The other people in the poem appear as disembodied parts or ghostly actions. They are metonymic 'faces', 'hands', 'arms' and 'eyes'. Both Prufrock, and the object of his desire, the 'you' who is partly addressed at the beginning of the poem, never fully come into focus. Instead, they are bits of bodies, implying the absence of a unified subject who could take control of his own fate and ask the overwhelming question. This poem is in fragments – of cultural reference, of different poetic metres, of human bodies – partly because Prufrock finds it difficult to step beyond these fragments and impose some kind of order, or structure upon them.

MODERNIST PROSE: JAMES JOYCE'S ULYSSES

James Joyce starts the final chapter of his epic modernist text *Ulysses* with the following words:

Yes because he never did a thing like that before as ask to
get his breakfast in bed with a couple of eggs since the *City
Arms* hotel when he used to be pretending to be laid up with
a sick voice doing his highness to make himself interesting
to that old faggot Mrs Riordan that he thought he had a
great leg of and she never left us a farthing all for masses for
herself and her soul greatest miser ever was actually afraid
to lay out 4d for her methylated spirit telling me all her ail-
ments she had too much old chat in her about politics and
earthquakes and the end of the world let us have a bit of fun
first God help the world if all the women were her sort down
on bathingsuits and lownecks of course nobody wanted her
to wear I suppose she was pious because no man would look
at her twice I hope Ill never be like her a wonder she didnt
want us to cover our faces but she was a welleducated woman
certainly and her gabby talk about Mr Riordan here and Mr
Riordan there I suppose he was glad to get shut of her and
her dog smelling my fur and always edging to get up under
my petticoats especially then still I like that about him polite
to old women[57]

James Joyce was born in Dublin, but he left home at the age of
twenty to travel to Paris, ostensibly to study medicine. He returned
to Dublin briefly in 1903 because of his mother's death, but quickly
departed for the Continent again in 1904, this time accompanied
by his lifelong partner, Nora Barnacle. There were a few trips back
to Dublin, but from this point on Joyce chose to live outside of
Ireland, first in Trieste, Rome and Zurich, and then later in Paris
(1920), where he lived during the 1920s and 1930s. He died in
Zurich in 1941.

Joyce had begun writing at school and university, but he started
his first novel, called *Stephen Hero*, and a collection of short stories,
Dubliners, in 1904. Joyce always had problems finding publishers
for his writing, mainly because of what was seen to be their obscenity. After many trials and tribulations with publishers and printers, *Dubliners* was finally brought out in 1914. In 1907 he started
rewriting *Stephen Hero*; it became Joyce's first novel, *A Portrait of
the Artist as a Young Man*, which was published in instalments in

the modernist magazine *The Egoist* from 1914, and as a complete book in 1916.

Joyce's brushes with censorship, however, certainly did not deter him. He immediately launched into the writing of *Ulysses*, the book which would not only transform the novel form, but which was hailed as the crowning achievement of modernist fiction. The first thirteen chapters of the book were published in instalments in the New York magazine the *Little Review* during 1917–18 before being suppressed for obscenity. The magazine's editors were taken to court in 1921 and *Ulysses* was banned from sale in the United States. Other countries, such as Britain, Australia and India, followed suit. It was not until 1933 that the book was taken through the US courts again, and released from censorship. It was published as a whole in Paris in 1922. Joyce went on to write his 'Work in Progress', which became *Finnegans Wake* on its publication in 1939.

The chapter from *Ulysses* from which the quotation above comes was entitled 'Penelope', after the heroine of Homer's *Odyssey*, and is based on a character called Molly Bloom. Apart from the fact that Joyce abandons punctuation in this piece of writing, it is also striking that there is no narrative voice to explain what is going on. The reader is not told who is speaking or even whether this *is* speech. There is no explanation as to who 'he' is or where the speaker is or what time it is. There are no characters as we might conventionally expect them, merely the mention of 'that old faggot Mrs Riordan' and the shadowy 'he'. There is no story; just a stream of disconnected statements about eggs, methylated spirits and bathing suits. There is no punctuation to structure her words and no obvious logic to the flow of ideas from one thing to the next: eggs connect to the City Arms hotel to Mrs Riordan to Mrs Riordan's spending habits, but the only thing that can possibly make these words cohere is the significance they have for the character of Molly. The writing is structured as though it were following her memories and mental connections.

A variety of words have been used to describe the particular features of this style of writing, the most significant of which are the terms 'stream of consciousness' and 'interior monologue'. Both refer to writing that is distinct from more conventional nineteenth-

and early twentieth-century narratives, which tend to use third or first person narration, or free indirect discourse.

Molly's monologue in *Ulysses* presents her unmediated and nascent thoughts prior to any logical organisation by syntax or punctuation. Others had developed similar techniques before Joyce: Dorothy Richardson, in her novel *Pilgrimage*, bases her writing on the psychological responses of her heroine Miriam Henderson, and the *fin de siècle* French writer Édouard Dujardin had produced a highly artistic version of this narrative form in his 1887 novel *Les Lauriers sont coupés*.

The attempt to write the unmediated thoughts, impressions or responses of characters was important for a number of modernist writers, but each writer created their own highly distinct techniques. The phrase 'stream of consciousness' was originally used by late nineteenth-century psychologists, such as William James, to describe how the mind functioned. James's 'Stream of Thought' chapter in *The Principles of Psychology* (1880) influenced the writing of his brother, Henry James, and Gertrude Stein. The term was first used in a literary context by May Sinclair to describe Dorothy Richardson's writing. The phrase 'stream of consciousness' works well to capture the flow of Molly's monologue here, but is a much less helpful term when applied to the more punctuated narratives of Woolf and Lawrence. It is for this reason that in this guide I will use the more mobile and generic term 'interior monologue' to describe a writing which structures itself as though it were mimicking the private mental connections and viewpoint of an individual character.

Writers in the 1910s and 1920s immediately heralded this writing style as a radical departure. May Sinclair, in her discussion of Dorothy Richardson's writing, announced that the prose merges with character: the author

> must be Miriam Henderson . . . Miriam is an acute observer, but she is very far from seeing the whole of these people. They are presented to us in the same vivid but fragmentary way in which they appeared to Miriam, the fragmentary way in which people appear to most of us.[58]

Valery Larbaud, in a discussion of *Ulysses* in 1922, reiterates the point about seeing and being: of the key characters in *Ulysses*, he suggests that it is like being 'Stationed in the intimacy of their minds . . . we see through their eyes and hear through their ears'.[59]

The Molly Joyce's writing will inhabit for the next forty or so pages of *Ulysses* is a mundane, catty, shameless, vain, anti-Christian, highly amusing, sexy and sexual middle-aged woman. She will be frank about the bodily functions, with descriptions of her period and her lover's penis. She will express irreverent thoughts about priests and the Church. In some senses her prose, as here, stays close to material objects and bodies, with references to Mrs Riordan's leg, money, bathing suits and lownecks. But God also features quite strongly. Molly considers Mrs Riordan's hypocritical Catholicism and piety, with a semi-conscious joke about her spirit being 'methylated'. Speaking, as here, is aligned to performance and action. The unidentified 'he' uses a 'sick voice' to 'do' his highness. It is uncertain whether it is Mr Riordan or Mrs Riordan's dog that wants to get up under Molly's petticoats. Similar kinds of humorous ambiguities pepper Molly's monologue, many of them centred on the desires and ridiculous activities of men.

The style was certainly new; but what does it open up? As with Eliot's poem, the writing is notable for what it lacks: it has no authorial narrative voice interpreting or guiding the reader. Sinclair's review, which positively embraces Richardson's new method, actually appears to pinpoint a number of its limitations: Miriam only sees fragments of the city or other people. The reader is confined to her view. In the case of this episode of *Ulysses*, one might argue that the reader is limited to Molly's unorganised perspective and understanding. As in a first person narrative, the reader is asked to enjoy dwelling in Molly's highly partial view of the world, rather than to take pleasure in the novelistic depiction of story development, character interaction or conflicting social forces.

But the style differs from first person narration in the way that character is staged. The Molly that we get to know in this chapter is contained in her vocabulary, jokes and views about the world. She is also importantly embodied in the rhythms of her language. One of the most striking things about this piece of writing is its lack of punctuation, the conventional means with which writers control the rhythm of their prose. The experience of reading this text, whether aloud or to oneself, is a breathless one. The reader is required to provide their own pauses, to construct their own line breaks.

Rather than describing a character called Molly Bloom from the outside, the writing inhabits her carelessly wandering words. Lawrence Edward Bowling helpfully suggests that interior monologue shifts literary attention from plot and narrative development to the uncensored and ungrammatical ways in which the mind works: attention is given to the 'meanderings of the mind, not as a means to an end, but as an important end in itself'.[60]

In some senses, one might see this as a limitation. Are we interested in following the drifting memories of Molly's mind? Does this focus reduce the scope of the novel? A number of critics have seen Joyce's writing in precisely this light, arguing that he has abandoned the attempt to understand and interpret the world, and instead chosen to reflect the mundane thoughts of a limited individual.

Others have seen this writing as a radically exciting new form of realism. Joyce has removed the narrative mediator separating character and reader. Not only does Joyce succeed in capturing the ways in which the mind works, and particularly, as here, the robust sexuality of the female mind, he also captures the linguistic texture of subjectivity.

The subjectivity that is revealed through Molly's monologue is a bit like the introspective smile described by Proust: just as a smile without a person to see it is a seemingly redundant physical expression, so Molly's voiceless words would seem to rebound silently around her bedroom, as though words are not means of communication; but the substance of thoughts.

Molly accuses the 'he' of this extract, a pronoun which during the course of the chapter will refer promiscuously to a number of different men in her life but which in this instance seems to signify her husband, Leopold Bloom, of putting on a 'sick voice' to impress Mrs Riordan. If there is one thing that Molly despises above all things, it is pretence. But her monologue could be seen as a pretence of a different kind. Molly's unspoken and unorganised monologue might lack an addressee, but her privacy, like Proust's introspective smile, is a fiction. Molly's individuality is both obliterated by this reduction of privacy to writing; and her personality is located in the texture, rhythm and content of writing.

Each of the three main characters in *Ulysses*, Stephen Dedalus, Leopold Bloom and Molly Bloom, is grammatically and linguistically distinct. Stephen's monologues are learned and punctuated, and sometimes pretentious. At other moments, in their rhythms and imagery, they are like beautiful prose poems. Episode three of *Ulysses*, called 'Proteus', starts like this:

> Ineluctable modality of the visible: at least that if no more, thought through my eyes. Signature of all things I am here to read, seaspawn and seawrack, the nearing tide, that rusty boot. Snotgreen, bluesilver, rust: coloured signs. Limits of the diaphane. But he adds: in bodies.[61]

The writing reveals Stephen in dialogue with Aristotle, the 'he' of the final line. In its dominant use of assonance and rhythm, the writing also pictures Stephen's words as poeticised. It communicates brokenly, as it requires a certain understanding of Aristotle's theory of knowledge and perception to know what 'limits of the diaphane' means. But beyond the specific engagements with philosophical texts, Stephen's words try to make sense of the everyday world – the tide, the boot, a sea which looks like the colour of snot – within a broader meditation on the nature of sight and vision.

Where Stephen's monologues are often questioning and philosophical, Leopold Bloom's words tend to be visual and empathetic:

> Mr Bloom, chapfallen, drew behind a few paces so as not to overhear. Martin laying down the law. Martin could wind a sappyhead like that round his little finger without his seeing it. Oyster eyes. Never mind. Be sorry after perhaps when it dawns on him.[62]

Bloom pulls back in order not to hear what Martin and others are saying about him, part of his sensitivity to the anti-Semitism he will experience throughout his day in Dublin. The interior monologue moves in and out of third person narration, 'Mr Bloom, chapfallen', and flashes of internal thoughts and responses: 'Martin laying down the law', 'Oyster eyes'. What is notable here is how Bloom's thoughts, ordinary and humane, are both responsive to and alienated from the conversations of other Dubliners. Whereas Molly's words combine memories and conversations, and Stephen's interpret the phenomenal world in relation to the history of philosophy and religion, Bloom's present-tense thoughts observe and respond to a busy urban environment.

The mind, in the hands of other modernist writers, reads differently. Richardson's prose weaves in and out of third person, free indirect discourse, and language which is a direct representation of thought, such as the word 'Chloroform' in the following paragraph: 'She must hide somewhere . . . She would not be wanted . . . If you were not wanted . . . If you knew you were not wanted – you ought to get out of the way. Chloroform.'[63] While Molly's monologue flows forwards in time, Richardson's, with its ellipses and punctuation, represents thought as impressionistic, broken and fragmented.

D. H. Lawrence's and Virginia Woolf's writing of interiority are less direct, working within, but pushing up against, the boundaries of free indirect discourse. Lawrence, in the following extract, creates a language of unconscious sexual communion shared between two characters, Rupert Birkin and Ursula Brangwen:

> She had her desire of him, she touched, she received the maximum of unspeakable communication in touch, dark, subtle, positively silent, a magnificent give and give again, a perfect acceptance and yielding, a mystery, the reality of that which can never be known, vital, sensual reality that can never be transmuted into mind content, but remains outside, living body of darkness and silence and subtlety, the mystic body of reality.[64]

Lawrence is particularly interested in bringing the unconscious, that which cannot be 'transmuted into mind content', into writing here. He does so by performing the ebbs and flows of sensual, felt and invisible energies. The effect of his diction is to create an idea of interiority which is both unconscious and mystical. This prose is very different from the chatty verbalism of Molly's monologue, but it is also distinct from more clear-cut uses of free indirect discourse.

Woolf, like Lawrence, creates a free indirect discourse that is so sustained and performative that it dips into interiority: 'It is, thought Peter Walsh, beginning to keep step with them, a fine training. But they did not look robust. They were weedy for the most part, boys of sixteen, who might, to-morrow, stand behind bowls of rice, cakes of soap on counters.'[65] Peter's thoughts, described from the outside, will carry the prose forwards for a full paragraph here. As the writing progresses it will stage the observational thoughts and rhythms of a man walking through London streets.

This brief foray into the different ways in which Joyce, Richardson, Woolf and Lawrence stage the unattended, 'meandering' thoughts of characters in key modernist texts reveals both a common fictional preoccupation with interiority, consciousness and unconsciousness, and how they effectively splinter apart the novel form into different styles.

The modernism of Eliot's 'Love Song of J. Alfred Prufrock' and Molly's monologue resides partly in their formal innovations – the poetic fragmentation, the ironic portrayal of inarticulacy, the partial and limited viewpoint of characters, bringing the psyche into language. It also lies in the preoccupations of these characters. The concerns of Prufrock, self-conscious, alienated and helpless, and Molly, sexually robust and shameless, are pointedly unimportant. He is anxious about his receding hairline. She is worried about whether to cook eggs for her husband in the morning. These texts foreground the uneventful details of human consciousness, but they do so while posing profound literary and philosophical questions: what is time? Is consciousness linguistic? Are there realms of human consciousness that are outside language? Is it possible to understand the culture in which one lives or merely to comprehend one's partial place within it? Can individuals mould and direct their lives, or do they merely respond to external pressures?

Virginia Woolf, in a discussion of modern fiction, made an important point about the interest writers had in the ephemeral technologies and objects of life. In a discussion of Proust's writing, she states that the

> commonest object, such as the telephone, loses its simplicity, its solidity, and becomes a part of life and transparent. The commonest actions, such as going up in an elevator or eating cake, instead of being discharged automatically, rake up in their progress a whole series of thoughts, sensations, ideas, memories which were apparently sleeping on the walls of the mind.[66]

Woolf suggests that a concentrated focus on commonplace objects releases a series of memories and ideas with important psychic resonance. Joyce and Eliot also attend to the philosophical significance of ephemera. Stephen Dedalus converses with an imaginary Aristotle to consider the significance of a rusty old boot and Prufrock appeals to Andrew Marvell's words to ponder his failures as a lover. Modernist texts often combine descriptions of the banal or bodily features of everyday life with philosophical reflection.

The brief discussion of 'The Love Song of J. Alfred Prufrock' and *Ulysses* has focused on the formal properties and possibilities of interior monologue, poetic fragmentation and the juxtaposition of the philosophical and the everyday. Literary texts always, to some extent, extend and alter the formal and thematic concerns of their predecessors. The description, in isolation, of these formal innovations thereby tells us very little about modernism. It is in the relationship between formal innovation and content or history that the modernism of these texts resides.

In the following five chapters of this guide, formal techniques will be read in relation to a number of contradictory and conflictual historical forces. In Chapter 1, there will be a focus on the literary and publishing networks which produced and disseminated modernism. Modernism, when seen in the light of these networks, will emerge as a writing practice which is abidingly and resolutely individualistic, and as something which is dependent on the promotional activities of the group. Chapter 2 focuses on the attempt to write about the geography of cities and the changing boundaries of nation states. Imaginatively, modernism will be seen as a writing which both beds itself in local streets and geographical locations and seeks an imaginative position outside the local and the national. In Chapter 3, modernism is seen as a site of moral conflict. It is that which writes directly and honestly about both sex and the unconscious. By so doing, it confronts and transgresses institutional forces of censorship. Chapter 4 considers the impact of expanding mass cultural forms such as publishing and the cinema on modernism. At once a fuel to modernist experiment and a danger to the cultural position of literature, mass culture both defines and drives modernism. The final chapter looks at modernism and politics. Modernism cannot be divorced from the political revolutions and utopian hopes of the period: communism, fascism and mass democracy all emerge as new political ideologies and realities in this period. But the modernist involvement in politics has been its most controversial element.

NOTES

1. Mina Loy, 'O Hell', in *The Lost Lunar Baedeker*, ed. Roger L. Conover (Manchester: Carcanet, 1996), p. 71.
2. Marshall Berman, *All that is Solid Melts Into Air: The Experience of Modernity* (Harmondsworth: Penguin Books, 1982); Peter Nicholls, *Modernisms: A Literary Guide* (Basingstoke: Macmillan, 1995).
3. Michael Levenson, *A Genealogy of Modernism: A Study of English Literary Doctrine, 1908–1922* (Cambridge: Cambridge University Press, 1984); Virginia Woolf, 'Character in Fiction', in Virginia Woolf, *Selected Essays*, ed. David Bradshaw (Oxford: Oxford University Press, 2008), p. 38. Graham Hough uses Woolf's essay to date 1910 as the beginning of modernism in *Image and Experience: Studies in a Literary Revolution* (London: Duckworth, 1960).
4. Rod Mengham and John Kinsella (eds), *Vanishing Points: New Modernist Poems* (Cambridge: Salt Publishers, 2004), p. xviii.

5. Peter Middleton and Nicky Marsh (eds), 'Introduction', *Teaching Modernist Poetry* (Basingstoke: Palgrave Macmillan, 2010), p. 4.

6. Laura Riding and Robert Graves, *A Survey of Modernist Poetry* (New York: Haskell House Publishers, [1927] 1969).

7. T. S. Eliot, *The Use of Poetry and the Use of Criticism* (London: Faber and Faber, 1933), p. 150.

8. I. A. Richards, *The Principles of Literary Criticism* (London: Routledge and Kegan Paul, 1924); F. R. Leavis, *New Bearings in English Poetry: A Study of the Contemporary Situation* (Harmondsworth: Penguin Books, 1932); Helen Gardner, *The Art of T. S. Eliot* (London: Faber and Faber, 1949).

9. Theodor Adorno, Walter Benjamin, Ernst Bloch, Bertolt Brecht and Georg Lukács, *Aesthetics and Politics: Debates Between Theodor Adorno, Walter Benjamin, Ernst Bloch, Bertolt Brecht, Georg Lukács* (London: Verso, 1980).

10. Hugh Kenner, *The Pound Era* (London: Faber and Faber, 1972).

11. Malcolm Bradbury and James McFarlane (eds), *Modernism: A Guide to European Literature, 1890–1930* (Harmondsworth: Penguin Books, 1976).

12. A number of books were published in the 1970s, 1980s and early 1990s which documented the political affiliations of modernist writers. See, for example, Fredric Jameson, *Fables of Aggression: Wyndham Lewis, the Modernist as Fascist* (London: University of California Press, 1979); Elizabeth Cullingford, *Yeats, Ireland and Fascism* (London: Macmillan, 1981); Cairns Craig, *Yeats, Eliot, Pound and the Politics of Poetry: Richest to Richest* (London: Croom Helm, 1982); Peter Nicholls, *Ezra Pound: Politics, Economics and Writing: A Study of 'The Cantos'* (London: Macmillan, 1984); David Ayers, *Wyndham Lewis and Western Man* (Basingstoke: Macmillan, 1992).

13. Ezra Pound, *Make It New* (London: Faber and Faber, 1934); T. S. Eliot, 'Tradition and the Individual Talent' (1919), in T. S. Eliot, *Selected Essays*, 3rd edn (London: Faber and Faber, [1951] 1986), pp. 13–22.

14. Mina Loy, 'O Hell', in *The Lost Lunar Baedeker* (1996), p. 71;

Ezra Pound, 'I Gather the Limbs of Osiris', in Ezra Pound, *Selected Prose: 1909–1965*, ed. William Cookson (London: Faber and Faber, 1973), p. 23.

15. Dorothy Brett claimed that D. H. Lawrence said this to her. See Dorothy Brett, *Lawrence and Brett: A Friendship* (London: Martin Secker, 1933), p. 79.

16. T. S. Eliot, 'The Metaphysical Poets' (1921), in Eliot, *Selected Essays*, p. 289; Mina Loy, 'Gertrude Stein', in *The Last Lunar Baedeker*, ed. Roger L. Conover (Manchester: Carcanet, 1982), p. 297.

17. T. S. Eliot, 'Tradition and the Individual Talent', in Eliot, *Selected Essays*, p. 17; Virginia Woolf, *The Essays of Virginia Woolf*, ed. Andrew McNeillie (London: Hogarth Press, 1986–), vol. 2 (1987), p. 436.

18. Woolf, *Essays of Virginia Woolf*, vol. 2, p. 59; T. S. Eliot, '*Ulysses*, Order, and Myth', in T. S. Eliot, *Selected Prose of T. S. Eliot*, ed. Frank Kermode (London: Faber and Faber, 1975), p. 177.

19. Virginia Woolf, 'Modern Fiction', in Woolf, *Selected Essays*, p. 6; D. H. Lawrence, *The Lost Girl* (Harmondsworth: Penguin Books, [1920] 1980), p. 59.

20. Woolf, *Essays of Virginia Woolf*, vol. 3, p. 429.

21. Virginia Woolf, 'Diary entry', 27 June 1925, in Virginia Woolf, *The Diary of Virginia Woolf*, vol. 3, ed. Anne Olivier Bell, assisted by Andrew McNeillie (London: Hogarth Press, 1980), p. 34.

22. James Joyce, *The Letters of James Joyce*, vol. 3, ed. Richard Ellmann (London: Faber and Faber, 1966), p. 146.

23. T. S. Eliot, 'The Function of Criticism', in Eliot, *Selected Essays*, p. 24.

24. Wyndham Lewis, *Tarr: The 1918 Version* (Santa Barbara: Black Sparrow Press, [1918] 1990), p. 13.

25. Mary Butts, 'Taking Thought', *Time and Tide*, 14.24 (17 June 1933), p. 738.

26. Mary Butts, 'Diary entry', 8 December 1919, in Mary Butts, *The Journals of Mary Butts*, ed. Nathalie Blondel (New Haven: Yale University Press, 2002), p. 121.

27. *The Lost Lunar Baedeker* (1996), p. 75.

28. D. H. Lawrence, *Lady Chatterley's Lover* (Harmondsworth: Penguin Books, [1928] 1961), p. 124.

29. Jean Rhys, *Good Morning, Midnight* (London: Penguin Books, [1939] 2000), p. 147.

30. See C. H. Rolph (ed.), *The Trial of Lady Chatterley: Regina v. Penguin Books, Ltd.* (London: Penguin Books, 1990), p. 25.

31. Ezra Pound, 'I Gather the Limbs of Osiris', in Pound, *Selected Prose: 1909–1965*, p. 23.

32. E. M. Forster, *Howards End* (London: Penguin Books, [1910] 1989), p. 213.

33. Marcel Proust, *Remembrance of Things Past*, vol. 2, trans. C. K. Scott Moncrieff and Terence Kilmartin (Harmondsworth: Penguin Books, 1981), p. 1029.

34. Wyndham Lewis, *The Revenge for Love* (Harmondsworth: Penguin Books, [1937] 1982), p. 354.

35. James Joyce, *Finnegans Wake* (London: Faber and Faber, [1939] 1975), p. 205.

36. Mary Butts, *Death of Felicity Taverner* (London: Wishart, 1932), p. 184.

37. Marcel Proust, *Remembrance of Things Past*, vol. 3, trans. C. K. Scott Moncrieff and Terence Kilmartin (Harmondsworth: Penguin Books, 1989), p. 95.

38. Virginia Woolf, *To the Lighthouse* (Oxford: Oxford University Press, [1927] 2000), p. 41.

39. Ezra Pound, 'A Retrospect' (1918), in Ezra Pound, *Literary Essays of Ezra Pound*, ed. T. S. Eliot (London: Faber and Faber, 1968), p. 8.

40. W. H. Auden, 'Here War is Simple like a Monument', in W. H. Auden, *Selected Poems* (London: Faber and Faber, 1979), p. 72.

41. Woolf, *Essays of Virginia Woolf*, vol. 2, p. 164.

42. E. M. Forster, *A Passage To India* (Harmondsworth: Penguin Books, [1924] 1979), p. 287.

43. Wilfred Owen, in Jon Silkin (ed.), *The Penguin Book of First World War Poetry* (Harmondsworth: Penguin Books, 1996), p. 193.

44. Virginia Woolf, 'Before Midnight', in Woolf, *Essays of Virginia Woolf*, vol. 2, p. 87.

45. Ezra Pound, 'Jean Cocteau Sociologist', in Pound, *Selected Prose: 1909–1965*, p. 403.

46. T. S. Eliot, 'Reflections on *Vers Libre*' (1917), in Eliot, *Selected Prose*, p. 91.

47. Eliot, 'Reflections on *Vers Libre*' (1917), in Eliot, *Selected Prose*, p. 88.

48. T. S. Eliot, *The Use of Poetry and the Use of Criticism* (London: Faber and Faber, 1933), p. 155.

49. Eliot, 'Reflections on *Vers Libre*' (1917), in Eliot, *Selected Prose*, p. 88.

50. The 'you' of this line has been variously interpreted. Maud Ellmann asks: 'Is the you, here, male or female, dead or alive? A lover or a friend? An alter ego or an effigy?' See Maud Ellmann, 'The Spider and the Weevil: Self and Writing in Eliot's Poetry', in Richard Machin and Christopher Norris (eds), *Post-Structuralist Readings of English Poetry* (Cambridge: Cambridge University Press, 1987), p. 380.

51. See the lines 'To have bitten off the matter with a smile, / To have squeezed the universe into a ball'.

52. T. S. Eliot, 'The Waste Land', l.38–40, in T. S. Eliot, *The Complete Poems and Plays* (London: Faber and Faber, 1969), p. 62.

53. T. S. Eliot, 'Four Quartets', in Eliot, *Complete Poems and Plays*, p. 202.

54. T. S. Eliot, 'Four Quartets', in Eliot, *Complete Poems and Plays*, p. 208.

55. T. S. Eliot, 'The Metaphysical Poets', in Eliot, *Selected Prose*, p. 65.

56. T. E. Hulme, 'Romanticism and Classicism', in *Speculations*, ed. Herbert Read (London: Routledge and Kegan Paul, 1960), p. 122.

57. James Joyce, *Ulysses: The Corrected Text*, ed. Hans Walter Gabler with Wolfhard Steppe and Claus Melchior (London: Bodley Head, 1986), p. 690.

58. May Sinclair, 'Review of *Pilgrimage*', in Vassiliki Kolocotroni, Jane A. Goldman and Olga Taxidou (eds), *Modernism: An Anthology of Sources and Documents* (Edinburgh: Edinburgh University Press, 1998), p. 352.

59. Valery Larbaud, 'The *Ulysses* of James Joyce', *The Criterion*, 1.1 (October 1922), p. 96.
60. Lawrence Edward Bowling, 'What is the Stream of Consciousness Technique?', *PMLA*, 65.4 (June 1950), p. 341.
61. Joyce, *Ulysses*, p. 31.
62. Joyce, *Ulysses*, p. 95.
63. Dorothy Richardson, *Pilgrimage* (London: Virago, 1979), vol. 1, pp. 244–5.
64. D. H. Lawrence, *Women in Love* (Harmondsworth: Penguin Books, [1921] 1979), p. 361.
65. Virginia Woolf, *Mrs Dalloway* (Oxford: Oxford University Press, [1925] 2008), p. 43.
66. Virginia Woolf, 'Phases of Fiction', in Virginia Woolf, *Collected Essays*, vol. 2 (London: Hogarth Press, 1966), p. 83.

CHAPTER I

Modernist Networks, 1914–28: Futurists, Imagists, Vorticists, Dadaists

Modernism, in its initial stages, was both vigorously individualistic and collaborative. The promotion and dissemination of Eliot's and Joyce's innovative writing did not take place in a vacuum. This book will use the word 'networks' to describe the artistic, social, publishing and communication links between writers in the years 1914–28. Other critics have created images of webs or pictorial diagrams to represent modernist ties.[1] The word 'network' aims to capture the loose but semi-institutionalised connections which informed the production and dissemination of modernist books.

Modernist networks were international. The focus of this chapter will therefore be on four years and three geographical locations: London, 1914, New York, 1917 and Paris, 1922; the chapter concludes with a discussion of a number of texts published in 1928. Modernist writers were more scattered and worked less collaboratively by the late 1920s. The chapter aims to capture the sheer range and innovativeness of literary experiment in the period.

The beginnings of modernism are to be found in the group activities of artists and writers. Some created labels for themselves and issued manifestos, or rules for writing. There were Italian and Russian Futurists, the London-based Imagists and Vorticists, Dadaists in Zurich and New York and Surrealists in Paris. Some of the groups are less well known or fall outside the remit of this book: the German Expressionists issued declarations about visual art and drama in the early 1910s, and an 'Eccentric Manifesto' was published to promote a group of Petrograd artists in 1922. Despite the wide range of groups, the individuals involved in these activities shared a number of aims. Many of the statements crafted in manifestos were deliberately outrageous and revolutionary. They aimed to offend, to tear up the literary styles of the past, to blur the divide between art and life, to say something new.

There were other ways of collaborating and forming group identities in the period. Some artistic connections and principles of composition were forged through the editorship of modernist journals. A huge number of new journals appeared in the 1910s and 1920s. They were often short-lived because of lack of funds or waning interest.[2] But these journals were often significant forums for the dissemination of new styles of writing and for the collection and promotion of groups of writers. They also made divergent claims about what made writing modern and which writers exemplified the modern spirit. For a time, for instance, Ford Madox Ford's London-based journal the *English Review* promoted new writing by Lawrence, Lewis, Yeats and Pound and seemed to be at the forefront of developments in English-language writing. But across the Atlantic there were competing claims. In 1917 the journal *Others* assembled together the work of four poets – Wallace Stevens, William Carlos Williams, Mina Loy and Marianne Moore. The journal announced that here were the writers leading developments in modern poetry.

Poems and novels were also legitimised through the lists of newly formed publishing firms. Numerous publishing houses sprang up in the 1920s and 1930s, often to bring out work that had been censored by the US or British authorities. Sylvia Beach created an entirely new firm, Shakespeare and Company, in order to publish a single book which had been banned for obscenity: James Joyce's *Ulysses*. Other Paris-based presses, such as Robert McAlmon's Contact Press and Jack Kahane's Obelisk Press, specifically published English-language books that had been suppressed by the US or English courts. Kahane's list included risqué works such as Henry Miller's *Tropic of Cancer* and avant-garde texts such as James Joyce's *Pomes Penyeach*.

The social and sexual connections between artists and writers were also significant. Modernism was partly a product of a café society in which writers from across the world would drink, talk and collaborate. With the entrance of financially independent women writers and artists into the public sphere, café society was sexualised, something that writers were keen to depict in novels and poems. Mina Loy describes the 'Eyes that are full of love / And eyes that are full of kohl' in her early poem 'Café du Néant' (1914).[3] In *Women in Love* Lawrence satirises the pretentious, hysterical and sexualised bohemian conversations in a London café: Gerald feels he is 'entering in some strange element, passing into an illuminated new region, among a host of licentious souls'.[4] The licentious element of café society is also a feature of Lewis's description of Lord Osmund's Lenten party in *The Apes of God* (1930). While the party descends into chaos as the general strike infiltrates the privileged world of aristocrats and artists, 'everyone raised contrary cries, some for and some against, and there was a drunken fight proceeding because one woman accused another of having stolen her man'.[5]

Literary, publishing and social networks were central to the international promotion and distribution of modernist writing. They also had a significant impact on the formal and thematic innovations of the period. But as this chapter will reveal, the collaborative efforts of modernists often seemed in tension with the experimental individualism of modernist texts.

LONDON, 1914

London's position as the financial and industrial capital of the world made it a magnet for writers, and a publishing centre, in the early 1910s. In 1914, English writers Ford Madox Ford (originally Hueffer), T. E. Hulme, and D. H. Lawrence were living in central London. But it was the foreign visitors to London, including F. T. Marinetti, Ezra Pound, H. D., Wyndham Lewis and T. S. Eliot, who were to shake things up in the poetry world. It was during 1914 that a number of important artistic collaborations were either initiated or came to fruition.

In September, Eliot went to visit Pound for the first time.

He showed him some of his poems and was flattered at Pound's positive response. Eliot remembered that 'in 1914 . . . my meeting with Ezra Pound changed my life'.[6] Pound was equally excited and immediately offered to help Eliot publish 'The Love Song of J. Alfred Prufrock' in the Chicago-based *Poetry* magazine. So began a literary friendship that would see Pound helping Eliot substantially with the composition of *The Waste Land*, an influence Eliot credited in the poem's dedication: 'For Ezra Pound, *il miglior fabbro*'.[7] The impact of Eliot's 'Love Song' was instantaneous. Here, Pound announced, was a poem which was genuinely new.

Pound's role as facilitator and energiser was also important for another new literary friendship. After many delays, Joyce's first collection of short stories, *Dubliners*, had finally been published by London publisher Grant Richards in 1914. In the same year, Pound used his position as literary editor of *The Egoist* to help bring out instalments of Joyce's first novel, *A Portrait of the Artist as a Young Man*. He also became involved in defending the realism of Joyce's writing, both in letters to publishers and in essays. In 'Dubliners and Mr. James Joyce', an essay published in *The Egoist* in July 1914, he discussed Joyce's short stories: 'he gives the thing as it is. He is not bound by the tiresome convention that any part of life, to be interesting, must be shaped into the conventional form of a "story".'[8] This statement champions the realism and narrative innovations of Joyce's writing. It also reveals Pound's own desire to shake off literary conventions and replace them with an understated and clear rendering of the external world.

Alongside the creation of literary connections with Eliot and Joyce in 1914, Pound was also at the centre of a London-based group of poets who were interested in modernising poetry. The oldest member of this group was Ford Madox Ford, who had started being published in the 1890s, but continued to write until his death in 1939. Ford's work bridges some of the more aestheticised concerns of *fin de siècle* writing and the social engagement of later modernism. He was an influential writer and publisher. He founded two important journals, the *English Review* in 1908, which published and promoted work by Lawrence, Yeats, Forster, Pound and Lewis, and the *Transatlantic Review* in Paris in 1923, which brought out risqué work by Pound, Joyce, Eliot, Rhys and

Hemingway. Another key figure on the London scene in 1914 was T. E. Hulme, who wrote a number of bold and provocative essays about modern art and poetry. His most influential essay, 'Romanticism and Classicism' (1912), controversially announced that the language and concerns of Romantic poetry were tired and outdated, and that England was ready for a 'new classicism' in the arts, a classicism he defined as linguistically concise and emotionally reserved. While the links between Joyce's fictional realism, Pound's 'thing as it is' and Hulme's poetic classicism might not seem obvious at first, there were shared concerns. Not only did all three writers want to promote a writing which was realistic, clinical and emotionally constrained, they were also keen to promote the novelty and modernity of this literary focus.

It was F. T. Marinetti's visits to London in 1910 and 1912, however, which were to galvanise these different poets into action. Marinetti, a young and wealthy Italian from Florence, engaged in a series of promotional lecture tours, art exhibitions and publications for his avant-garde movement, Futurism. He had first set out his artistic and linguistic principles in 'The Founding and Manifesto of Futurism' in 1909, in which he declared that art, rather than being something created and legitimated in institutional contexts such as the museum, the art academy and the university, is a product of the spontaneous and anarchic energies of metropolitan streets and crowds. Rather than looking backwards at the literary tradition for ideas of beauty, writers should celebrate and embody the products and processes of modernisation. His manifesto demands that art be audacious, revolutionary and absurd. He promotes what he calls the 'inhuman' artistic energies of the crowd, arsenals, shipyards, electricity, factories, cars and locomotives. Marinetti is specifically interested in the unpredictable and thereby 'futuristic' activities and tendencies of groups. This is an aesthetic that, by extolling the modern, seeks to embody it.

Marinetti's manifesto was a hybrid form declaring war on the establishment. He called for a new freedom in words and acts, and for the destabilisation of boundaries between visual and linguistic art, high and low, art and life. His aesthetic was grotesque, obscene and dynamic. While his manifestos set out their artistic aims as though the Futurists were a political party, they also narrate stories about the activities of Marinetti and what he calls his Futurist 'friends'. We are told details about their youth, energy, arguments and 'frenzied scribbling', as though their collective artistic impulses are so vigorous and overwhelming they have no choice but to run into the streets and express themselves. Marinetti creates pictures of the artist plunging headlong into the city's crowds, mess and energy: 'Fair factory drain! I gulped down your nourishing sludge'.[9] *Zang Tumb Tuuum* (1912–14) exemplifies more forcefully this Futurist aesthetic absorbed in both the details of machines and movement, and in the mechanical organisation of words on the page: 'exploding roasting + speed + ferocity of the tires coal dust of the street thirst thirst of the rubber cactus'.[10]

Marinetti addressed crowds by insulting them, and thereby attempting to jolt them out of habits of thought. His was a theatrical aesthetic, which emerged from performances in concert halls and vaudeville palaces. His *Variety Theater Manifesto* (1913) sought to transform theatre into 'a theatre of amazement, record-setting and body-madness'.[11] When he spoke to a London audience in 1910, he accused the English of snobbery, anti-intellectualism and puritanism. But, he also commended the English love of liberty, struggle and pugilism. London's status as the financial and political centre of the world meant that is was, as Marinetti declared, the Futurist city 'par excellence'.

Marinetti launched an exhibition of Futurist paintings in London in 1912 and his activities were covered in the mainstream press. His success sparked intense debate among Hulme, Pound and Wyndham Lewis. Why not an Anglo-American equivalent? If English-language writers wanted to promote their activities, did they need a collaborative manifesto in order to do so? And could they tap into the advertising possibilities of being oppositional and futuristic, as Marinetti had achieved so successfully?

H. D. recalled, in a later novel, *Bid Me To Live*, 'It was a time of isms', and Pound launched the first Anglo-American 'ism', Imagism, in 1914 to promote a classical and succinct poetry.[12] There were four annual anthologies published between 1914 and 1917, *Des Imagistes* (1914) and three follow-up volumes titled *Some Imagist Poets* (1915, 1916, 1917), a manifesto in 1915 and a much later anthology brought out by American poet Amy Lowell in

1930. F. S. Flint and Pound had also published earlier essays about Imagism in the American *Poetry* magazine in 1913. Seven people were significantly connected with the movement: Pound, H. D., Aldington, Lowell and Flint, as well as John Gould Fletcher and D. H. Lawrence.

Des Imagistes included a slightly eclectic mix of poems, but the group name allowed Pound to tap into and promote a collective poetic style. He claimed for the Imagists a novelty and importance that challenged the power and values of existing publishers, reviewers for newspapers such as *The Times* and journals, such as the newly formed *Times Literary Supplement*.

Pound's two essays 'A Few Don'ts by an Imagiste' (1913) and 'Preface to *Some Imagist Poets*' (1915) set out a number of literary aims for the group. He suggested that poets use the 'language of common speech', create new rhythms, enjoy the liberty of free verse and make the image central to the poem. These rules were designed to demarcate a clinical and streamlined modern aesthetic distinct from Romantic poetry.

The most successful Imagist poet was H. D., who had been briefly engaged to Pound in America in 1907. She had travelled to England in 1912 and married an English poet, Richard Aldington. After the breakdown of their marriage, she met the wealthy heiress Winefred Ellerman, who called herself Bryher, with whom she lived for the next forty years. Her first volume of poems, *Sea Garden* (1916), was followed by *Red Roses for Bronze* (1931), *Trilogy* (1944–6) and *Helen in Egypt* (1961), and novels, including *Her* (written 1927; first published 1981) and *Bid Me To Live* (written 1927; first published 1960).

When H. D. arrived in London in 1912, she both renewed her friendship with Pound and created one of the first Imagist poems, 'Hermes of the Ways' (1914). It begins:

> The hard sand breaks,
> and the grains of it
> are clear as wine.
> Far off over the leagues of it,
> the wind,
> playing on the wide shore,

> piles little ridges,
> and the great waves
> break over it.[13]

H. D.'s is a very different kind of free verse to that of 'The Love Song of J. Alfred Prufrock'. Her poetic lines, free as they are, often rely on the incantatory repetition of words or grammatical conjunctions. These rhythmical connections bind together the images which are the basic unit of significance. Some of her images are unusual and rely on the shock of unlikely connections, such as her images of sea and wind in another poem, 'Oread' ('Whirl up, sea – / whirl your pointed pines').[14] Yet others are more notable for their visual clarity and emotional restraint, such as this opening stanza of 'Hermes of the Ways'. By restricting its focus to the minute particulars of sand, the poem invites us to respond to the visual dimensions of language. By removing any linguistic excess, each word is isolated and highlighted. H. D. applies this attention to nouns, as in the wind above, and adjectives: a later stanza detaches the activities of the Greek god Hermes as 'Dubious / facing three ways'.

Many readers have commented that her poems read as though they are like translations from Greek poetry. The words in H. D.'s poems feel both pristine and estranged, a bit like translated words. The effect is to create an arresting and alienated temporal dimension: her lines both refer to Greek poetry and seem bleached of history.

As she developed her precise and timeless poetic and prose voice over the next two decades, H. D. would use the clear-cut diction of these early Imagist poems to penetrate and describe the mind. Rather than representing the psyche as a source of value or order, H. D.'s poems tend to represent it as torn, scattered, and unstable. In another early poem 'Mid-day' she pictures a psyche raw with exposure to external stimuli:

> The light beats upon me.
> I am startled –
> A split leaf crackles on the paved floor –
> I am anguished – defeated.
> A slight wind shakes the seed-pods –

my thoughts are spent
as the black seeds.
My thoughts tear me[15]

H. D.'s visually arresting images of the leaf which crackles and the
seed-pods that shake are juxtaposed with an 'I' in various states
of abjection. The lines rest on implied similes, with the images of
the leaf and seeds carrying the visual meaning of the psychological trauma. In his 'rules' for poets, Pound commented on the way
that Imagist techniques could give a new and significant access to
psychological states. He claimed that 'An "Image" is that which
presents an intellectual and emotional complex in an instant of
time' and indicates that he uses the word complex 'in the techni-
cal sense employed by the newer psychologists'.[16] H. D.'s images
embody references to being 'split', cracking and shaking, movements created by the external power of wind and light. By being
juxtaposed with mental states these external images evoke the
mind's uncontrollable, and unconscious, energies. The mind is
certainly split apart in this poem – 'my thoughts tear me' – but it is
the natural imagery which communicates an almost visceral sense
of mental discomfort. H.D.'s poems are notable for the economy
of their language, their startling imagistic juxtapositions and
psychic intensity. She would go on to use these poetic techniques
to explore classical and psychological themes, often focusing on
Greek gods or goddesses and gendered dynamics.

Pound's Imagist poems tend to be less psychological. 'In a Station
of the Metro' has a clinging wet petal, rather than a leaf, which
represents the fragile and transitory dimensions of the moment:

The apparition of these faces in the crowd;
Petals on a wet, black bough.

There are visual connections between the pale faces in the crowd
and the petals on the black bough, but the poem is grounded in the
momentary juxtaposition of unlike urban and natural images. The
poem's effects lie in the new linguistic connections that are forged
out of lines which conflict with each other in space and time.

Pound's rules for writing, and the poems in the Imagist

anthology, look tepid and careful when placed next to Marinetti's Futurist manifestos, but the differences reveal limitations on both sides. Marinetti's iconoclastic transgressions were fundamentally different to the aims of Pound, H. D., Eliot and Lawrence, who were interested in re-interpreting and repositioning the words of the past. For Pound, modern poetry was always a more scholarly and less celebratory affair than the absurd and transgressive Futurist avant-garde. He had begun his poetic career as a translator of poems from medieval and Romance languages, and his early poems in *A Lume Spento* (1908), *Personae* (1909) and *Exultations* (1909) are often studies in the spirit of translation on subjects ranging from the Provençal troubadour Peire Vidal (1175–1215) to the texts of Browning and Yeats. H. D. and Eliot, in their focus on Greek writing and seventeenth-century poetry, also sought to make the words of the past live in the present.

Yet, Futurism, by clearly signalling its relationship to metropolitan and technological energies, had an enviable excitement and boldness that Imagism clearly lacked. It was partly for this reason that Pound's Imagist phase did not last long. There was also a simplicity about his rules in 'A Few Don'ts by an Imagiste' that served both to popularise the movement and to dilute its ambitions. When Amy Lowell tried to take control of the group, Pound quickly jumped ship and belittled her aims by calling the movement 'Amygism'. He, in any case, was already involved with a new collaborator, Wyndham Lewis, and a new movement, Vorticism.

Wyndham Lewis was born in Canada, but educated in England. After travelling in Europe and studying in Paris in the early 1900s, he settled in London in 1908. Lewis was an accomplished painter, as well as a prolific writer. He produced groundbreaking First World War paintings and was connected to other visual artists such as Edward Wadsworth, Jacob Epstein, Cuthbert Hamilton and the sculptor Henri Gaudier-Brzeska through the Rebel Art Centre. The group concretised its aims when it published an audaciously pink and large avant-garde journal called *Blast* in 1914. Lewis went on to write a number of innovative novels, including *Tarr* (1918), *The Childermass* (1928), *The Apes of God* (1930) and *The Revenge for Love* (1937), as well as works of criticism and philosophy, such as *Time and Western Man* (1927) and *Men Without Art* (1934).

The Vorticists, unlike the Imagists, synthesised ideas about the modernity of literature and visual art, and their manifestos present a theory of writing that was essentially spatial. The word 'Vorticist' comes from physics and generally denotes a whirling motion of a fluid, or atoms whose movement forms a cavity in the centre. The Vortex is a 'radiant node or cluster . . . a VORTEX, from which, and through which, and into which, ideas are constantly rushing'.[17] The Vorticists argued that painting, poetry and prose should include a raw kind of energy, balanced or controlled by an organisational still point at its centre. The writing in *Blast* effectively embodies ideas of energy by manipulating the visual qualities of typography, page layout and capitalisation, as well as the violent expression of vitriolic sentiments. The words, then, seem to shout out of the page:

BLAST First (from politeness) **ENGLAND**
CURSE ITS CLIMATE FOR ITS SINS AND INFECTIONS
DISMAL SYMBOL, SET round our bodies,
        of effeminate lout within.
VICTORIAN VAMPIRE, the LONDON cloud sucks
        the TOWN'S heart.[18]

The journal 'blasts', or criticises, an impressively wide array of things: nation states, people, historical periods, human emotions and objects. The typography, parataxis and cursing owe a lot to Marinetti's manifestos and Futurist texts. Like Marinetti's 'Founding and Manifesto of Futurism', *Blast* also expresses a strident iconoclasm which challenges English class divisions and snobbery, education, academic knowledge and the art establishment. Modern art, in place of these moribund institutions, should tap into the 'crude energy' and 'unconsciousness of humanity'.[19]

The lines above picture the airs of London as unhealthy and vampiric, surrounding and penetrating the individual body. Unlike Marinetti's desire to jump into the factory sludge of industrial London, the city's energies have a sinister edge here, threatening to suck the life out of its inhabitants. The idea that the artist needs both to embrace the crude energies of the metropolis and to defend him or herself from its swirling energies is helpful in understanding the Vorticist balancing act between the avant-garde activities of the group and its individualistic philosophy. *Blast*, Lewis declares, both appeals 'TO THE INDIVIDUAL' and celebrates an artistic individualism: the moment 'a man feels or realizes himself as an artist, he ceases to belong to any milieu or time'.[20] At the same time, however, the Vorticists made claims for themselves as a group distinct from the Futurists. With a pugilistic nod to Marinetti's claim that London was a Futurist city, Pound described living in the 'vortex' of London. The opening manifesto accuses the Futurists of wanting to 'change the appearance of the world'.[21] The Vorticists criticise the Futurists for an artistic passivity in their response to the visual world. Marinetti's leap into the crowds and speeding machines of the metropolis merely results in the documentation of accelerated energies and objects. The task, according to Lewis and Pound, is to control or make sense of them. The claim that Vorticist art occupies a still point in the midst of the unconscious energies of modern life is helpful when considering the visual art in *Blast*. In Lewis's paintings and Gaudier-Brzeska's sculptures there is a balance between the realistic depiction of the human form or city crowds and a stylistic abstraction or non-mimesis. The two elements are fused in the painting, which expresses and contains an object which seems to strain at its edges.

It was less clear in *Blast* how Vorticist principles could be realised in writing. The journal included some poems by Pound whose Vorticist energy seems to rest largely on slinging insults at the literary establishment. 'Salutation the Third' declares: 'Let us deride the smugness of "The Times": / GUFFAW! / So much the gagged reviewers'.[22] *Blast* also published an instalment of Ford's novel *The Good Soldier* and Rebecca West's 'Indissoluble Matrimony'. These texts, however, failed to match the novelty of the visual art in the journal. It is perhaps Wyndham Lewis's Expressionist play *The Enemy of the Stars* which comes closest to creating a radical writing practice working with Vorticist principles. It focuses on two characters, Arghol and Hanp, who fight and argue in the midst of swirling universal energies. But a question mark is left hanging with regard to *Blast 1*: how might the Vorticist principles that had been so clearly and loudly shouted from the journal be realised in poetry and prose?

Just a few months after the appearance of *Blast*, however, the world was at war, and the Imagist and Vorticist groups began to disintegrate, either because individuals went to fight or because they sought to escape London. But the literary connections that were forged in London in 1914 would prove central to subsequent artistic projects. The publication of *Des Imagistes* and *Blast*, the close poetic friendship between Pound and Eliot, as well as Pound's collaboration with Joyce, Lewis and H. D. were vital to future texts. The composition of *The Waste Land* and the publication of *Ulysses* in the *Little Review* were partly a result of friendships formed in 1914. The literary principles that had been discussed and promoted in 1914 would also prove significant. The promotion of a new classicism in poetry, the focus on restrained imagery, free verse and the unconscious would all be developed in future texts. The anti-establishment thrust of 1914 modernism was also foundational for modernist writing. Pound, Eliot and Lewis developed a clear understanding of the artistic value of claims to literary novelty and transgression. They also realised the importance of creating the means with which to disseminate and promote their work. All three would go on to edit journals and write essays to promote their own versions of what modern writing should look like. Their visions would, as it turned out, be very different.

NEW YORK, 1917

The First World War scattered the individuals who had been involved in artistic activity in London in 1914, and broke up the Imagist and Vorticist groups. Many of the key figures of London intellectual life fought in the war, and many of them died. Ford Madox Ford, Wyndham Lewis and Richard Aldington all went to the front and limped home. The sculptor Henri Gaudier-Brzeska and the philosopher and art critic T. E. Hulme died there. Lewis succeeded in issuing one more *Blast*, what he called a 'war number', but the war damaged the diversity of its essay and picture contributions.

While artistic and literary activity continued during the war, wartime conditions made international publishing and communication more difficult. The war also had a profound impact on the parameters and themes of literature. It destabilised already fragile class and gender hierarchies, and made the aggressively militaristic rhetoric of Futurists and Vorticists seem inappropriate. Marinetti's statement, for instance, that war is the 'world's only hygiene' sat awkwardly with writers who now confronted war at first hand. A number of writers who did not fight, either because they were declared to be physically unfit to do so, such as Lawrence and Eliot, or because they were not eligible, such as most of the women modernist writers, engaged with the war in their writing of the 1910s and 1920s.[23]

There were also a host of writers and artists who wanted to escape the fighting, and who eschewed the militaristic rhetoric that had featured in Futurist and Vorticist manifestos. A new movement came to prominence during 1915 which was specifically anti-war. Neutral Zurich offered a safe place for German and Romanian writers and artists such as Hugo Ball, Richard Huelsenbeck and Tristan Tzara, and the famous Café Voltaire became the meeting-place that spawned a name – Dada – and a number of manifestos and declarations.

Dada was pacifist, anarchic, anti-bourgeois and facetiously anti-art. André Breton declared that Dada describes, not a politics or a particular artistic school, but 'a state of mind'.[24] In his 'Dada Manifesto' of 1918, Tzara evoked the contours of this new aesthetic:

DADA; the elegant and unprejudiced leap from one harmony to another sphere; the trajectory of a word, a cry, thrown into the air like an acoustic disc; to respect all individualities in their folly of the moment, whether serious, fearful, timid, ardent, vigorous, decided or enthusiastic[25]

Tzara expresses a delight in the graceful gesture and the just word. His leaps, cries, throws and follies tap into the aesthetic pleasures of linguistic spontaneity and aestheticised bodies.

Groups that were loosely connected to Dada sprang up across

Europe, with centres in Barcelona, Berlin and Paris. But the most significant unofficial Dada city was New York, which, until America entered the war in 1917, was also a safe haven from military conflict. The artists and writers who collected in New York from 1915 to 1917 did not officially use the word Dada until the publication of the journal *New York Dada* in 1921. But they comprised a loose Dada group. They included European expatriates Marcel Duchamp, Francis Picabia, Mina Loy, Elsa von Freytag-Loringhoven and Arthur Cravan and Americans Man Ray, William Carlos Williams, Djuna Barnes, Wallace Stevens, Alfred Kreymborg and Carl Van Vechten. The organisational heart of this group was the wealthy poet Walter Arensberg, who opened up his apartment to groups of artists and writers from 1915 to 1918.

In 1915, Duchamp, newly arrived from Paris, turned up at Arensberg's apartment in the middle of a snowstorm. He promptly produced a snow shovel that he had bought at a hardware shop, and called it 'Advance of the Broken Arm'. It was his first American 'readymade', a term that simply designates the process of taking or buying an object, giving it a name and placing it in an artistic space: a gallery, a café or an apartment full of artists. By so doing, the significance of the object, and the space in which it is placed, are transformed. Like Marinetti's Futurists, this gesture seeks to destabilise the values and boundaries of the art gallery or the museum. But where Marinetti's actions are destructive and hostile Duchamp's art objects transgress by way of humour and irony.

Duchamp's most famous readymade appeared in the Independents Exhibition at the Grand Central Palace in April 1917, just before America sent its first troops to fight in the war.[26] Called 'Fountain', it was a urinal placed on a black pedestal, and signed 'R. Mutt'. Not only did this controversial object incite debate about the proper boundaries of art, the means by which this was achieved were groundbreaking. Duchamp's anonymity was assured by his use of a pseudonym, 'R. Mutt', a gesture that blocked any attempt to relate questions about the artistic status of the object back to its creator. The effect was to remove the artistic aggressor of Futurist writing and art, and leave a space in which the art object speaks for itself. The art work raised a number of questions: if not the artist, then who or what serves to frame questions about its artistic value? Does the gallery legitimate the object as art? Is it the case that everyday objects such as the urinal have aesthetic qualities if looked at with an artistic eye? Does this process of repositioning destroy the associations of the object with human waste and disgust?

These questions and artistic gestures feed the poetry, drama and fiction of the period. One of the most exciting of the new writers was Mina Loy, a London-born poet who travelled from Florence to New York in 1917. She published a number of poems in the New York journal *Others*, and was declared to be one of the most important of the new generation of poets in the journal in 1917. Here was an English-language modernism distinct from the aesthetic values espoused by the London-based Imagists and Vorticists.

Loy, who had lived in Florence in the early 1910s, had originally been connected to the Italian Futurists, and had a brief affair with Marinetti. She humorously described this experience as like having sex with a piston, a statement that captures some of the features of her writing: she produced sexually explicit, feminist, free verse and witty poems. Her subjects were fellow artists, love, sex, the cultural status of art, the position of women and the anti-Semitism experienced by her Jewish father at the hands of petty bourgeois Londoners. Her 'Aphorisms on Futurism' were published in the New York journal *Camera Work* in 1914, and they playfully asked readers to 'Live in the Future' and to 'LOVE the hideous in order to find the sublime core of it'.[27]

Her first poems, such as 'Parturition', 'Virgins Plus Curtains Minus Dots', and 'Three Moments in Paris', were Futurist and feminist satires. In the first four of her 'Love Songs', which were published in the New York journal *Others* in 1915, she removed the narrative frame that had featured in these early satires, and created poems defined by their visually arresting form. Here is the first stanza of Love Song 1:

> Spawn   of   Fantasies
> Silting the appraisable
> Pig Cupid   his rosy snout
> Rooting erotic garbage

"Once upon a time"
Pulls a weed   white star-topped
Among wild oats   sown in mucous membrane[28]

The lines are like a poetic version of a Cubist painting. The phrases are organised paratactically – which means arranged without connectives – rather than causally connected. It is as though Loy has thrown onto the page a number of different phrases related to the themes of love and song. In accordance with its cubistically spatial form, the registers of these lines are also deliberately distinct from one another. Scientific words such as spawn and mucous membrane sit next to Romantic narrative clichés, such as 'Once upon a time'. Loy includes witty and obscene imagery: Pig Cupid is a visually arresting conflation of pigs and cupids which alters our view of both. The Cupid's 'rosy snout / rooting' both disrupts conventions and synthesises sex and waste, a register enforced in the phrase 'erotic garbage'. The lines also shift abruptly from the microcosmic and low – the spawn, the mucous membrane – to the elevated 'star-topped', and act as a corollary to her statement that the 'sublime core' lies within the hideous.

But Loy's writing is distinct from the Futurism of Marinetti. Unlike Marinetti's avoidance of introspection, Loy was keen to incorporate a language of selfhood, particularly some of the new psychological terms developed by Freud, into these poems. The concluding stanza of 'Love Song 1' has the lines: 'I must live in my lantern / Trimming subliminal flicker'. Loy leaves it open whether this subliminal light is another bit of romanticised rhetorical garbage akin to 'Once upon a time' or part of a new psychoanalytic language of the self.

Loy's participation in the artistic group of Duchamp and Arensberg in 1917 prompted her to mark clearly her distance from the Futurists with whom she had once collaborated. In 'Lion's Jaws' (1920) she ridicules the gender politics of the 'flabbergast movement / hurled by the leader Raminetti' into the art circles of Europe, and also sends herself up, describing a 'flabbergast child' hiding behind various Duchamp-esque pseudonyms: 'Nima Lyo, alias Anim Yol, alias / Imna Oly / (secret service buffoon to the Woman's Cause)'. There was an element of childishness and buffoonery to Dada gestures and texts which was distinct from the vitriolic elements of Futurism and Vorticism. Here, Loy's tone, like that of Duchamp's objects, is both ironic, and gentle, working to ridicule herself, as much as anyone else. The cubistic form of her 'Love Songs' specifically refuses to create an overarching poetic authority to order her linguistic fragments.

PARIS, 1922

The post-war world was both unrecognisable from the one that had preceded it, and radically uncertain. The Russian revolution of 1917 unleashed a revolutionary politics that would change the balance of power in nation states across the globe. In the immediate post-war period, political revolution spread across eastern Europe. In 1919 Soviet-style workers revolts were declared in Germany. In 1921, Mussolini's Italian fascists marched on Rome and seized political power. Unsatisfactory political settlement was reached at Versailles in 1919, and political upheaval and uncertainty was to mark the next two decades until war broke out again in 1939.

Writers registered the war and these wider shifts in multiple ways. Virginia Woolf, in the character of Septimus Warren Smith in *Mrs Dalloway* (1925), records military conflict as unrecognised, brutalised and isolated psychological trauma. Ford Madox Ford, in *Parade's End*, depicts war as psychological amnesia: when Tietjens loses his memory in a bomb blast, a slice of British history and tradition is obliterated at a stroke. Pound, in 'Hugh Selwyn Mauberley', angrily identifies the real causes of the First World War as financial. The soldiers return 'home to old lies and new infamy / usury age-old and age-thick'. D. H. Lawrence wearily describes the spiritual breakdown and fragmentation unleashed by the war. In his novel *Kangaroo* he writes:

> The spirit of the old London collapsed. The city, in some way, perished, perished from being the heart of the world, and became a vortex of broken passions, lusts, hopes, fears, and horrors. The integrity of London collapsed, and the genuine debasement began.[29]

With the end of the war, artists and writers were also on the move again. Many who had travelled from Europe to New York journeyed back again. Most ended up in the city that would be the centre for modernist and avant-garde activity in the 1920s: Paris. Paris had long been the focus of European artistic and literary activity in the nineteenth century, but in the 1920s its famous Left Bank became the place where English-language writers lived and worked, and the publishing centre for modernist writing. There were a number of reasons for this. The US economy was booming in the 1920s and the strength of the dollar encouraged American writers to travel to Europe, where they could live incredibly cheaply.

There were also artistic reasons for seeking the communities of the Left Bank. In 1922, André Breton announced that Dada was dead, and convened a 'Congress of the Modern Spirit', which sought to forge a new artistic group. Within two years the Surrealists had a name and a manifesto. The Surrealists were the first avant-garde group to take Freud's ideas seriously, although Freud himself was bemused by their interpretation of his work. Breton argued that art and writing, by depicting the uncanny object, the chance encounter and the slip of the tongue, could unleash unconscious processes with radical aesthetic, moral and political possibilities. As he put it in his 'Surrealist Manifesto' of 1924, Surrealism is interested in unlocking 'the actual functioning of thought. Dictated by thought, in the absence of any control exercised by reason, exempt from any aesthetic of moral concern'.[30] Breton encouraged writers to record impulses, feelings, impressions, unregulated by reason and morality. Surrealist ideas and groups had a significant impact on some English-language modernist writers, often in a fairly loose way. Djuna Barnes, Mina Loy, Henry Miller, Anaïs Nin, Jean Rhys and Leonora Carrington can all be seen to incorporate elements of Surrealist ideas.

Writers also migrated to Paris because of the repressive censorship rules in Britain and America. In 'How to Read' (1928), Ezra Pound describes how he 'sought the banks of the Seine' because of his inability to find a British publisher.[31] Modernist writing was not only formally experimental; it was also often sexually explicit. Prohibition had severely curtailed literary freedom in America in the 1910s and early 1920s, and many publishers were wary of taking on the potentially expensive risk of bringing out risqué works. New publishers emerged, partly in order to avoid US and British censors, and in the 1920s, many of the key modernist texts were disseminated from Paris.

Pound arrived in Paris in 1921 and became acquainted with Ernest Hemingway, e. e. cummings, Jean Cocteau, Constantin Brâncuşi, Mina Loy, Djuna Barnes and Gertrude Stein, as well as renewing existing friendships with Joyce and others. Stein, who played host to a large number of the significant writers in Paris in the 1920s, had settled in the city decades before, declaring that 'Paris was where the twentieth century was'. She arrived in Paris in 1903, quickly made friends with Picasso and Matisse, and opened her house to most of the key writers and artists of the 1900s, 1910s and 1920s, experiences she recorded in her most commercially successful novel, *The Autobiography of Alice B. Toklas* (1933). The text shifts between quite specific and humorous descriptions of meeting writers such as Pound, Eliot, Loy, Barnes and Hemingway in the early 1920s and sentences which are boldly unspecific. Of Pound she wrote 'he was a village explainer, excellent if you were a village, but if you were not, not'. Juxtaposed next to these funny snippets about artistic personalities, she produces sentences which resist concrete reference: 'In those days you met anybody everywhere'.[32]

Stein had partly developed the latter of these styles of writing through her encounter with the avant-garde painting of Matisse, Picasso and Braque. Just as these visual artists can be said to adjust the focus of their painting from the depiction of external objects to the painterly properties of shape, light and colour on the canvas, so her writing concentrates on the texture of language. Her first two extended pieces of writing, *Three Lives* (written 1904–5 and published in 1909) and the monumental *The Making of Americans* (written in 1906–8; published in 1925), create rhythmical sentences to focus attention on the unfolding differences within repetition in spoken language. In 'Melanctha', the second of the three lives which form the substance of her first text, she creates a prose that inhabits the stereotyped speech rhythms of a working-class black woman:

I certainly don't think you got it all just right in the letter, I just been reading, that you just wrote me. I certainly don't think you are just fair or very understanding to all I have to suffer to keep straight on to really always to believe in you and trust you.[33]

Loy, in an interesting essay on Stein published in the *Transatlantic Review* in 1924, argues that she produces two contrary writing practices. Her prose works, such as *Three Lives*, focus on language whose meanings are revealed through the differences within verbal repetition. According to Loy, Stein's poetry, or prose poems, in contrast, are static: 'she ignores duration and telescopes time and space and the subjective and objective'.[34] This second kind of writing is exemplified in *Tender Buttons*, a series of radical prose poems published in 1914. Stein declared that while prose should eschew the noun, poetry should be based on it.[35] Here is one of her tender poetic buttons:

PASTRY
Cutting shade, cool spades and little last beds, make violet, violet when.[36]

Tender Buttons takes nouns that refer to domestic entities and then undercuts the ways in which the noun might map an object. Some of the words that follow the highlighted pastry are echoes of pastry-like elements: the action of cutting, the sensation of cool-ness, the shape of a bed. But the words 'make violet, violet when' do not connect obviously to pastry. Looked at in another way, the reader might find that the drift of these words is sideways, so that cutting, spades, last beds and violets connect together by a gardening motif. The poetry rests on the associative relationships between nouns. It is not, however, that there is a hidden key in and behind these words: that, if the reader were to understand more about Stein's pastry-making practices, they might discover in what way 'violet when' relates to pastry. Stein is interested in unleash-ing thinking that moves in another direction: not inwards to the poet or concrete referent behind the ruling noun, but outwards to the word-associations within the language system. Whether there are gardening or cooking registers in the writing, grammatically, semantically and syntactically, the sentence blocks sense. It asks the reader to take pleasure in the way the words slip and slide in their relationship to the world.

Stein was an importantly influential figure on the international art scene. Her early writing experiments succeed in creating texts which embody some of the elements demanded by early avant-garde manifestos. This is a writing which clears away all linguistic clichés, is spatial and non-mimetic, refuses any kind of introspection and is radically new. Initially, however, her experiments were simply too strange to appeal to a large number of readers and she struggled to find publishers for her writing. She brought out *Three Lives* at her own expense. While she had a number of prominent fans, who instantly hailed her as an important writer, her reputation did not really grow until the 1920s.[37] She was invited to lecture at Oxford and Cambridge Literary Societies in 1926, and the lecture 'Composition as Explanation' was subsequently published by Virginia and Leonard Woolf's Hogarth Press.

Fame and influence, however, were to be awarded to two other writers, whose work combined some of the radical features embodied in Stein's word-experiments with a full-scale engagement with the historical, the temporal and the urban. There were two books published in 1922 which captured the public mood of the post-war generation, and which sealed the fame and cultural importance of the new developments in English-language writing: T. S. Eliot's *The Waste Land* and James Joyce's *Ulysses*. While *Ulysses*, which records the events of a particular day, 16 June 1904, only engages with the war tangentially, *The Waste Land*, with descriptions of demobbed husbands, dead lands and revolutionary hordes, is, in some respects, a war poem.

The Waste Land has stylistic similarities with 'The Love Song of J. Alfred Prufrock'. Both poems splice together past and present, high and low, ironic and portentous registers. But, the subject matter has shifted dramatically: not the hesitations and anxieties of an ineffectual modern man, but the past and possible future of a post-war world. The techniques of earlier poems, such as the rhythmical free verse and the fragmentation of Prufrock's universe, open a space for the epic dimensions of *The Waste Land*. Eliot retrospectively, and rather coyly, described the poem as 'the relief of a personal and wholly insignificant grouse against life; just a piece of rhythmical grumbling'. Rhythm does form the focus of the poem's energy, but Eliot's range of reference stretches much further than a partial complaint against life.

The land that has been laid waste incorporates the devastated landscapes of the war, the monotonous rituals of London commuters, the splintering nation states of post-war Europe, the threat to authority of revolution and class and gender mobility, the religious and communal beliefs that have been hollowed out by war and capitalism. Everyday lives, those of the tarot card reader Madame Sosostris, the women in the pub and the typist who entertains her uninspiring young man, are framed by portentous questions and statements. What, the poem asks in its opening lines, might grow out of this 'stony rubbish'?

The poem's energy resides in its international scope, which creates the extraordinary linguistic and rhythmical effects, fuels the global references to different religious faiths, and taps into the transnational political inclinations of the post-war period.

> Shall I at least set my lands in order?
> London Bridge is falling down falling down falling down
> *Poi s'ascose nel foco che gli affina*
> *Quando fiam uti chelidon* – O swallow swallow
> *Le Prince D'Aquitaine à la tour abolie*
> These fragments I have shored against my ruins
> Why then Ile fit you. Hieronymo's mad againe.
> Datta. Dayadhvam. Damyata.
> Shantih shantih shantih[38]

Eliot's scholarly interest in the anthropological works of James Frazer and Jane Harrison, as well as different religious traditions, most notably Buddhism and Hinduism, which he had studied at Harvard, feed into these lines. The reader is asked to connect 'fragments' of Buddhist and Hindu scripture, as well as lines from a nursery rhyme about London Bridge, Dante's *Purgatorio*, Gerard de Nerval's sonnet 'El Desdichado' (The Disinherited), and the subtitle *Hieronymo is Mad Againe* of Thomas Kyd's Elizabethan play *The Spanish Tragedy*.

The poem brings together different languages: Sanskrit, French, Latin, Greek. It juxtaposes distinct linguistic registers: nursery rhymes, biblical phrases, Renaissance drama, contemporary jazz songs. It requires the reader both to register the presence of these different genres and religious traditions, and to experience the shock of their juxtapositions. The nursery rhyme refrain 'London Bridge is falling down' reveals the poem's focus on London's collapsing financial and imperial power. The subversive hooded hordes who 'swarm' across mountains earlier in 'What the Thunder Said' constitute another modernising energy, this time one that is pictured as anonymously threatening and destructive.

The Waste Land unleashes the multilingual forces of modern life. Here, in some respects, was a full-blown poetic expression of the verbal energy proclaimed by the Vorticists. But readers have asked where is the still point at the centre of the whirling fluid energies of *The Waste Land*? In an essay on *Ulysses*, Eliot suggested that myth might be seen to order the chaos of 'history', as he put it, a comment that has been sometimes read as helping us to understand *The Waste Land* rather than *Ulysses*.[39] There is certainly a plethora of myths and mythical figures in the poem. The words of the prophetic sibyl at Cumae, generally renowned for her wisdom, form the substance of the poem's epigraph; the opulence of Cleopatra's 'burnished throne' makes a lavish appearance in 'A Game of Chess'; Tiresias is resurrected from the dead so that he can witness a deathly sexual encounter in 'The Fire Sermon'; and the medieval Christian legend of the Grail Quest is central to 'What the Thunder Said'.

While the poem, like 'The Love Song of J. Alfred Prufrock', asks many questions, particularly whether any faith might 'grow' out of the lives, objects and lands of the post-war world, it importantly does not provide any conclusive answers. In a discussion of the urban poetry of mid-nineteenth-century French poet Baudelaire, Eliot argued that Baudelaire made sordid city imagery 'represent something much more than itself'. But in his own descriptions of contemporary London, he seems to use myth to make waste significant as a symbol of cultural loss.[40] The interpenetration of past and present serves to mourn the loss of meaning. The modern love scene depicted in 'The Fire Sermon', for instance, is seen by the blind Greek prophet Tiresias, who not only evokes all the other love scenes in the history of Western culture, but also sees into and fore-suffers future trysts. Her assault at the hands of the spotty young man is spliced with the song of Olivia from Oliver Goldsmith's *Vicar of Wakefield*: 'When Lovely Woman Stoops to Folly'.

The line from Goldsmith reveals the repetitive nature of human desires and actions, as well as the recurring themes of literary texts. But the juxtaposition of lines also pirouettes on a question. While Olivia's song in Goldsmith's novel goes on to lament her melancholic guilt and shame at her seduction, such emotions are notably absent from the typist's responses. Instead, she experiences boredom, fatigue and indifference. In this instance, the presence of the past in the present reveals both the repetitive cycles of the human body, and a notable emptiness in the moral substance of contemporary lives.

Joyce's *Ulysses*, set in 1904, asks no specific questions about the war, or the post-war world. But the impact of its thematic and stylistic modernity was no less significant. Despite its retrospective setting, fellow writers proclaimed the book's novelty in radical terms, Eliot declared that it was 'in advance' of its time, and that, in its formlessness, the book signalled the end of the novel form.[41]

Like *The Waste Land* the book is remarkable for its epic scale and ambition, and for its balancing of realistic detail and mythic parallels. The action is confined to a single day in Dublin, specifically 16 June 1904. It starts at eight o'clock in the morning, and ends in the early hours of the next day. The narrative is largely structured in accordance with the regular forward movement of time. The reader initially follows the thoughts and experiences of Stephen Dedalus, who wakes up, teaches a history lesson and walks on the beach at Sandymount Strand. The book then shifts focus to Leopold Bloom, who cooks breakfast, goes shopping and attends a funeral. It concludes with Molly Bloom lying in bed musing about her life and loves.

The book is many things. It is, in some respects, a love story, as well as a book which explores themes of friendship, paternity and maternity. It also describes a young man's desire to become a modern artist. The book was declared to be a disgusting mass of obscenity at the time of its publication. It is most notorious now, however, for its stylistic innovations. In the Introduction to this guide, I discussed Joyce's innovative use of interior monologue in *Ulysses*. But this attempt to write the mind's responses was merely one style among many. The book incorporates historical, religious and philosophical debates about time, space and subjectivity, and a number of languages, most notably Greek, Latin, French and Italian. It also reproduces, parodies and pastiches a wide range of different styles of languages, such as newspaper journalism, religious scripture, play-script and colloquial slang. The book is also a series of puzzles. Joyce prophetically stated, 'I've put in so many enigmas and puzzles that it will keep the professors busy for centuries arguing over what I meant, and that's the only way of insuring one's immortality.'[42]

Some of the puzzles relate to its handling of mythic parallels. In 1920 and 1921, Joyce created two 'schemas' for *Ulysses* which he sent to two friends, Carlo Linati and Valery Larbaud, thereafter known as the Linati and Larbaud schemas. They were designed to help readers negotiate the mythic parallels in *Ulysses*. They indicated that episode three, for instance, is called 'Telemachus', after Odysseus' son, who at the beginning of the *Odyssey* dreams of his father returning home from the Trojan War. We are also told that the art of the episode is theology, its colours are white and gold and its symbol is 'heir' and so on. Episode seven is called 'Aeolus', after Homer's *Odyssey*, and it begins like this:

IN THE HEART OF THE HIBERNIAN METROPOLIS
Before Nelson's pillar trams slowed, shunted, changed trolley, started for Blackrock, Kingstown and Dalkey, Clonskea, Rathgar and Terenure, Palmerston park and upper Rathmines, Sandymount Green, Rathmines, Ringsend and Sandymount Tower, Harold's Cross. The hoarse Dublin United Tramway Company's timekeeper bawled them off[43]

The first thing we notice about this piece of writing is its use of capitalisation, as though the writing is mimicking the structure of a newspaper in which headlines announce and summarise the text that follows. The words positioned below the title do, indeed, take us to the 'Heart of the Hibernian Metropolis', with their focus on Nelson's pillar, which sits at the centre of Dublin, and the trams going in and out. The writing also captures the rhythms and sounds of moving trams: 'Right and left parallel clanging ringing a double-decker and a singledeck moved from their railheads, swerved to the down line, glided parallel.'[44] This sentence does not neutrally describe a double-deck and single-deck tram moving parallel to each other. Instead, it performs the movement and sounds by which the two trams move from their railheads, swerve inwards and glide parallel.

Both the capitalisation and the performative nature of single sentences create a writing which mimics, to some extent, the language of newspapers. But there are other layers to this writing, many of which are humorous. Joyce labelled this section of the book 'Aeolus', after Book 10 of Homer's *Odyssey* in which Odysseus reaches an island called Aeolia, ruled by Aeolus, whom Zeus had made 'warden of the winds'. Aeolus entertains Odysseus and tries to help him by confining all the unfavourable winds in a bag, which Odysseus stows in his ship. Within sight of Ithaca, Odysseus 'nods' at the tiller. His men suspect him of having hidden some treasure in the bag. They open it, release the winds, and the ships are driven back to Aeolia, where Aeolus refuses any further help to Odysseus and drives him away as a 'man the blessed gods detest'.[45]

The focus on trams coming in and out of central Dublin looks slightly different in the light of our knowledge of the mythic parallels. The movements and sounds of the modern city are like a modern-day version of Homeric seas, in which individuals struggle to journey home. The words used to describe this movement could also be seen to apply both to trams and to boats. In the third section, 'Gentlemen of the Press', for instance, there is a description of barrels bumping, floating and rolling, like a ship on the sea: 'Grossbooted draymen rolled barrels dullthudding out of Prince's stores and bumped them up on the brewery float. On the brewery float bumped dullthudding barrels rolled by grossbooted draymen out of Prince's stores.'[46] These two sentences are not only notable for their references to rolling and bumping, but also for the fact that the barrels are rolled twice, but with minor differences, so that both the mechanical movement of trams, and the physical movements of draymen, are described in their repetitions. The emphasis on the blustery and windy movement of bodies and machines runs through the episode, with a breathless focus on speed and sound: 'Thumping, Thump'.[47]

As *Ulysses* progressed, its style became increasingly experimental. Section eleven, called 'Sirens', has mythic parallels with the scene in *The Odyssey* in which Odysseus, in trying to get home, must sail past two Sirens whose beautiful voices bewitch sailors. In order that he might hear the wondrous sounds of their voices, but succeed in sailing past, Odysseus blocks the ears of his sailors with wax and ties himself to the mast of his ship. In *Ulysses* Bloom ducks into the Ormond Street Hotel to have a bite to eat and keep his eye on his rival, Blazes Boylan. The episode is written as a kind of musical prose. It begins with phrases which, as in a musical score, introduce the musical motifs of the ensuing piece:

> Bronze by gold heard the hoofirons, steelyringing.
> Imperthnthn thnthnthn.
> Chips, picking chips off rocky thumbnail, chips.[48]

Each of these lines will be repeated in the main body of the chapter. The first line, for instance, will become 'Bronze by gold, Miss Douce's head by Miss Kennedy's head, over the crossblind of the Ormond bar heard the viceregal hoofs go by, ringing steel'.[49] Both sentences emphasise the acoustical elements of combined words. The chapter does deal with plot and character development to some extent, but at times the language disintegrates into seemingly meaningless, if sonorous, letters: 'Imperthnthn thnthnthn'.

Not all of Joyce's readers were convinced by this radical linguistic experimentation. Pound was worried that Joyce had lost aesthetic focus with 'Sirens', and complained that the proliferation of stylistic experimentation in the second half of *Ulysses* was distracting and unnecessary. He wrote to him, 'even the assing girouette of a postfuturo Gertrudo Steino protetopublic dont demand a new style per chapter. If a classic author "shows steady & uniform progress" from one oeuvre to ensanguined next, may be considered ample proof of non-stagnation of cerebral Rodano.'[50] Pound's desire for steady narrative progress, rather than a new style for each chapter, reveals just how strange Joyce's book appeared to his contemporary readers.

Such anxieties on the part of his editors and publishers, however, did not deter Joyce. Instead, *Ulysses* became more, rather than less, experimental after 'Sirens'. Episode fourteen, called 'Oxen of the Sun', is set in Dublin's maternity hospital. While a woman gives birth to a child upstairs, a group of men, including Stephen Dedalus and Leopold Bloom, get drunk downstairs. These events are narrated in a range of different styles of writing which move chronologically forwards from the Latin prose styles of Roman historians, through middle English, the style of Thomas De Quincy and up to the present, which is represented as a cacophony of Irish New York slang: 'Change here for Bawdyhouse. We two, she said, will seek the kips where shady Mary is. Righto, any old time.'[51] 'Oxen of the Sun' exploits the humorous and experimental possibilities of contemporary urban slang.

The publications of *The Waste Land* and *Ulysses* reveal much about the cultural status of modernist writing by 1922. No poem or novel had ever looked quite like this before. These texts were new, learned and epic, and this combination of elements meant that they had an immediate and significant impact on world literature. They had a cult status for ambitious writers of the 1920s and 1930s, influencing the work of experimental writers such as Djuna Barnes and more mainstream writers such as F. Scott Fitzgerald. More generally, however, they ensured the wider cultural significance of modernism. Lawrence Rainey's book *Institutions of Modernism* (1998) has documented Pound's, Eliot's and Joyce's careful and canny negotiations with publishers and agents in order to secure lucrative prices for the two texts. Sylvia Beach, Joyce's publisher, manipulated the new fame and status of modernist writing by publishing three different editions of *Ulysses*, one of which was a luxuriously printed deluxe edition designed as a collector's item. Rainey suggests how this strategy encouraged purchasers to invest in modernist writing, an investment that in turn served to legitimise the movement.

The publication of *Ulysses* through Beach's Shakespeare and

Company publishing firm also reveals another significant element of the social status of modernism in 1922. Because *Ulysses* had been banned for obscenity in America and then across the globe, it was brought out in Paris, and then smuggled around the world through private subscription lists. The combination of obscenity and experimentalism sealed Joyce's reputation after 1922 as an international literary celebrity. Modernism had become significant, controversial and lucrative.

1928

This section focuses on a year – 1928 – but not a place. The reason for doing so is to highlight the way in which the first generation of Anglo–American modernist writers, by the late 1920s, had dispersed. Modernism was less a product of group activities based in particular cities, and more a series of scattered international publishing events.

In 1928 a number of important modernist books were published. Pound brought out a deluxe edition of *A Draft of The Cantos 17–25* in Paris and *Selected Poems*, edited by Eliot and published by Faber and Gwyer in London. 'Anna Livia Plurabelle', the most famous section of Joyce's *Finnegans Wake*, was published as a separate volume in New York. D. H. Lawrence's hugely controversial and obscene book *Lady Chatterley's Lover* was printed by a small publishing firm based in Florence and then smuggled to readers in America and Britain by means of private subscription lists. Djuna Barnes's sexually and formally experimental *Ladies Almanack* was published anonymously by the Darantière Press in Dijon, while the New York based publisher Horace Liveright produced and disseminated her novel *Ryder* before it was censored for obscenity. Radclyffe Hall's *The Well of Loneliness*, which was to cause an international stir, not because of its form but because of its depiction of a lesbian relationship, came out with Jonathan Cape in London before operations were transferred to Paris to avoid the censor. Virginia Woolf published her novel *Orlando* through her own Hogarth Press in London.

These writers were now scattered across Europe. Pound and

Lawrence were living fairly isolated lives in Italy. Joyce had been in Paris for eight years, and Barnes for seven, but Joyce was suffering from severe eye troubles and Barnes was in the middle of the traumatic breakup of her relationship with Thelma Wood. Eliot and Woolf were established figures in London literary life, with Eliot editing the important international literary journal *The Criterion*, and Woolf helping to run the Hogarth Press.

These publications also reveal much about the shifting coordinates and divergent directions of modernism in the 1920s. Pound's *The Cantos*, which he had begun in 1917 and would continue to write until his death in 1972, and Joyce's 'Anna Livia Plurabelle', which was part of the book that was finally published as *Finnegans Wake* in 1939, represent the most formally experimental strands of Anglo–American modernist poetry and prose.

After much hesitation, rewriting and self-doubt, Pound, after a false start in 1917, had begun the final version of *The Cantos* in 1922. His earlier struggles to synthesise his scholarly interest in the poetic materials of the past, the question of time and visionary qualities had come to fruition in *The Cantos* which present a collage of 'luminous' details, idioms, registers and images.

A Draft of XVI Cantos creates a poetic language in which images and ideas, both contemporary and ancient, local and global, are splintered into fragments and then brought together in a new synthesis. The themes addressed in the early Cantos comprise the economic causes of the First World War and the status of art. For Pound, these questions involve trawling backwards to the origins of European conflicts and values. He brings to life the extensive religious and governmental disputes over what was called usury, the practice of charging interest on loans, and the sponsorship and denigration of art in the history of European nations.

Pound writes a history which, rather than documenting past events, unfolds in the present. In Canto IX he describes Federigo da Montefeltro, first duke of Urbino in the early to mid fifteenth century, and Galeazzo Malatesta, nicknamed the 'inept' because he was hopeless in battle: 'through the wangle of the Illus. Sgr. Mr. Fedricho d'Orbino / Who worked the wangle with Galeaz' (Canto IX, 35). Federigo is of interest to Pound, and should be remembered and commemorated in *The Cantos* because he was a great Italian patron of the arts, although Pound also signals his position in the chain of power: he was Sigismundo Malatesta's 'Amy Lowell'.

Pound writes about these entangled disputes of Renaissance Italy, not by preserving the facts of the past, but by bringing the details of fifteenth-century battles, financial deals and artistic projects alive in the present. The poem overlaps past and present, historical facts and mythical stories, direct quotation and anecdote, seeking to present and not to privilege one kind of language over another. The poem as a whole moves in an out of the detailed presentation of Renaissance individuals and their actions, and lyrical, visionary registers. Canto XVII, the first of the series published in 1928, departs from the Purgatory of Canto XVI and enters what Pound described as 'a sort of paradise terrestre'. It begins:

> So that the vines burst from my fingers
> And the bees weighted with pollen
> Move heavily in the vine-shoots:
>   Chirr – chirr – chir-rikk – a purring sound,
> And the bird sleepily in the branches.
>   ZAGREUS! IO ZAGREUS![52]

Canto XVII, like Homer's *Odyssey* starts in medias res, or in the middle of things. Here the lines delight in the synthesis of the natural world and mythical vision. Zagreus, another name for the god Dionysus, who was the divinity of wine in late Greek tradition, signifies to Pound a religious ecstasy connected to the rites of spring. As in Loy's 'Love Song', these lines are organised like a collage, but where her poem's Cubistic qualities function with a present-tense immediacy, Pound uses these techniques to create an epic poem of mythical vision which signals the centrality of time through the contrast of past and present.

The layering of languages in these Cantos creates a poetic vision through the precise rendering of the past, and an endless proliferation of connections and meanings. This openness was significant to Pound, and constituted a key difference between the direction in which his own work was heading and that of Eliot's *The Waste Land*. Canto VIII half quotes from Eliot's poem: 'These fragments you have shelved (shored). / "Slut!" "Bitch!" Truth and Callipe / Slanging each other sous les lauriers'.[53] By undermining Eliot's scholarly use of literary fragments as a kind of defence against the modern, Pound suggests the differences in his own use of poetic fragments. He wants to make them live again – to 'burst from' his 'fingers'.

The Cantos also memorialises the achievements of other one-time artistic collaborators. In Canto XVI he writes of those who fought in the war: 'And Wyndham Lewis went to it / With a heavy bit of artillery'.[54] Pound also refers to other one-time collaborators:

> And Henri Gaudier went to it,
> And they killed him,
> And killed a good deal of sculpture,
> And ole T.E.H. he went to it[55]

Henri Gaudier-Brzeska and T. E. H. (which refers to T. E. Hulme), both of whom died in the war, are memorialised through the poem. The lines, when situated next to Pound's references to Greek and Renaissance poetry, serve to legitimise the activities of a select group of contemporary writers.

Alongside the publication of Pound's The Cantos Joyce had begun bringing out parts of what he called his 'Work in Progress', first in Ford's journal, the Transatlantic Review, in 1924, and then more consistently in the Paris-based journal transition from April 1927 to 1929. 'Anna Livia Plurabelle' forms the eighth part of 'Work in Progress', which was eventually published as Finnegans Wake in 1939.

There is no plot as we would conventionally understand it in Finnegans Wake, but there are characters of sorts. There is Finnegan, whose wake forms the basis of the first part of the book, and who rises up to have one last drink. There is Harold or Humphrey Chimpden Earwicker, otherwise referred to as HCE or Here Comes Everybody, whose hazy misdemeanours in the Phoenix Park form the basis of much speculation and gossip. There is his wife, Anna Livia Plurabelle, whose activities and numerous lovers also prompt extraordinarily vibrant stories, chatter and gossip.

These characters are the ghostly bones on which Joyce hangs an entirely new writing practice. 'Anna Livia Plurabelle' begins:

> O
> Tell me all about
> Anna Livia! I want to hear all
> About Anna Livia. Well, you know Anna Livia? Yes, of
> course, we all know Anna Livia. Tell me all. Tell me now.
> You'll die when you hear. Well, you know, when the old cheb
> went futt and did what you know. Yes, I know, go on. Wash
> quit and don't be dabbling. Tuck up your sleeves and loosen
> your talktapes. And don't butt me – hike! – when you bend.
> Or whatever it was they threed to make out he tried to two in
> the Fiendish park. He's an awful old reppe. Look at the shirt
> of him! Look at the dirt of it! He has all my water black on
> me. And it steeping and stuping since this time last wik.[56]

The excitement, humour, creativity, repetitions and pleasures of gossip and hearsay are central to the writing of *Finnegans Wake*, and to this breathless beginning to 'Anna Livia Plurabelle'. Here, we are presented with Anna through the chatter and imagination of two washerwomen talking to each other across the River Liffey in Dublin.

The most obvious thing to note about this writing is its linguistic invention. New words, combinations or echoes of ones with which we are familiar, form the substance of *Finnegans Wake*. Many of these new words are comic. The word 'stuping' in the extract above, for instance, echoes with stupid, and stooping, which would connect to the back in the 'black' of the previous line. Both words are present in 'stuping', and both would apply to HCE. The text takes pleasure in, and asks the reader to take pleasure in, these comic inventions.

The status of knowledge and language is also immediately referred to in these words. The women discuss Anna's husband, Humphrey Earwicker, or HCE, whose activities in the Phoenix Park have been the basis for much rumour since the second section of *Finnegans Wake*: 'Well, you know, when the old cheb went futt and did what you know'. As it happens, the reader does not know what the narrative voice declares that 'you know'. Questions about the status of what the reader might know continue to inform the episode. Let us take the phrase 'loosen your talktapes' in the sentence above: one might conventionally allude to loosening one's tongue, and there is an echo of a tongue in talktapes. Tapes also gives a mechanical resonance to the idea of memory as repetition. If she is going to loosen her talktapes, we might expect to hear a fixed story that has been played before. If the reader lets his or her eye drift into the next couple of sentences, further acoustical connections can be seen: 'Or whatever it was they threed to make out he thried to two in the Fiendish park.' If read aloud, these words both connect to 'Tuck up' and talktapes, and move in other directions: threed echoes with tried, two with do; but the issue of numbers three and two, which are in dispute in the rumours about ECH's activities in the Phoenix or fiendish park, are maintained. There is also the hint of a lisp in the sentence.

Joyce creates single words which both juxtapose ideas or images, and combine them. They do not function by means of substitutions: there is no other word for 'talktapes' which would make it more intelligible through familiarity. The word reveals something about the power of gossip to become factual through repetition. But it is significant that as a whole *Finnegans Wake* points in the other direction. Language, far from being that which is a repetition of a tape that we have heard before, bursts onto the page in all its novelty and excitement. Like these opening lines of 'Anna Livia Plurabelle', *Finnegans Wake* bridges the gap between words that we know and words that we do not, and invites us to interpret and invent. Later in this episode, we have the words 'O gig goggle of gigguels. I can't tell you how! It's too screaming to rizo, rabbit it all!', which is an extraordinarily inventive way of depicting giggling gossips.[57]

While Pound in *The Cantos* laments the loss of fellow artists and writers through the First World War, Joyce also refers frequently, and largely affectionately, to the works of his contemporaries in *Finnegans Wake*. Pound appears as 'unbluffingly blurtubruskblunt as an Esra, the cat'.[58] *The Waste Land* is quietly ridiculed, as Eliot's own quote from Goldsmith is quoted again: 'when lovely wooman stoops to conk him'. Yeats's poem 'When I am Old And Gray' is transformed into 'when you are old I'm grey fall full wi sleep'.[59]

Joyce also refers in *Finnegans Wake*, more tangentially, to the writing of Wyndham Lewis. By the 1920s, Lewis had jettisoned the impulses of collaborative artistic enterprise as they had been expressed in *Blast* and was instead styling himself as 'the enemy'. He criticised Joyce's *Ulysses*, Pound's poetry and Stein's writing.[60] Along with his caustic judgements on the experimental endeavours of his contemporaries, Lewis also provided a more compelling reason for this shift from modernism as group activity to modernism as individual experiment. In *Time and Western Man* he describes the early days of *Blast*. The Vorticists, he suggests, attempted to destroy 'the academic of the Royal Academy tradition' in English culture. This necessary work of destruction, he declares, has succeeded: this tradition is now 'completely defunct'. In place of academic control, artists enjoy 'freedom of expression', as long as they have enough money to indulge in this freedom.[61]

The story Lewis tells in *Time and Western Man* (1927) about the preceding fifteen years of modernist writing is perceptive in its claim that avant-garde activity cleared the ground for the freedom of the individual. These freedoms had allowed Pound and Joyce to produce texts which pushed poetic and prose language in new directions. Other writers pursued liberty of expression in a different direction. The modernity of *The Well of Loneliness*, *Orlando* and *Lady Chatterley's Lover* resides in the exploration and exposure of sex, sexuality and the language of sex. This was an aspect of modernism that was just as transgressive and controversial as the modernist's experiments with form.

Radclyffe Hall's *The Well of Loneliness* was published in London by the reputable publisher Jonathan Cape in July 1928. It was not an experimental piece of writing in terms of form. But, in its focus on a lesbian relationship, it was to incite the fury of the purity campaigner James Douglas and the British Home Secretary, Sir William Joynson-Hicks. It was taken to court for obscenity, a violation of Hall's freedom to publish that was opposed by a number of writers, including Virginia Woolf, T. S. Eliot, Rebecca West and Djuna Barnes.

It was not the only contentious book to be published in 1928. D. H. Lawrence's novel *Lady Chatterley's Lover* was an explicitly obscene text which includes vivid descriptions of the sexual relationship between Lady Connie Chatterley and her gamekeeper, as well as the use of colloquial terms such as 'cunt' and 'fuck'. Lawrence did not even attempt to get the book published in England or America. Woolf's depiction of the cross-gender Orlando and Barnes's representation of Natalie Barney's lesbian Parisian salon in *Ladies Almanack* and *Ryder* also test the boundaries of writing about sex and sexuality.

The writing of Djuna Barnes was perhaps the most interesting in this regard because it combined sexual explicitness and formal experimentation. Barnes, who earned her money as a journalist, had been involved in the New York Dadaist circles in the war years. When she arrived in Paris in 1921, she renewed her friendship with Mina Loy and soon became close to Joyce, Stein, Pound and others. She worked as a journalist for a number of publications, including *Vanity Fair*, and interviewed an eclectic array of contemporaries, including writers such as Joyce, and celebrities, such as Coco Chanel and the boxer Jack Dempsey.

Her book *Ladies Almanack* (1928) is partly based on the lesbian salon of the American heiress Natalie Barney who had set up both a home and a literary salon in Paris in 1909. The salon was a meeting place for women, and in particular lesbian, writers. But Barney also hosted and collaborated with Pound, Ford, Eliot, Williams, Gide, Max Jacob, Louis Aragon and others in the 1920s. She was a committed feminist, setting up an Académie des Femmes (Women's Academy) in 1927 to honour the work of women writers. The list of esteemed writers included Stein, Loy and Barnes. She is also famous for the number of her love affairs.

Barnes celebrates both of these characteristics in her affectionate portrayal of Dame Evangeline Musset in *Ladies Almanack,* describing her as having a heart which is 'one Grand Red Cross for the Pursuance, the Relief and the Distraction, of such Girls as in their Hinder Parts, and their Fore Parts, and in whatsoever Parts did suffer them most'.[62] Barnes uses this outré subject matter as the basis for an extraordinarily inventive text of female desire. The book is sexually explicit, open in its description of lesbian desire, and intensely witty. She presents fragmented female bodies through a luxuriously abundant and inventive lexicon. Some references are seemingly explicit; many are playfully euphemistic. She refers to 'Countess Clitoressa' and 'that Lesbian eye'.[63] She also describes, by means of a pointed arrow directed at the picture of a woman's body, 'the love of life'; she refers to 'the rowdy part', the 'Matter', 'front to front', a 'hone to my blunt', the 'little Difference which shall be alien always', and many more.[64]

There is a correlation between Barnes's desire to push linguistic boundaries and the metaphoric or substitutive nature of her writing. She analyses this quite explicitly. In the July section of her *Almanack* she suggests that there is an absence of words to describe what women say to women: nowhere 'can be gathered the vaguest Idea of the Means by which she puts her Heart from her Mouth to her Sleeve, and from her Sleeve into Rhetorick, and from that into the Ear of her beloved'.[65] This is a wonderful description of a feeling or impulse or desire journeying from heart to heart. The thing that travels has the taste of a sensation because it is one that stops at various parts of the body – heart, mouth, sleeve – before being translated into rhetoric and poured into the beloved's ear. Language as rhetoric has a secondary function here, a status mirrored in the grammar of Barnes's prose. She tends to focus on nouns, often capitalised nouns, that stand in for sensations: it is, after all, the 'Heart' that originates the energy that then travels towards the other's Heart. But she also describes something that originates here in the Heart that then necessarily travels outside it, thereby capturing the inherent mobility of love and language. Within the terms of such relationships, the language system is not static. The meaning of words is often dependent on the words that sit alongside, just as the desire that is described jumps from place to place. The slipperiness of the words in Barnes's lexicon, then, creates the lesbian desire it names.

Barnes wittily explores the legally obscene and culturally absent language of female desire, sex and homosexuality. Joyce, in *Finnegans Wake*, creates a familiar, but only half-understood new language to describe a mythic history of Dublin. Pound makes the past live in the present by splicing together dissimilar images and idioms in *The Cantos*. These texts push the boundaries of literary conventions. Their authors imply that these experiments are somehow appropriate responses to a modern world characterised as chaotic, revolutionary or impenetrable. Understandings of the modern world, and the writer's place within it, were central to the formal innovations described in this chapter.

Chapters 2 to 5 will bring this world to light by discussing literary texts in relation to four different historical contexts, all of which have figured prominently in recent literary criticism. The focus of the following chapters will be on a history of ideological conflict.

In Chapter 1, I have suggested that modernism emerged from contradictory impulses. While modernism was dependent on the promotional and collaborative aims of the group, it also led writers in stylistically individualistic directions. Chapter 2 considers modernism in relation to geography, looking at how nationalism, imperialism and migration affected poems and fiction. Here the writing of geography involves the creation of new techniques to capture the local and the particular. The changing nature of national and urban borders, and the creation of new technologies, however, also prompted literary visions and techniques which are both aerial and global. Chapter 3, called 'Sex, obscenity, censorship', focuses on both the centrality of sex and sexuality to modernist writing and the strict censorship rules which aimed to control this writing. The attempt to write the body produced profound moral and cultural clashes. Chapter 4 considers the centrality of new mass cultural forms for the innovative techniques of modernism, and the concomitant attempt to control or to distance the literary object from these technologies. Chapter 5, called 'Modernism and politics', discusses the polarised political beliefs which marked the 1920s and 1930s. Here, modernism is seen as both fundamentally and inescapably involved in politics, and as a writing which attempts to extract the writer from political authority.

SUMMARY OF KEY POINTS

- Early modernism is a product of artistic collaborations in publishing and manifestos.
- Modernism also incorporated a range of highly individualistic styles of writing.
- The origins of Anglo-American modernism lie in the collaborative efforts of writers in London in 1914.

- During the First World War, the geographical centre and artistic tenor of modernism shifted to New York Dada.
- In the 1920s, the centre of modernist activity was in Paris. Eliot's *The Waste Land* and Joyce's *Ulysses* were published in 1922, and they altered the status of modernism.
- By 1928, modernism has become a less collaborative and more experimental affair.
- Modernism was controversial for its stylistic innovations and for its sexual explicitness.

NOTES

1. See, for instance, Bonnie Kime Scott, *The Gender of Modernism: A Critical Anthology* (Bloomington: Indiana University Press, 1990) and Steven Watson, *Strange Bedfellows: The First American Avant-Garde* (New York: Abbeville Press, 1990), pp. 16–17, 60–1, 74–5, 132–3, 290–1.

2. For a full discussion of modernist journals see Peter Brooker and Andrew Thacker (eds), *The Oxford Critical and Cultural History of Modernist Magazines: vol. 1, Britain and Ireland, 1880–1955* (Oxford: Oxford University Press, 2009).

3. Mina Loy, 'Three Moments in Paris', in Mina Loy, *The Lost Lunar Baedeker*, ed. Roger Conover (Manchester: Carcanet, 1996), p. 16.

4. D. H. Lawrence, *Women in Love* (Harmondsworth; Penguin Books, [1921] 1979), p. 68.

5. Wyndham Lewis, *The Apes of God* (Harmondsworth: Penguin Books, [1930] 1965), p. 626.

6. T. S. Eliot, *Letters of T. S. Eliot, Volume 1: 1898–1922*, ed. Valerie Eliot (New York: Harcourt Brace Jovanovich, 1988), p. xvii.

7. T. S. Eliot, *The Complete Poems and Plays* (London: Faber and Faber, 1969), p. 59.

8. Ezra Pound, '*Dubliners* and Mr James Joyce', in Ezra Pound, *Literary Essays of Ezra Pound*, ed. T. S. Eliot (London: Faber and Faber, 1968), p. 400.

9. F. T. Marinetti, 'The Founding and Manifesto of Futurism', in Vassiliki Kolocotroni, Jane A. Goldman and Olga Taxidou (eds), *Modernism: An Anthology of Sources and Documents* (Edinburgh: Edinburgh University Press, 1998), p. 250.

10. F. T. Marinetti, *Zang Tumb Tuuum*, quoted in Jerome Rothenberg and Pierre Joris (eds), *Poems for the Millennium*, vol. 1 (Berkeley: University of California Press, 1995), p. 205.

11. *Poems for the Millennium*, p. 207.

12. H. D., *Bid Me To Live* (London: Virago, 1983), p. 7. Written 1927; first published 1960.

13. H. D., *Collected Poems, 1912–1944* (New York: New Directions, 1983), p. 37.

14. H. D., *Collected Poems*, p. 55.

15. H. D., *Collected Poems*, p. 10.

16. Ezra Pound, 'A Few Don'ts by an Imagiste', in Peter Jones (ed.), *Imagist Poetry* (Harmondsworth: Penguin Books, 1972), p. 130.

17. *Poems for the Millennium*, p. 372.

18. Wyndham Lewis, *Blast* (Santa Barbara: Black Sparrow Press, 2008), p. 11.

19. Wyndham Lewis, 'Long Live the Vortex', in Lewis, *Blast*, p. 7.

20. Wyndham Lewis, 'Long Live the Vortex', in Lewis, *Blast*, p. 7.

21. Wyndham Lewis, 'Long Live the Vortex', in Lewis, *Blast*, p. 7.

22. Ezra Pound, 'Salutation the Third', in Lewis, *Blast*, p. 45.

23. Eliot tried to join the US Navy when America entered the war in 1917.

24. André Breton, *Les Pas perdus* (Paris: Gallimard, 1979), p. 64.

25. Tristan Tzara, 'Dada Manifesto', in *Modernism: An Anthology*, p. 280.

26. America declared war on 6 April 1917.

27. Mina Loy, 'Aphorisms on Futurism', in Loy, *The Lost Lunar Baedeker*, p. 149.

28. Mina Loy, 'Songs to Joannes, 1', in Loy, *The Lost Lunar Baedeker*, p. 53.

29. D. H. Lawrence, *Kangaroo* (Cambridge: Cambridge University Press, [1923] 1994), p. 220.

30. André Breton, 'The First Manifesto of Surrealism', in Kolocotroni, Goldman and Taxidou (eds), *Modernism: An Anthology of Sources and Documents* (Edinburgh: Edinburgh University Press, 1998), p. 309.

31. Ezra Pound, 'How to Read', in Pound, *Literary Essays*, p. 18.

32. Gertrude Stein, *The Autobiography of Alice B. Toklas* (Harmondsworth: Penguin Books, [1933] 1966), p. 217, p. 213.

33. Gertrude Stein, *Three Lives* (Harmondsworth: Penguin Books, [1909] 1990), p. 103.

34. Mina Loy, 'Gertrude Stein', in Mina Loy, *The Last Lunar Baedeker*, ed. Roger Conover (Manchester: Carcanet, 1982) p. 290, p. 291.

35. Gertrude Stein, 'Poetry and Grammar', in Gertrude Stein, *Look at Me Now and Here I Am* (Harmondsworth: Penguin Books, 1984), p. 138.

36. Gertrude Stein, 'Tender Buttons', in Stein, *Look at Me Now and Here I Am*, p. 192.

37. Ann Charters, 'Introduction', in Stein, *Three Lives*, p. xviii.

38. T. S. Eliot, 'The Waste Land', in Eliot, *Complete Poems and Plays*, pp. 74–5.

39. T. S. Eliot, '*Ulysses*, Order and Myth', in *Selected Prose of T. S. Eliot*, ed. Frank Kermode (London: Faber and Faber, 1975), p. 177.

40. T. S. Eliot, *Selected Essays*, 3rd edn (London: Faber and Faber, [1951] 1986), p. 426.

41. T. S. Eliot, '*Ulysses*, Order and Myth', in Eliot, *Selected Prose*, p. 177.

42. See Richard Ellmann, *James Joyce* (1959; rev. edn 1982; corr. New York: Oxford University Press, 1983), p. 521.

43. James Joyce, *Ulysses: The Corrected Text*, ed. Hans Walter Gabler with Wolfhard Steppe and Claus Melchior (London: Bodley Head, 1986), p. 96.

44. Joyce, *Ulysses*, p. 96.

45. See Don Gifford with Robert J. Seidman, *Ulysseys Annotated: Notes for James Joyce's Ulysseys* (Berkeley: University of California Press, 1988), p. 128.

46. Joyce, *Ulysses*, p. 96.
47. Joyce, *Ulysses*, p. 98.
48. Joyce, *Ulysses*, p. 210.
49. Joyce, *Ulysses*, p. 211.
50. Ezra Pound, Letter to Joyce, 10 June 1919, in Pound, Ezra, *Pound/Joyce*, ed. Forrest Read (London: Faber and Faber, 1967), p. 157.
51. Joyce, *Ulysses*, p. 349.
52. Ezra Pound, *The Cantos* (London: Faber and Faber, 1986), p. 76.
53. Pound, *The Cantos*, 28.
54. Pound, *The Cantos*, p. 71.
55. Pound, *The Cantos*, p. 71.
56. James Joyce, *Finnegans Wake* (London: Faber and Faber, [1939] 1975), p. 196.
57. Joyce, *Finnegans Wake*, p. 206.
58. Joyce, *Finnegans Wake*, p. 116.
59. Joyce, *Finnegans Wake*, p. 170.
60. Wyndham Lewis, *Time and Western Man* (Santa Rosa: Black Sparrow Press, [1927] 1993), pp. 67–8.
61. Lewis, *Time and Western Man*, p. 38.
62. Djuna Barnes, *Ladies Almanack* (Manchester: Carcanet, [1928] 2006), p. 6.
63. Barnes, *Ladies Almanack*, p. 8, p. 35.
64. Barnes, *Ladies Almanack*, p. 66, p. 43, p. 44, p. 57.
65. Barnes, *Ladies Almanack*, p. 43.

CHAPTER 2

Modernism and Geography

Modernist texts engage with the geographical instabilities of the early twentieth century. New nation states were emerging, cities were expanding, natural landscapes were disappearing and the geographical boundaries of nation states were redrawn. These shifts had a profound impact on how modernist writers engaged with the 'real', thematically and formally.

Many modernist texts locate their action in the streets of cities and new writing techniques, such as interior monologue and poetic fragmentation, were developed to depict the urban experience. Joyce's *Dubliners* (1914), *A Portrait of the Artist as a Young Man* (1916) and *Ulysses* (1922), Virginia Woolf's *Mrs Dalloway* (1925) and *The Years* (1937), Dorothy Richardson's *Pilgrimage* (1938) and T. S. Eliot's *The Waste Land* (1922) embed their writing in the geography of Dublin and London. The importance of the city for modernist writing has long been a preoccupation of critical accounts. Walter Benjamin, in an unfinished and monumental critical work written during the late 1920s and 1930s (he died in 1940) focused on the mid-nineteenth-century French poet Charles Baudelaire, and argued that modern subjectivity, and hence poetry, was essentially urban.[1] He adopted Baudelaire's own term, the *flâneur*, to capture the spirit of a lone, and lonely, subject who wanders the city streets, giving himself up to the chance seductions of prostitutes and commodities in shop windows. In Benjamin's theory, the *flâneur*, in his estrangement both from other individuals and from commodities, is a subject who encounters the alienated relations of mid-nineteenth-century capitalism. Baudelaire's poems bring this alienation into language, both thematically and formally. They focus on isolated poetic figures who expose themselves to the pleasures and the dangers of the city, and these encounters are written by way of the distanced and estranged tones of irony, rather than through empathetic or sentimental registers.

The subject matter of Baudelaire's city poems and his play of ironic tones were influential on mid- to late-nineteenth-century poetry, and on the writing of Marinetti, Eliot, Pound and others. Benjamin's account of the *flâneur* has also proved tenacious as a way of understanding the urban texts of English-language modernism. The wandering characters of Woolf's, Joyce's, Barnes's, and Richardson's fiction have been interpreted as *flâneur*s, whose isolation and alienation in the city exposes the economic or commodified structures of Dublin, London and Paris.[2]

The *flâneur* occupies a necessarily partial perspective on the cities through which he or she wanders, a narrative perspective that has significantly informed postmodern theories of space. French theorist Michel de Certeau, in *The Practice of Everyday Life* (1984), distinguishes between two different literary ways of mapping places. There are stories which create static and ordered landscapes, in which the narrator is largely immobile and surveys and maps an observed material world. Then there are narratives which are grounded in a character's experiential discourse in which spaces come to life through movement, what de Certeau calls 'the actualization of space'. De Certeau argues that this is not a firm opposition, and that most narratives comprise both perspectives. But the distinction has been seen as helpful in understanding the partial and experiential features of the *flâneur*'s construction of cities.[3]

Theorists of geographical space, including de Certeau, Michel Foucault and others, argue, in addition, that places – streets, buildings, landscapes – are not inert matter, but part of a nexus of historical power relations. These theories are helpful when considering modernist texts which not only write carefully about specific and 'real' city streets – Joyce, for example, famously wrote *Ulysses* with a Dublin map on his desk – but also create geographical metaphors to imagine national borders, politics and the psyche. The modernist techniques of interior monologue discussed in the Introduction to this book, when considered in the light of Benjamin's ideas of the *flâneur* and de Certeau's work on space, can be seen to be informed by historical ideas of nationalism, imperialism, race, class and gender.

The theoretical understanding of place and space allows us to read and understand the more political features of interior monologue. It also opens up other elements of modernist writing, particularly the depiction of the historical forces and technologies which work to fragment and dislocate land.

While city streets were seen as the focal point for modern experience, there were also significant explorations of the uncertain boundaries of the city. A number of writers pictured an expanding city and a concomitant idea of shrinking natural landscapes. In Mary Butts's novel *The Death of Felicity Taverner* (1932) the sinister character Kralin threatens to destroy the Dorset landscape by building a leisure complex with a golf club.[4] This picture of metropolitan sprawl also features in Aldous Huxley's dystopian futuristic novel *Brave New World* (1932), which creates an aerial view of London as a vast urban conglomeration. Henry Foster and Lenina Crowne fly over London and look down on it from above: 'They were flying over the six kilometre zone of parkland that separated Central London from its first ring of satellite suburbs . . . Near Shepherd's Bush two thousand Beta-Minus mixed doubles were playing Riemann-surface tennis.'[5] This vision incorporates both the urban spread necessitated by overcrowding and the geographical perspective afforded by the new technology of the aeroplane (the first Atlantic flight was in 1919). D. H. Lawrence, in *Lady Chatterley's Lover* (1928), depicts land as obliterated by industrialisation, arguing that:

> This is history. One England blots out another. The mines had made the halls wealthy. Now they were blotting them out, as they had already blotted out the cottages. The industrial England blots out the agricultural England. One meaning blots out another.[6]

The meaning Lawrence attaches to shifts in the landscape are also evident in Woolf's *Between the Acts* (1941), which describes the historical layering of landscape from an aerial perspective. Mr Oliver states that 'from an aeroplane' you could 'still see, plainly marked, the scars made by the Britons; by the Romans; by the Elizabethan manor house.'[7] This recurrent image of landscape as a palimpsest of historical 'scars' is important for the panoramic writing of geography, which involves an attention to a historically fragmented material world. The 'scars' are made more sinister by their suggestion of future invasions – the Romans are precursors to the aerial threat of German planes in *Between the Acts*.

If the boundaries separating urban and natural domestic geographies were seen as disturbingly mobile, the geographical frontiers of nation states were even more fragile. After the First World War, the frontiers of both the Austrian Empire and Germany were broken up in the Treaty of Versailles. The geographical relationship between Western imperial centres and colonial frontiers were also in transit. In the case of the most powerful imperial centre, London, the scope of its geographical power shifted considerably: Ireland became independent in 1922; Britain continued to hold power over India (which was a vast geographical landmass incorporating present-day Pakistan, India and Bangladesh), but its authority changed, as the movement for Indian independence gained momentum. After the First World War Britain was granted control over another huge landmass in the Middle East, which it split into two states, Palestine (which included modern-day Israel) and Mesopotamia (incorporating the regions around Baghdad). The Balfour Declaration of 1917 had pledged for the establishment of a national home for Jews in Palestine, a commitment that Britain enshrined in 'The Palestine Mandate'.

The changes to European and Middle Eastern geographical boundaries shifted perceptions of national identity which, in turn, had a significant impact on writing. Some writers engaged directly with national conflicts. W. B. Yeats, in his poems 'Easter 1916' and 'Sixteen Dead Men' (both published in *Michael Robartes and the Dancer*, 1921), memorialised the Irish nationalist leaders James Connolly and Padraic Pearse and their involvement in the bloody history of the Easter massacre in Dublin. His 'Meditations in Time of Civil War' (published in *The Tower*, 1928), along with novels such as Elizabeth Bowen's novel *The Last September* (1929), engaged with the Irish civil war.

Nationalism and Irishness are staged in a rather different way in Joyce's *Ulysses*: 'Do you know what a nation means?', asks John Wyse Nolan. Bloom, an Irish Jew, answers by privileging the connections between people and land: 'A nation is the same people living in the same place'. When everyone in the pub laughs at this statement, Bloom changes tack: 'Or also living in different places'.[8] Bloom's seemingly simplistic focus on the nationalism of people and place betrays anxieties about his own position in Irish society. But it also attests to the core coordinates defining different kinds of nationalisms in the period. Irish nationalism involved the assertion of the right to geographical and political self-determination and independence from English rule, a principle that had been enshrined in the founding protocols of the League of Nations which was created after the First World War. The Jews, in contrast, might be said to constitute a nation of people 'living in different places', who sought to legitimate their national identity through land. The political nationalism of the Italian fascists, meanwhile, involved the aggressive assertion of existing national borders and identities.

A number of writers were interested in the deeper causes of nationalism and imperialism, seeing London's expanding and changing landscape as a result of its global economic exploitation of other lands. Eliot's *The Waste Land* focuses on London as a place which is marked by the interrelationships of stock market flows, shifting geographical borders, and fragile national identities. Pound, in *The Cantos*, meanwhile, brings to life the historical and contemporary links between financial speculation, military conflict and cultural production.

MODERNISM AND REALISM

Before considering the writing of Woolf, Richardson and Joyce, I want to turn to an important precursor to their narratives of the city, Ford Madox Ford's *The Soul of London* (1905). *The Soul of*

London creates a partial and fragmented description of the city, and highlights the fact that these techniques are partly a response to London's imperial status. By 1905, London was the largest city in the world. Ford captures both the excitement and the feelings of isolation and disconnection, of being in the modern metropolis. A host of writers in the mid to late nineteenth century had engaged with London as an enlarging geographical entity and site of technological, financial and cultural modernisation. The psychological consequences of industrialisation and expansion had also become a preoccupation of sociologists and psychologists in the late nineteenth and early twentieth century. Gustave Le Bon wrote a famous account of the terrifyingly unconscious impulses of city crowds in *The Crowd: A Study of the Popular Mind* (1895), in which he argued that the sensual activities of large urban groups reveal the unpredictability and irrationality of modern democratic politics. Georg Simmel, in *The Metropolis and Mental Life* (1903), describes the individual in the city as experiencing a sensory overload which produces either an unconscious hypersensitivity to external stimuli, or a protective intellectual attitude, what he labels a 'blasé metropolitan attitude'.[9]

Ford's *The Soul of London* engages with both a rich fictional heritage and the tenor of Le Bon's and Simmel's attempts to bridge psychology and sociology. *The Soul of London* experiments with and destabilises the boundaries separating fiction and criticism by creating a hybrid text which documents, rather than fictionalises, the city, and privileges the narrator's personality as a source of experience and meaning.

Ford and his co-writer Conrad labelled their work Impressionism in order to promote its novelty. The word deliberately referenced the Impressionist painting of the late nineteenth century, such as works by Pisarro, Degas, Cézanne, Manet, and, in particular Monet, whose painting 'Impression' (1872) occasioned the coining of the term. The principles of Impressionism as a term applied to writing, rather than painting, are described in Conrad's preface to *The Nigger of the 'Narcissus'* (1897) and Ford's essay 'Impressionism' in 1914. Both writers emphasise the artistic significance of an isolated narrative moment involving a heightened experience of space and time. Ideas of the author's or narrator's sincerity and tenacity were significant in revealing the moment's 'secret', as Conrad put it, ideas that are set out in the opening paragraph of *The Soul of London*:

> Most of us love places very much as we love what, for us, are the distinguished men of our social lives. Paying a visit to such a man we give, in one form or another, our impressions to our friends: since it is human to desire to leave some memorial that shall record our view of the man at the stage he has reached. We describe his manners, his shape, his utterances: we moralise a little about his associates, his ethics, the cut of his clothes; we relate gossip about his past before we knew him, or we predict his future when we shall be no more with him. We are, all of us who are Londoners, paying visits of greater or less duration to a Personality that, whether we love it or very cordially hate it, fascinates us all. And, paying my visit, I have desired to give such a record.[10]

Ford uses a number of significant words in this opening paragraph – 'impressions', 'Personality', 'view', 'love', 'desire', 'form' and 'record'. He begins by suggesting that London, a geographical place, is actually more like a person than an area of land. This anti-materialism is evident in *The Soul of London* in a number of ways. The personal note of the narrator's relationship to London is maintained throughout and the text does not present a factual description of the city's geography or history. Instead, it creates vignettes about random individual lives or experiences, or presents isolated images of the different elements that make up the London that the narrator loves and hates. Ford labels these pictures 'Impressions' because their pictorial qualities are central to the writing: along with his reference to 'view' in his opening paragraph, he also describes his desire to 'cast a light upon modern London', or to present the 'details' which 'strike at the eye'.[11] These phrases both situate agency in the narrator who will illuminate London and suggests that the details of the external world are perceived, even organised, pictorially. It is the narrator's subjectivity, a subjectivity which is 'passionate in its attempt after truth of rendering', as he puts it, which will bring life to these isolated elements, and make them meaningful.[12] While Ford uses the words 'love', 'personality', 'desire' and 'passion' to capture the intensity and predilections of his narrator's focus, Conrad, in his 'Preface' to *The Nigger of the 'Narcissus'* refers to the sincerity and integrity of the author.

Ford gives a number of reasons for presenting a London that is both painterly and personal. At the beginning of Chapter 1 he states that London is simply too big to visualise as a whole. This is because of its position at the heart of the British imperial state, whose geographical boundaries reside, not in the suburban outskirts of London geography, but in the outer reaches of India or Africa. The representation of London, then, would merely create an account that is either a list of uninteresting facts, or an abstraction. Any attempt to depict the city, he argues, will be necessarily partial, and the individualistic parameters of Impressionism are therefore an artistic response to the sprawling geography and historical complexity of the modern imperial city. The coordinates of Ford's response to the modern metropolis involve a self-reflexive discussion of the values and ideas which mediate the relationship between narrator and urban space.

As in Ford's *The Soul of London* the city is thought of as personal to Dorothy Richardson and Virginia Woolf. Their focus on individual perspective and psychic responses to the city raised significant questions about what the novel could reasonably seek to represent, questions which concerned the nature of narrative form and literary realism. Literary realism is a complicated and heavily disputed term. As a starting point one might say that literary realism aims to represent experiential reality through the accurate portrayal of details about character, time and place. Literary realism, however, is a shifting category, because the understanding of what constitutes reality, as well as the means by which a writer might capture this entity, vary according to time and place. The formal experiments of modernist texts might be seen to be distinct from the aims and parameters of literary realism. Techniques discussed in the Introduction and the previous chapter, such as Stein's prose experiments or Joyce's *Finnegans Wake*, could, reasonably enough, be said to distort the coordinates of literary realism, and the 'real' geographical spaces of cities.

Some modernist writers, however, claimed that their work,

particularly their use of interior monologue, represented a new kind of realism. 'What is reality?' Virginia Woolf asked in 'Character in Fiction', and 'who are the judges of reality?'[13] Woolf did not want to dispense with literary realism, but to re-invent it to fit modern concerns. In her essay 'Modern Fiction', she distinguished between a factual and a psychic account of external realities, and pulled apart the presuppositions and parameters of what she called the 'materialist' style of popular contemporary realist novelists Arnold Bennett, H. G. Wells, and John Galsworthy.[14] Bennett, in particular, is singled out as the key contemporary exponent of conventional literary realism, mainly because he is the most successful of these writers. Woolf argued that his realistic narratives arrange a series of materialistic details in an immobile narrative structure with a predictable beginning, middle and end and in doing so fails to respond to and capture the thing they seek: 'Whether we call it life or spirit, truth or reality, this, the essential thing, has moved off, or on, and refuses to be contained any longer in such ill-fitting vestments as we provide.' Bennett, she implies, is looking at the wrong thing. Look 'within', Woolf demanded, and examine 'an ordinary mind on an ordinary day'. This ordinary mind, she claims, drifts and responds, rather than develops. The task of the modern writer is to capture the mind's movement, both in its responses to the world and in its shifting ability to see or feel its own desires because 'the point of interest, lies very likely in the dark places of psychology'.[15]

Dorothy Richardson also argued that her writing of consciousness gave access to a heightened kind of 'contemplated reality' in which psychic realism replaces artificial plot structures. She had set out in 1908–12 to write a new kind of novel which explored a woman's quest for independence within the patriarchal society of the late nineteenth century, with the first volume, *Pointed Roofs*, appearing in 1915. The book focalised attention on the female protagonist's point of view and was instantly hailed by critics as the instigator of a new kind of 'psychological' novel. Subsequent volumes of *Pilgrimage* were published quickly through the 1910s, with *Backwater* (1916), *Honeycomb* (1917), *The Tunnel* (February, 1919), *Interim* (December 1919), *Deadlock* (1921) and *Revolving Lights* (1923). Later chapters took longer to write, and Richardson's reputation, which was at its height when *Interim* was appearing in *The Little Review* in 1919, started to wane.[16]

The novel dispenses with the conventional structure of the novel form – the beginning, middle and end – and replaces it with a narrative composed from the point of view of an individual's experiences through chronological time. Richardson's understanding of space and reality was informed by gendered power relations. Similarly to Woolf, Richardson wanted to oppose the style exemplified by Arnold Bennett's novels; in her 1938 'Foreword' to *Pilgrimage*, which looked back at her first forays into print, she expressed the need to create a 'feminine equivalent' to the 'current masculine realism'.[17] *Pilgrimage* follows the life of its protagonist, Miriam Henderson, as she develops from young adulthood to maturity. *Pointed Roofs* begins with Miriam leaving school and travelling to Germany to complete her education. Volume four, *The Tunnel*, focuses on Miriam's working life in London. Miriam experiences the financial and psychological freedoms and anxieties of being a woman in London. One night, walking along Euston Road she hears the voice of an invisible woman:

'Dressed up – he was – to the bloody death . . .' The words echoed about her as she strolled down the street controlling her impulse to flinch and hurry. The woman was there, there and real, and that was what she had said.[18]

Richardson's writing is generally fragmentary in style, often adopting ellipsis to suggest the impressionistic movement of the mind. Miriam's anxiety is a core aspect of her response to the city. The writing, in its nervousness about the intentions of a woman who can be heard but not seen, implies that there is a sense-certainty to visual information, a solidity that will make the woman 'real'. *Pilgrimage* describes in meticulous and unadorned language Miriam's consideration of the visual information and conversations which she sees or hears.

The novel also probes her protagonist's introspective thoughts about selfhood, masculinity and femininity. Like Joyce, who documents the semi-conscious thoughts that flit across Bloom's mind, she is interested in unconscious or lapsed forms of consciousness. At the end of Chapter 3, for instance, Miriam leaves the dental surgery where she works in Wimpole Street, forcibly restraining her impulsive desire to run. Chapter 4 begins 'When she came to herself she was in the Strand'. The movement through the intervening space and the thoughts she has had, remain blank: 'She wondered what she had been thinking since she left Wimpole Street, and whether she had come across Trafalgar Square without seeing it or round by some other way.'[19] The city that is created through this voice is explicitly partial, dependent on gaps in the writing which mirror the absences in Miriam's consciousness.

Richardson, in her 'Foreword', worried about what kind of reality she had given birth to in *Pointed Roofs*. She is anxious that the movement inwards to the 'reconstruction of experience focused from within the mind of a single individual' has created a writing which lacks objectivity. It has 'a hundred faces', all of which cancel each other out.[20] But in many respects this fragmented reality is one of the novel's strengths, as the focus on the individual and the splintering of the objective world forms part of the 'actualisation of space' described by de Certeau. It takes the reader into the texture of a woman's walk through London, which includes precise references to streets and buildings, and considerations of the relationship between reality, gender and consciousness. After arriving at her new flat at the beginning of *The Tunnel*,

> she was surprised now at her familiarity with the detail of the room . . . that idea of visiting places in dreams. It was something more than that . . . all the real part of your life has a real dream in it; some of the real dream part of you coming true. You know in advance when you are really following your life. These things are familiar because reality is here. Coming events cast *light*.[21]

The self as an entity defined in and through time – Miriam's lived part, dream part, and future part – competes with the self as something realised through objects. Reality is both connected to that which is familiar – the room, the streets of the city – and to forms of self-understanding which involve an ability to see the history and the trajectory of one's life clearly.

But what about Richardson's claim that there is something 'feminine' about her focus on the mind? Richardson herself complicated the idea that psychological fiction was 'feminine' in some way by admitting that Proust's and James's novels also attend to the interior life. But one could argue that her writing is 'feminine' in a different sense. When Miriam wanders into an A.B.C. (a chain of tearooms, named after the Aerated Bread Company, popular in the late nineteenth and early twentieth century) to have supper, she considers the freedom of her fellow diners, and of herself: 'No one who had never been alone in London was quite alive . . . I'm free – I've got free – nothing can ever alter that, she thought, gazing wide-eyed into the fire, between fear and joy.'[22] The femininity of the writing resides partly in its focus on a woman's self-reflexive sense of the novelty of her urban and financial freedoms: it is as a woman that she has 'got free'. Richardson's writing of Miriam's psychic responses to the London landscape does attend to a female experience of the city, in which the individual is the object of a sexualised gaze, and in which a sexualised 'fear' and anxiety is never far away from the 'joy' of independence.

A sense of the historically recent freedoms of wandering women in the city is also central to Woolf's *Mrs Dalloway* (1925). Elizabeth Dalloway, Mrs Dalloway's daughter, drifts through the streets of London and experiences an unconscious and impulsive freedom where 'Elizabeth stepped forward and most competently boarded the omnibus, in front of everybody . . . She was delighted to be free'.[23] Despite their shared focus on female independence, however, the London that Virginia Woolf writes in *Mrs Dalloway* is very different to the city we are presented with in *Pilgrimage*. Woolf's novel tells the story of a day in the life of a woman in her fifties preparing for an evening party. Mrs Dalloway's map of London geography is fairly contained and restricted to a privileged part of the city: the writing follows Clarissa as she leaves her house in Westminster, crosses Victoria Street, reaches St James's Park, looks at buses in Piccadilly, and then walks towards Bond Street.

Like *Pilgrimage*, Woolf's writing captures the interior life of her protagonist. But the means with which she does so are distinctive.

In contrast to *Pilgrimage*, the writing moves seamlessly in and out of subjective and objective viewpoints:

> But everyone remembered; what she loved was this, here, now, in front of her; the fat lady in the cab. Did it matter then, she asked herself, walking towards Bond Street, did it matter that she must inevitably cease completely; all this must go on without her; did she resent it; or did it not become consoling to believe that death ended absolutely? But that somehow in the streets of London, on the ebb and flow of things, here, there, she survived, Peter survived, lived in each other, she being part, she was positive, of the trees at home; of the house there, ugly, rambling all to bits and pieces as it was; part of people she had never met; being laid out like a mist between the people she knew best, who lifted her on their branches as she had seen the trees lift the mist, but it spread ever so far, her life, herself.[24]

In the passage above the linguistic movement into Clarissa's memories and opinions is intermittently drawn back to the streets through which she walks. Rather than presenting a psyche that responds to external stimuli, sentences such as 'Did it matter, then, she asked herself, walking towards Bond Street' inhabit the rhythms of a mind thinking while walking. Woolf's free indirect discourse moves so close to the 'ebbs and flows' of Clarissa's thoughts that the reader is placed inside the words of the 'she' who loves, resents, consoles and survives. This interior monologue is less visual than that of Richardson and Joyce. The reader is not allowed to see what it is that Clarissa sees. Instead, she is permitted to learn what it is that Clarissa loves: it seems to be more important that the city is 'this, here, now, in front of her' rather than that she has seen something specific that gives her pleasure. While some concrete details are provided, other aspects of the external world are more general. Woolf writes as much about Mrs Dalloway's feeling about the city, as she does about the city itself.

Woolf represents Clarissa Dalloway's thoughts about the fragments of her presence in geographically distant trees, in houses in her accidental eye line, in people she has never met, as well as those she has. There is something ghostly about this idea of the intermixture of a subject and the objects or individuals she has encountered, as well as in the way that the writing transports the reader across space and time. This ghostliness is partly a product of Clarissa's thoughts about what kind of presence she might have in the world after she is dead. But Woolf was more generally interested in the self as an apparition that could glide in and out of external entities. In an earlier text, called 'Street Haunting: A London Adventure', Woolf explicitly connects city wandering with haunting. The text focuses on a woman who leaves her room and goes into the city in order to buy a pencil. She describes herself as 'a central oyster of perceptiveness, an enormous eye', an eye which 'floats' around the streets of the city, observing, empathising briefly and then sliding on.[25] In the passage above from *Mrs Dalloway*, the tempo and reach of the writing is ghostly in this way; it also floats, touches and glides. Woolf's writing sees the mind as contained in its rhythmical movement in and out of introspective thoughts or memories.

In *To the Lighthouse* (1927), Woolf also depicts apparitional characters who haunt the present, but the novel is set in a natural, rather than urban landscape, and the characters are largely static. Landscape is something to be looked at in this novel, not walked through, and the contemplative aspect of the novel produces different effects. A focus on the organisational principle of time continues to structure the narrative: *To the Lighthouse* follows the thoughts of Mrs Ramsay (in Part One) as she goes about her domestic duties, and Lily Briscoe (in Part Three) as she paints her picture through time. But Mrs Ramsay and Lily sit and look at the lighthouse on the horizon, and the novel is preoccupied with how that external entity can be made meaningful. Woolf repeats the distinction between facts and feeling: while for Mr Ramsay, the reality of the lighthouse is of uncompromising facts; for Mrs Ramsay and Lily the real is a product of feeling.

Lily Briscoe, on returning to the house at the beginning of the third part of *To the Lighthouse*, considers:

She had no attachment here, she felt, no relations with it, anything might happen, and whatever did happen, a step outside, a voice calling (It's not in the cupboard; it's on the landing', someone cried), was a question, as if the link that usually bound things together had been cut, and they floated up here, down there, off, anyhow. How aimless it was, how chaotic, how unreal it was, she thought, looking at her empty coffee cup. Mrs Ramsay dead; Andrew killed; Prue dead too – repeat it as she might, it roused no feeling in her. And we all get together in a house like this on a morning like this, she said, looking out of the window – it was a beautiful still day.[26]

The unreality Lily experiences is connected to feeling and form. The novel as a whole balances the chaos and disconnection here described by way of Lily's voice, and the imposition of form and significance. The repetition of the factual language of death rouses no feeling in Lily; she seeks recognition of loss through other means. But if the aimless happenings of life are 'unreal' to Lily, then the novel, or at least Lily as a character, locates reality in an idea of a true perception of life; in a more heightened awareness, perhaps, or a visionary artistic experience. The sudden declaration - 'it was a beautiful day' – is the result of an impulsive shift of perspective from the coffee cup to the scene outside the window. Such moments occur frequently in Woolf's prose, and in *To the Lighthouse* in particular, and their significance lies in the real, because impulsive, nature of feeling. Towards the end of the first episode, Prue experiences a sudden realisation of Mrs Ramsay's truth: '"That's my mother", thought Prue. Yes; Minta should look at her; Paul Rayley should look at her. That is the thing itself, she felt, as if there were only one person like that in the world; her mother.'[27]

Here, 'the thing itself', which Pound had seen in Joyce's depiction of ordinary lives in *Dubliners*, surfaces to demarcate reality as heightened experience. The idea that reality is formed by way of an intense perception conforms to Woolf's argument in 'Modern Fiction' that reality is an 'essential thing' or spirit, caught at a moment of psychic intensity.

DUBLIN

Alongside London, another city was to play a significant part in the modernist imaginary: Dublin. All of Joyce's novels are grounded in the geography of Dublin, but the way in which geography is made into language changes radically from the short stories about ordinary lives of his first book *Dubliners*, to the linguistic distortions of *Finnegans Wake*. The precise references to streets and areas reveal class affiliations in *Dubliners*: Mr James Duffy, in 'A Painful Case', lives in Chapelizod because 'he found all of the other suburbs of Dublin mean, modern and pretentious.'[28] At the beginning of 'Anna Livia Plurabelle' in *Finnegans Wake*, meanwhile, the Phoenix Park becomes a 'Fiendish park' in the voice of one of the washerwomen.[29] Geographical location is still significant, but the particularities of place are only one level of reference: the texture of the words used to refer to geography have now become subject matter to be played with and distorted.

The terms of this Joycean trajectory from literary realism to modernist experiment, from geography as specific street names to geography as distorted language, are complex, however. The opening lines of 'A Painful Case' both imply and produce a collective register: by assuming a consensus about the class significance of living in certain Dublin suburbs, they construct Chapelizod within a class hierarchy. The feelings Mr Duffy has about his Dublin suburb, however, are more revealingly personal than the language implies. By the end of the story, the careful description of Mr Duffy's suburb, 'sombre house' and lonely room become key signifiers of his psychic reality. After he has refused intimacy with the lonely Mrs Sinico, he experiences a sudden realisation of his own isolation. Mr Duffy, in trying to separate himself from the mean and the modern, has become a potent image of ungenerous and small-minded modernity. The notion that Chapelizod is isolated from the suburban qualities he despises, it seems, is partly a product of his personal perspective. The idea of a consensus about geography becomes blurred. The movement between geography as a bearer of collective signifiers and geography as the product of personal interpretation structures the book as a whole.

In another story in *Dubliners*, 'Two Gallants', the narrative maps the city by following the precise geographical contours of Lenehan's and Corley's walk through Dublin. They go 'down the hill of Rutland Square', pass 'along the railings of Trinity College', stroll 'along Nassau Street' and then turn 'into Kildare Street', before reaching 'Stephen's Green'. When Lenehan separates from Corley, the location of his perambulations become even more specific: he walks as far as the 'Shelbourne Hotel', past the 'railings of the Duke's Lawn', and then drifts down 'Grafton Street'.[30] Other stories, such as 'Eveline', focus on fantasies of escape from the grinding poverty and familiarity of Dublin.

The way in which Joyce writes about geography in *Dubliners* takes us, as it did in Woolf's and Richardson's work, into questions about the parameters and meaning of realism. He provides some clues about how we might read the realism of his writing in a lecture of 1912 about Daniel Defoe and William Blake called 'Realism and Idealism in English Literature', in which he examines their opposed ways of writing about the real. According to Joyce, it is in Defoe's writing that 'the soul of the modern realist novel can be glimpsed'.[31] This is a realism of what he calls 'admirable clarity' in which 'the star of poesy is, as they say, conspicuous by its absence'. In addition to the absence of lyricism and sentiment in the writing, Defoe's work involves a particular kind of approach to the world: his writing has the 'precision and innocence of a child's questions.' Blake, in contrast, is a visionary writer who searches for the meaning behind or beyond the visible world: 'the soul must not look *with* but rather *through* the eye'. His writing, according to Joyce, annihilates 'space and time' and denies the 'existence of memory and the senses' because he is focused on the supernatural. His style is to move 'from the infinitely small to the infinitely big, from a drop of blood to the universe of stars'.[32]

Joyce's thoughts on the differences between Defoe and Blake are helpful in understanding the way he writes about geography. It is not the case that Defoe's writing is less carefully constructed or artificial than Blake's, nor that it is less personal. It is more that the thing that is being looked at, and the way that it is being regarded, is different. Defoe, according to Joyce, dissects the world, in both its geographical and supernatural guises, from the point of view of an innocent rationalist; hence the idea of a 'child's questions'. Defoe's narratives build a picture of the real through an encyclopaedic attention to the details of the material universe, whether this involves describing the phenomenology of wind or the geographical details of Crusoe's island.

Blake's focus, according to Joyce, is different. He is not interested in the phenomenal world and its spatial and temporal dimensions: he aims to look through 'the eye' of streets, buildings or bodies, to their supernatural and visionary significance. Joyce's writing tends to look 'with' rather than 'through' the body, but aspects of Blake's visionary aesthetic are also an essential part of Joyce's early writing. He adopted a religious word to describe these visions – epiphany – and the stories in *Dubliners* centre on them.

Joyce's lectures are interesting not only for what they say about Defoe and Blake, but also for the way they split the history of literature into two opposed camps of realism and visionary poetry. These divergent approaches to the real, according to Joyce, also, importantly, involve an understanding of nationality and empire. Defoe, Joyce argues, is the first English writer to 'instil a truly national spirit into the creations of his pen'. Defoe's innocence and precision is that of the imperialist cartographer abroad – the approach of 'the Anglo-Saxon in the presence of the Celt' and of a 'realist in the presence of the unknown'.[33] Its spirit involves a need to map an alien geography. Blake's visionary aesthetic, in contrast, is connected to an Enlightenment politics of revolution and self-determination. It is grounded in a stable material universe that looks beyond.

Joyce's own early writing, and the particular blend of his modernism, bridges Defoe's realism and Blake's visionary imagination. Joyce's epiphanies, in contrast to Blake's visions, centre on unostentatious or everyday objects or revelations: an epiphany, Joyce wrote, is the instantaneous 'revelation of the whatness of a thing', when 'the soul of the commonest object . . . seems to us radiant'.[34] In 'A Painful Case', when Mr Duffy suddenly realises at the end of the story that he has withheld life from both Mrs Sinico and himself, he feels his world falling to pieces, but his true understanding of this moral failure comes by way of his body. He recognises that he is alone and thinks he feels the voice of Mrs Sinico 'touch his ear'. He then gazes down at Dublin from the top of Magazine Hill and notices a goods train winding its way 'like a worm' through the darkness and hears the sound of the engine 'reiterating the syllables of her name'. He has a sudden realisation of his true isolation when the sound of the train disappears:

'He could hear nothing: the night was perfectly silent. He listened again: perfectly silent. He felt that he was alone.'[35] When Mr Duffy is finally able to 'feel', rather than simply comprehend his isolation, he realises his disconnection from his body.

Like *Dubliners*, Joyce's second book, *A Portrait of the Artist as a Young Man*, balances geographical realism and epiphanic moments. Unlike *Dubliners*, however, it shifts the parameters of its realism inwards. *A Portrait of the Artist as a Young Man* literally begins from the point of view of a child: 'Once upon a time and a very good time it was there was a moocow coming down along the road and this moocow that was coming down along the road met a nicens little boy named baby tuckoo . . .'.[36] The 'Portrait' that Joyce sketches in the novel is one that views the phenomenal world 'with' the eyes of his artist as he develops from a boy thinking in nursery rhymes to a young intellectual who has started to think independently and is about to leave home. Joyce has shifted the focus of his writing from stories which gesture towards the way in which Dubliners see the city, to the manner in which language structures external objects and landscapes. When Stephen Dedalus wanders 'up and down the dark slimy streets peering into the gloom of lanes and doorways', the Dublin he presents, a Dublin composed of sinister and indecipherable darkness, is the one that matches his psychic and linguistic reality at this stage of the book. When he is kissed by a prostitute, his body encounters the linguistic counterpart to these gloomy doorways: he feels her lips 'as though they were the vehicle of a vague speech'.[37]

The proximity of geographical and psychic registers controls the writing. At the beginning of the next chapter, Joyce writes that 'It would be a gloomy secret night'.[38] The word 'gloomy' has become a kind of psychic trigger signifying sexual promiscuity. The picture that the novel presents of Stephen's development as an artist depends, to some extent, on the contours of these geographical signifiers. Much later in the book, Stephen experiences an epiphanic realisation of the nature of secular beauty through the contemplation of a girl wading in the sea. Here the geography of a natural landscape, in its ability to offer up seascape metaphors of wildness, flight and delicacy, allows Stephen to realise his artistic nature: 'He was alone and young and wilful and wildhearted, alone amid a waste of wild air and brackish waters'. In his contemplation of the girl, he considers that 'She seemed like one whom magic had changed into the likeness of a strange and beautiful seabird.'[39] The sordid and sexualised Dublin streets and the liberated and romanticised beach of Stephen's imagination combine the realities of geography – Stephen is unlikely to see a wild seabird on Grafton Street – and the artifice of styles of writing. The assonantal connections between wilful, wildhearted, waste, wild and waters are partly the product of Stephen's romanticised poetic sensibility at this stage of the novel. Language, the book teaches us, constructs, rather than reflects, geography.

There is an implication that Stephen's words at the end of the novel constitute a more realised artistic register. They are precise about Dublin streets: 'Met her today point blank in Grafton Street. The crowd brought us together.' They are also, however, significantly replete with the imaginative and artistic temptations of unknown and abstract foreign geographies: 'the white arms of roads, their promise of close embraces and the black arms of tall ships that stand against the moon, their tale of distant nations'.[40]

In *Ulysses*, Joyce mocks his own earlier interest in epiphanies. As his two key protagonists wander around the city, the text carefully pins itself to the names and dimensions of streets and buildings, as well as the time it would take to travel from one place to another. With the introduction of interior monologue as one of the many linguistic styles in *Ulysses*, however, the shift of focus takes a further turn inwards. The interior monologues of Bloom and Stephen present the city as psychic material: 'Mr Bloom came to Kildare street. First I must. Library.'[41] Kildare Street in Dublin is flanked by the National Museum to the south and the National Library to the north. While third person narration guides us into Kildare Street, the word 'Library' is a signifier of Bloom's direct encounter with the external world. But Joyce's technique of interior monologue necessarily produces a city that is filtered through the personal preoccupations, political and religious affiliations and intellectual interests of his characters.

Despite the cartographic accuracy of geography in *Ulysses* the city that is written by means of interior monologue is individualised and psychically charged. Immediately after Bloom turns into Kildare Street and faces the Library, he sees something that troubles him: a 'Straw hat in sunlight'.[42] The straw hat is one of the key signifiers of Bloom's sexual rival, Blazes Boylan, who later in the day will go to Bloom's house to have sex with Molly Bloom. The straw hat in sunlight serves, at this point in the text, to distort Bloom's response to geography: 'His heart quopped softly. To the right. Museum. Goddesses.' Bloom distracts himself from his troubled heart by turning round and fixing his eyes and his mind on the museum and its statues. For the benefit of Boylan, Bloom also puts in a psychic performance of scrutinising the goddesses, as though his mind imagines itself being observed. The feelings of anxiety and jealousy that animate this performance are not fully articulated by Bloom: the writing implies that they take place just beneath the surface of Bloom's conscious mind: 'Making for the museum gate with long windy strides he lifted his eyes. Handsome building. Sir Thomas Deane designed. Not following me?'[43] Here, Bloom's mind pretends to be interested in the impressive building in front of him, but he is mainly preoccupied with whether Boylan is pursuing him. Whereas Bloom is generally observant about the external world, his perspicacity here breaks down in the face of emotional pressure. 'Handsome building' has the echo of something one might read on a brochure; while Sir Thomas Deane did not design the National Museum; his grandson did.

Other episodes fragment the city further. As we saw in the previous chapter, 'Aeolus' begins in the middle of the city. This description of trams coming in and out of Sackville (now O'Connell) Street is mediated, not by Stephen's or Bloom's interior lives, but by an excitable journalistic style, a style that is no more objective than Bloom's response to the museum. Joyce employs many other recognisable discursive styles in *Ulysses*. An oral culture of Dublin slang and nationalism informs the writing of 'Cyclops', which focuses on Bloom having a drink in a pub and talking to an anti-Semitic Irish nationalist; in 'Circe' Joyce writes about the red-light district of Dublin in the form of a Surreal playscript; in 'Ithaca', as Stephen and Bloom wander home through deserted Dublin

streets in the early hours of the morning, he writes their conversations in the style of both the catechism and a school textbook of
encyclopaedic knowledge by Richard Magnall called *Historical and
Miscellaneous Questions*.

At the heart of the Hibernian metropolis sits the statue of an
English admiral, Nelson, and the trams that transport Dubliners
in and out of the city congregate around it. The statue occupies a
commanding view over the main thoroughfare in Dublin, Sackville
Street, which was the site of Dublin Lockout gatherings in 1913
and the Easter Rising of 1916. It was originally named after
Lionel Cranfield Sackville of Dorset, Lord Lieutenant of Ireland,
but was renamed O'Connell Street in 1924, in honour of Daniel
O'Connell, a nineteenth-century Irish Nationalist leader. The
streets of Dublin bear the marks of England's authority in Ireland,
and Ireland's subjection to English rule features significantly in
Ulysses.

Despite the fact that *Finnegans Wake* distorts place names
through playful and comic invention, it also writes a kind of map
of Dublin. The text begins in midstream with a description of the
River Liffey: 'riverrun, past Eve and Adam's, from swerve of shore
to bend of bay, brings us by a commodious vicus of recirculation
back to Howth Castle and Environs'.[44] Margot Norris, in an essay
on *Finnegans Wake*, suggests that the opening of the book 'drops
us, without map, clock, compass, glossary, or footnotes, into an
unknown verbal country'.[45] The topography around Dublin and
reference to Howth Castle and the Adam and Eve pub, orientates
the language in the Irish landscape. But the circular sweep of the
language involves a panoramic, almost cinematic, view of landscape, a lofty perspective which informs the playful self-reflexivity
of the language. In a later section of *Finnegans Wake* Joyce evokes
this landless cinematic quality more explicitly:

It scenes like a landescape from Wildu Picturescu or some
seem on some dimb Arraz, dumb as Mum's mutyness, this
mimage of the seventyseventh kusin of kristansen is odable
to os across the wineless Ere no oedor nor mere eerie nor liss
potent of suggestion than in the tales of the tingmount.[46]

The dumb actions of silent cinema are mixed with fantasy film studios – Wildu Picturescu – in the creation of a medium of expression which reaches 'across the wineless' Ere, a word which suggests sea, Eire, and ear. This phrase incorporates the winedark sea of Homer's Odyssean epic, and what was seen as the universal, because silent, power of cinema in the 1920s, as well as the new wireless technologies which were revolutionising the representation of geography and time. The sentence above, situated as it is in the middle of an episode which mentions 'television', 'telephony' and the movies, might be said to both incorporate reference to cutting-edge technologies, and gesture forwards in time: perhaps this is what Joyce thinks is 'potent' about their suggestiveness.

Joyce refers to those things that the movies cannot do: they are dumb and odourless. The bodily sensations of vocal noises, smell and touch are qualities that Joyce had once seen as significant to one kind of literary realism, as we saw above. The phrase 'scenes like a landescape' is helpful when considering the writing of geography in *Finnegans Wake*. Like the 'potent' technologies of cinema, the book is able to splice together images of different geographies and time zones in the creation of a seamless present tense.

EXILED WRITING

I wanted to free myself of repetitive thoughts and experiences – my own and those of many of my contemporaries. I did not specifically realize just what it was I wanted, but I knew that I, like most of the people I knew, in England, America and on the Continent of Europe, were drifting . . . Where? I did not know but at least I accepted the fact that we *were* drifting.[47]

H. D., in *Tribute to Freud*, describes her generation as 'drifting'. Alongside the drifting writers of the 'lost generation', as it was known, however, there were more politicised accounts of the experience of artistic exile or national estrangement, accounts which involved writing techniques distinct from the psychological or cinematic focus discussed in the previous two sections. Both Wyndham Lewis and D. H. Lawrence were overtly hostile to the interior monologue styles of Woolf, Richardson and Joyce. They sought to create, in disparate ways, a spatial or visual writing which emphasised other elements of the historical conflicts of geography and space.

At the same time as Wyndham Lewis was producing *Blast* 1 and 2, he also wrote his first novel, *Tarr*, which was published in *The Egoist* in instalments from 1916 to 1917. It is embedded in the geography of Paris and written from the point of view of an artistic exile attuned to the way that class and money fragment the urban landscape:

> The Knackfus Quarter is given up to Art. = Letters and other things are round the corner. = Its rent is half paid by America. Germany occupies a sensible apartment on the second floor. A hundred square yards at its centre is a convenient space, where the Boulevard du Paradis and Boulevard Pfeifer cross with their electric trams. = In the middle is a pavement island, like vestige of submerged masonry. = Italian models festoon it in symmetrical human groups; it is also their club. = The Café Berne, at one side, is the club of the 'grands messieurs Du Berne.' So you have the clap-trap and amorphous Campagna tribe outside, in the Café twenty sluggish commonsense Germans, a Vitagraph group or two drinking and playing billiards. There as the most permanent tableaux of this place, disheartening and admonitory as a Tussaud's of The Flood.[48]

This writing is precise about the arrangement of specific city streets and cafés. But it also depicts, with a remarkable economy of means, the layers of associations that construct these city spaces. Lewis is attuned to way that economics, nationality and class fragment the streets and buildings of Paris. Paris is depicted as both the centre of international artistic activity – America, Germany, Italy and England are all here – and as splintered apart by national associations and characteristics.

It is as though this is written from the perspective of an anthropological and exiled observer who considers the odd group behaviour and rituals of strangers. The narrative voice, then, is alienated from the human activity it observes and satirises. At the same time, however, the writing relies on the instant cultural significance of labels, whether these relate to commodified technologies, literary works or nationalities. Immediately prior to this paragraph, Lewis refers to Henri Murger's 'Vie de Bohème'. Murger's *Scènes de la vie de bohème* (1847–9) focused on his experiences of poverty in the streets of mid-nineteenth-century Paris. The 'Campagna tribe' is a catchy way of referring to a group of Romans. The Vitagraph group playing billiards, conjures up the nature of film production. By 1907 the American Vitagraph was one of the most significant of the American studios.

While the paragraph documents the economic niceties of Paris real estate, it also participates in the commodified language which is partly a product of this economics. The 'Art' that these individuals give themselves to, then, is a complex entity comprising nationality, money and new technology. *Tarr*, which is based on a character of that name, focuses on the attempt to create a different notion of art, one that stands outside these interests – which might be described as a kind of vortex of modernising elements – and controls its energies. Lewis's language is spatial in its juxtapositions of unlike urban and natural imagery, economic realities and journalistic stereotypes, anthropological and literary registers.

While Lewis's spatial language is visual, Lawrence created a different metaphorical language of exile. After the war, he travelled to Sicily, Ceylon (Sri Lanka) and Australia, before setting up home in New Mexico in 1924, partly in order to escape from an England that he felt had persecuted him during the war. In his writing self-exile creates a series of spatial metaphors in which psychic and spatial emptiness is imagined by way of landscape. At the end of *Women in Love*, Lawrence's four main characters, Gerald, Gudrun, Birkin and Ursula, escape England and travel to Austria. Their exilic fantasies of a new world are mapped onto a pristine, timeless snowscape. Ursula, coming through the snow at night-time, uses this landscape to play with thoughts of her past, and future:

> She looked round this silent, upper world of snow and stars and powerful cold. There was another world, like views on a magic lantern; The Marsh, Cossethay, Ilkeston, lit up with a

common, unreal light. There was a shadowy, unreal Ursula, a whole shadow-play of an unreal life. It was as unreal, and circumscribed, as a magic-lantern show. She wished the slides could all be broken . . . She wanted to have no past. She wanted to have come down from the slopes of heaven to this place, with Birkin, not to have toiled out of the murk of her childhood and her upbringing, slowly, all soiled . . . She knew herself new and unbegotten, she had no father, nor mother, no anterior connections, she was herself, pure and silvery, she belonged only to the oneness with Birkin, a oneness that struck deeper notes, sounding into the heart of the universe, the heart of reality, where she had never existed before.[49]

In this passage the icy European landscape furnishes a language for Ursula's fantasies of autogenesis and new life. The writing incorporates both Ursula's individual perspective on her home, and a narrative view of the 'common, unreal light' which illuminates England. Her fantasy of rebirth thereby extends outside herself. The idea of the snowscape as a timeless landscape is shared by other characters. The image of the heart – or centre – of the universe echoes with Gudrun's view that the snowscape is the 'centre, the knot, the navel of the world'.[50] Lawrence's writing seeks to synthesise the fate of individual characters and the shared cycles of life.

In the passage from *Women in Love* quoted above, the material qualities of a landscape separate from English soil, proffers a language uncontaminated by history and memory. This foreigner's perspective of a geographical *tabula rasa* allows Ursula to look back at her old life in England and see its unreality, as though she is viewing herself as an image on a screen projected by the light from a magic lantern. While the vision relates to Ursula's personal memories, there is also an implication that England itself partakes of this unreality. A bit earlier in the chapter, Birkin declares: 'Any hope of England's becoming real? God knows. It's a great actual unreality now, an aggregation into unreality. It might be real, if there were not Englishmen.'[51] Birkin expresses his world-weary disgust at the political democratisation, industrial expansion and cultural stagnation of England, a view which was shared to a large extent by Lawrence himself. Here, the real is about being able to touch or feel the land; a language of touch that is disconnected from the historical weight of nationality, and attached instead to a mind or geography bereft of human contamination. There is something futuristic about the idea of the 'new reality' Ursula will forge with Birkin in the Austrian mountains.

In this passage, and in the chapter 'Continental' as a whole, the words 'reality' and 'unreality' are repeated and repositioned. Ursula perceives the pristine and new Alpine landscape as the 'heart of reality' because they are unencumbered by English culture. This history-less landscape is a backdrop to the novel's conclusion, in which the four characters find space and time to ponder their possible futures. Yet, just as this passage documents Ursula's struggle to discard her past, so the pristine new world of self-invention is a fantasy. Gerald and Gudrun's murderous relationship concludes with Gerald's death, and Birkin and Ursula end up back in England bickering about love.

In Lawrence's post-war novels *The Lost Girl* (1921) and *Kangaroo* (1923), he extends the exploration of new subject positions by way of new geographies. Alvina Houghton, the protagonist of *The Lost Girl* descends in social class after her father opens a cinema in the Midlands mining town of Woodhouse before she escapes to Italy. She finds herself an outsider to the community in which she was raised, and Lawrence registers this by way of a cartographic metaphor: 'She was off the map: and she liked it'.[52] The protagonist of *Kangaroo*, the Englishman Richard Somers, ends up in Sydney, Australia, specifically in order to escape a politically exhausted post-war Europe: 'In Europe, he had made up his mind that everything was done for, played out, finished, and he must go to a new country. The newest country: young Australia!'[53] There are moments in the novel when this new country facilitates images of a clear and unencumbered psychic space: 'For he was always aware of the big empty spaces of his own consciousness: like his country, a vast empty "desert" at the centre of him.'[54] This image of empty landscape, however, furnishes a metaphor for psychic vacancy which is also nihilistic. The novel is actually more concerned with the fact that this image of the new world is a fantasy and that rather than being a pristine landscape which will furnish a new community, it is merely a geographical space scarred with the labels and values of imperial London: 'In Martin Place he longed for Westminster, in Sussex Street he almost wept for Covent Garden and St. Martin's Lane, at the Circular Quay he pined for London Bridge. It was all London without being London.' This London abroad is a simulacrum: 'The London of the southern hemisphere was all, as it were, made in the five minutes, a substitute for the real thing.'[55] London is imagined from a position outside England, a perspective which allows the narrative to look back on a city made 'real' through exile. Here is a spatial imagination of a particular kind, one which registers both the desire to escape England and Englishness – to be 'off the map'– and confronts the world's inescapable interconnections.

Other writers in the 1920s and 1930s wrote importantly about troubled, and racially determined, experiences of migration, exile and diaspora. Djuna Barnes's *Nightwood* (1936) focuses on a group of deracinated and loosely connected characters, including the Jewish Felix Volkbein, who wander the night-time streets of Paris and Berlin. In *Voyage in the Dark* (1934) Jean Rhys represents a young woman from the West Indies encountering the cold streets of London. Rhys describes Anna's schizophrenic experience of the city: 'Sometimes it was as if I were back there and as if England were a dream. At other times England was the real thing and out there was the dream, but I could never fit them together.'[56]

Mina Loy, in her long poem 'Anglo–Mongrels and the Rose' (1923–5), mixes up some of the different techniques described in this chapter in her depiction of Jewish wandering. The poem concentrates on a Jewish man called Exodus who travels from Budapest to London, marries an anti-Semitic English woman called Ada, otherwise ironically nicknamed the 'English Rose', and has a child, Ova, who is partly based on Loy herself. The poem collects together a number of different images of Jews: there is the Hungarian Jewish patriarch; the Jewish father, misunderstood by his racist English wife; the poor Jews of Kilburn in London, spurned by Ova's nurses; and the London Jewish tailor, who is figured as a modern deity at the end of the poem. The key motif of the poem, however, is its depiction of Jewish wandering, in particular its reinterpretation of the Wandering Jew, the punished figure doomed to wander in the wilderness forever for his crimes against Christ. The poem references a kind of *flâneur* figure, but, in his position as enforced migrant, the terms of urban wandering are complicated. Exodus

> paces
> the cancellated desert of the metropolis
> with the instinctive urge of loneliness
> to get to 'the heart of something'
>   The heart of England[57]

Here the Jewish wanderer does not drift freely around the urban streets; instead he is in search of some kind of centre or heart that will make the blank desert of the city cohere. His hope that an encounter with Englishness will either eradicate his alienation or centre the city, however, is in vain. While he does find an English 'Rose' in the country hedgerows, she will, through her anti-Semitism, enforce rather than relieve his estrangement. Exodus' encounter with the 'new world' of London is very different to Somers' experience in Sydney. Rather than mapping the landscape from above and using land as a basis for images of psychic regeneration, however complicated, Exodus tries hopelessly to find a perspective above the chaos of the city:

> (The) unperceived
> conquerer   of a new world
>   Exodus   lifts his head
>   over the alien crowds
>   under the alien clouds[58]

This ironised 'conquerer' of a strange land sends out rejected 'tentacles' to touch his fellow Londoners, an image which enforces the impossibility of an elevated perspective on the city.[59] Exodus' knowledge, then, is confined to his anonymous and submerged position in the crowd.

> The dumb philosophies
> of the wondering Jew

> fall into rhythm   with
>   long unlistened to   Hebrew chants[60]

In the lines above, Exodus' philosophies are mute both to others and to himself, so that the knowledge he possesses, and passes on to his daughter, is contained in an idea of the body's rhythm. Ova's philosophical and physical inheritance is not a specific body of textual knowledge; more an unconscious state of mind or a condition of the body. It is in the gait of the wanderer, the contours of the mind's rhythm. While this figure has similarities with the women who walk the streets of London in *Pilgrimage* and *Mrs Dalloway*, Loy's focus on the estranged need to search for inclusion or acceptance has more obvious connections to Joyce's depiction of Bloom in *Ulysses*.

The general trends described in this chapter, inwards to the 'dark places of psychology' as Woolf described it, and outwards to the panoramic view of land afforded by new technologies and by positions of exile, as well as the estranged perspectives of enforced migration, created a tension or crisis in the meaning of realism. Modernist texts embody the historical conflicts over land, imperialism and national belonging.

SUMMARY OF KEY POINTS

- The geographical boundaries of cities and nation states changed significantly in the early twentieth century.
- Modernist authors write the city by way of the partial perspective of the *flâneur*.
- Ford Madox Ford captures the impact of London's imperial status on the parameters of writing.
- Virginia Woolf, Dorothy Richardson and James Joyce create new techniques of interior monologue to capture the psychic responses to the city.
- Modernist texts also write the city and natural landscapes from an aerial perspective.
- Other modernist writers, such as D. H. Lawrence, Wyndham Lewis and Mina Loy, write about geography with regard to themes of travel, diaspora and exile.

NOTES

1. Walter Benjamin's unfinished project was edited and translated into English in 1999; Walter Benjamin, *The Arcades Project*, trans. Howard Eiland and Kevin McLaughlin (Cambridge: Harvard University Press, 1999). Three essays from the project had been previously translated and published in 1973. See Walter Benjamin, *Charles Baudelaire: A Lyric Poet in the Era of High Capitalism*, trans. Harry Zohn (London: Verso, 1976).
2. See, for example, Deborah Parsons, *Streetwalking the Metropolis: Women, the City, and Modernity* (Oxford: Oxford University Press, 2000).
3. See Andrew Thacker for a comprehensive account of theories of space with regard to modernist writing: Andrew Thacker, *Moving Through Modernity: Space and Geography in Modernism* (Manchester: Manchester University Press, 2003).
4. Mary Butts, *Death of Felicity Taverner* (London: Wishart, 1932).
5. Aldous Huxley, *Brave New World* (London: Harper Collins, [1932] 1994), p. 55.
6. D. H. Lawrence, *Lady Chatterley's Lover* (Harmondsworth: Penguin Books, [1928] 1961), p. 163.
7. Virginia Woolf, *Between the Acts* (Harmondsworth: Penguin Books, [1941] 1992), p. 5.
8. James Joyce, *Ulysses: The Corrected Text*, ed. Hans Walter Gabler with Wolfhard Steppe and Claus Melchior (London: Bodley Head, 1986), p. 271, p. 272.
9. Extracts from both texts can be found in Vassiliki Kolocotroni, Jane A. Goldman and Olga Taxidou (eds), *Modernism: An Anthology of Sources and Documents* (Edinburgh: Edinburgh University Press, 1998), p. 55.
10. Ford Madox Ford, *The Soul of London* (London: Orion, [1905] 1998), p. 3.
11. Ford, *The Soul of London*, p. 4, p. 42.
12. Ford, *The Soul of London*, p. 3.
13. Virginia Woolf, 'Character in Fiction', in Virginia Woolf, *Selected Essays*, ed. David Bradshaw (Oxford: Oxford University Press, 2008), p. 43.

14. Virginia Woolf, 'Modern Fiction', in Woolf, *Selected Essays*, p. 7.
15. Virginia Woolf, 'Modern Fiction', in Woolf, *Selected Essays*, p. 8, p. 9, p. 11.
16. Dorothy Richardson, *Pilgrimage*, vols 1–4 (London: Virago, 1979).
17. See Richardson, 'Foreword', in *Pilgrimage*, vol. 1, p. 9.
18. Richardson, *Pilgrimage*, vol. 2, p. 30.
19. Richardson, *Pilgrimage*, vol. 2, p. 75.
20. Richardson, *Pilgrimage*, vol. 1, p. 10.
21. Richardson, *Pilgrimage*, vol. 2, p. 13.
22. Richardson, *Pilgrimage*, vol. 2, p. 76.
23. Virginia Woolf, *Mrs Dalloway* (Oxford: Oxford University Press, [1925] 2008), p. 115.
24. Woolf, *Mrs Dalloway*, p. 8.
25. Virginia Woolf, 'Street Haunting: A London Adventure', in Woolf, *Selected Essays*, p. 178.
26. Virginia Woolf, *To the Lighthouse* (Oxford: Oxford University Press, [1927] 2000), pp. 198–9.
27. Woolf, *To the Lighthouse*, p. 81.
28. James Joyce, *Dubliners* (Harmondsworth: Penguin Books, [1914] 2000), p. 103.
29. James Joyce, *Finnegans Wake* (London: Faber and Faber, [1939] 1975), p. 196.
30. Joyce, *Dubliners*, p. 43, p. 47, p. 48, p. 50.
31. James Joyce, 'Realism and Idealism in English Literature (Daniel Defoe – William Blake)', in James Joyce, *James Joyce: Occasional, Critical, and Political Writing*, ed. Kevin Barry (Oxford: Oxford University Press, 2000), p. 168.
32. Joyce, 'Realism and Idealism', in Joyce, *James Joyce: Occasional, Critical, and Political Writing*, p. 170, p. 171, p. 181, p. 182.
33. Joyce, 'Realism and Idealism', in Joyce, *James Joyce: Occasional, Critical, and Political Writing*, p. 164, p. 171.
34. Quoted in Richard Ellmann, *James Joyce* (Oxford: Oxford University Press, 1966), p. 87.
35. Joyce, *Dubliners*, p. 114.
36. James Joyce, *A Portrait of the Artist as a Young Man* (Oxford: Oxford University Press, [1916] 2000), p. 5.

37. Joyce, *A Portrait of the Artist*, p. 83, p. 85.
38. Joyce, *A Portrait of the Artist*, p. 86.
39. Joyce, *A Portrait of the Artist*, p. 144.
40. Joyce, *A Portrait of the Artist*, p. 212, p. 213.
41. Joyce, *Ulysses*, p. 150.
42. Joyce, *Ulysses*, p. 150.
43. Joyce, *Ulysses*, p. 150.
44. Joyce, *Finnegans Wake*, p. 3.
45. Margot Norris, 'Finnegans Wake', in Derek Attridge (ed.), *The Cambridge Companion to James Joyce* (Cambridge: Cambridge University Press, 1990), p. 161.
46. Joyce, *Finnegans Wake*, p. 53.
47. H. D., *Tribute To Freud* (Oxford: Carcanet, [1956] 1971), p. 20.
48. Wyndham Lewis, *Tarr: The 1918 Version* (Santa Rosa: Black Sparrow Press, [1918] 1996), p. 21.
49. D. H. Lawrence, *Women in Love* (Harmondsworth: Penguin Books, [1921] 1979), p. 460.
50. Lawrence, *Women in Love*, p. 450.
51. Lawrence, *Women in Love*, p. 445.
52. D. H. Lawrence, *The Lost Girl* (Harmondsworth: Penguin Books, [1920] 1980), p. 146.
53. D. H. Lawrence, *Kangaroo* (Cambridge: Cambridge University Press, [1923] 1994), p. 13.
54. Lawrence, *Kangaroo*, p. 40.
55. Lawrence, *Kangaroo*, p. 20.
56. Jean Rhys, *Voyage in the Dark* (London: Penguin Books, [1934] 2000), pp. 7–8.
57. Mina Loy, 'Anglo-Mongrels and the Rose', in Mina Loy, *The Last Lunar Baedeker*, ed. Roger Conover (Manchester: Carcanet, 1986), p. 116.
58. Loy, 'Anglo-Mongrels', in Loy, *The Last Lunar Baedeker*, p. 117.
59. Loy, 'Anglo-Mongrels', in Loy, *The Last Lunar Baedeker*, p. 119.
60. Loy, 'Anglo-Mongrels', in Loy, *The Last Lunar Baedeker*, p. 117.

CHAPTER 3

Sex, Obscenity, Censorship

In the early twentieth century, the claim that the obscenity of literary texts could corrupt the minds of the young and impressionable fuelled the censorship of huge numbers of books, making it one of the most tightly controlled periods in the history of literary expression. A number of novels were taken to court. D. H. Lawrence's *The Rainbow*, which features a lesbian relationship, extramarital sex and Ursula Brangwen's miscarriage, was confiscated by the legal authorities in London and debated in the Houses of Parliament in 1915. In James Joyce's *Ulysses* Leopold Bloom goes to the toilet, masturbates while gazing at a seventeen-year-old virgin, engages in sadomasochistic fantasies about being whipped by a prostitute and has thoughts about being turned into a woman. It was suppressed by a New York judge in 1921 and was subsequently banned in other parts of the world, including England. Radclyffe Hall's novel *The Well of Loneliness*, which is a sensitive, but not sexually explicit, portrayal of the anxieties of a woman involved in a lesbian relationship, was condemned by journalists, seized by police in 1928, taken to court in London and banned.

Alongside these famous court cases there were a whole raft of less institutionalised kinds of censorship, by printers, postmen, customs officials, circulating libraries and publishers, which worked to control the dissemination of modernist texts. Two printers meddled in the format and language of Joyce's *Dubliners* and Pound's 1916 collection of poems, *Lustra*, because of their perceived obscenity. Editions of the *Little Review* which published Lewis's short story, 'Cantleman's Spring Mate' were stopped by a postman in 1917.[1] Djuna Barnes was forced by her publisher to alter the text of *Ryder* in 1928 to avoid prosecution for obscenity.[2] The agents of censorship in these cases – printers, publishers, postmen – comprised a scattered network of interconnected individuals who made private decisions about the production and dissemination of modernist texts. During the period of the early twentieth century these individuals had the responsibility and the power to decide the fate of twentieth-century literature.

Not only do these legal events and censorship networks reveal much about the culturally unacceptable side of modernist writing, they also highlight the desire by writers in this period to write about sex, sexuality and the bodily functions. This literary interest dovetailed with other cultural developments. Alongside changes in the financial and employment opportunities for women, there were significant intellectual shifts in the understanding of male, female and childhood sexuality by psychological and psychoanalytic writers as well as a new openness about feminist issues such as birth control. In these ways, Modernism brought into the open the anxieties and conflicts of modern sexuality.

LAW AND LITERATURE

During the mid to late nineteenth century, legislators argued that obscene writing was capable of creating moral harm. Lord Campbell's Obscene Publications Act of 1857 made it illegal to publish and distribute obscene fiction which was capable of 'corrupting the morals of youth.[3] In 1868, Lord Chief Justice Cockburn interpreted Campbell's law in the decision of *Regina v. Hicklin*, and laid down a famous obscenity ruling 'whether the tendency of the matter charged as obscenity [i.e., the isolated passages to be examined] is to deprave and corrupt those whose minds are open to immoral influences and into whose hands a publication of this sort may fall.[3] Lord Campbell's Act and the Hicklin ruling created an extremely broad definition of obscene writing, and were the basic legal coordinates for the censorship of fiction in the late nineteenth and early twentieth century.

The conflict between modernist literature and the law, however, was not simply connected to changes in the laws on obscene writing. It was also because of developments in the European novel form, most significantly a new kind of openness in describing sex and sexuality in realist and naturalist fiction. The literary naturalism of Émile Zola, in his series of novels collectively entitled *Les Rougon-Macquart* (published 1871–93), documented with dispassionate observation and meticulous detail the squalid environmental influences and instinctual nature of interrelated characters. In 'Naturalism on the Stage' (1880), he argued that the 'naturalistic novel' is 'impersonal'. The novelist, he claims, is 'but a recorder who is forbidden to judge and to conclude'. 'Here is the truth; shiver or laugh before it, draw from it whatever lesson you please, the only task of the author had been to put before you true data.'[4] The impersonal narrator of naturalist fiction, as well as the 'data' of described sexual activity, influenced English-language writers such as George Moore and Thomas Hardy, whose *Jude the Obscure* (1895) exposed and criticised marriage and institutionalised religion, a stance that prompted the Bishop of Wakefield famously to burn his copy of the novel in 1895. Alongside personal objections to developments in the novel form in the late nineteenth century, there were legal conflicts. The London publisher Henry Vizetelly, who published a translation of Zola's novel *La Terre* (*The Earth*) in 1888, was taken to court and fined £100 for obscene libel. Vizetelly tried to bring out Zola's writing again in 1889, and this time was fined £200 and thrown in jail for three months.

Joyce's *Dubliners* and Lawrence's early novels, such as *Sons and Lovers*, were written, to some extent, in the spirit and style of literary naturalism. Joyce's problems with printers and publishers over *Dubliners* were connected largely to the text's naturalistic details – his inclusion of colloquial words such as 'bloody', and his depiction of a boy's perspective on the creepy man with half-understood sexual inclinations in 'An Encounter' – although there were also complaints about its blasphemy and anti-monarchism. These brushes with censorious printers and publishers, however, did not deter Joyce in his pursuit of naturalistic detail. In *A Portrait of the Artist as a Young Man* Stephen Dedalus is pictured visiting prostitutes in Dublin's red-light district. In *Ulysses* descriptions of Bloom defecating, masturbating and urinating form part of the text's naturalistic physical 'data' of everyday life. It was the second of these physical activities that would prove problematic for the New York authorities.

The editors of the American magazine the *Little Review* had been bringing out instalments of Joyce's *Ulysses* from 1917. There were murmurs of complaint about some of the earlier instalments, but it was the 'Nausicaa' episode (episode thirteen), which created offence and sparked the court case. It depicts Bloom sitting on a beach masturbating while looking at a seventeen-year-old girl called Gerty. In Homer's *Odyssey* Nausicaa is a princess whom Odysseus encounters in the land of the Phaeacians. Odysseus sleeps in a thicket to keep himself hidden, and he awakes to see Princess Nausicaa and her maids-in-waiting who have come to a river to do the laundry. In the course of a game, the Princess loses a ball, and Odysseus then reveals himself to Nausicaa. Rather than grasp her knees in supplication, he uses his eloquence to persuade her to help him, praising her beauty.

The bare bones of the Homeric story structure Joyce's episode. Leopold Bloom, like Odysseus, sits on a beach observing the activities of a group of maidens, but in *Ulysses* they are teenage girls, Cissy Caffrey and Edy Boardman, who are looking after a baby and two toddlers. There is also a third girl, Gerty MacDowell, the Nausicaa figure of the episode, who is 'as fair a specimen of winsome Irish girlhood as one could wish to see'. Cissy and Edy play a game with a ball, while Gerty bends backwards and clutches her knees. If Gerty is partly Nausicaa, she is also likened to the Virgin Mary at a number of points, and the entire episode takes place to the sound of a Catholic church choir singing.

Along with the references to Homer's *Odyssey* and Catholicism, aspects of the episode are also based on another text: a hugely successful mid-nineteenth-century Romantic novel by Maria Cummins called *The Lamplighter*, whose main protagonist is a young orphan girl called Gerty who is adopted by a kind old lamplighter. By the end of the novel she not only finds love with her childhood sweetheart, Willie, but she is also reclaimed by the mysterious Mr Philips, who, it turns out, is her long-lost father.[5] Joyce's 'Nausicaa' includes traces of this plot. Gerty whimsically fantasises about a boy on a bike called Reggie Wylie. Bloom, who takes on the role of Cummins's Mr Philips, meanwhile, looks at Gerty penetratingly, just as Mr Philips does. Above all, however, it is Cummins's narrative style of sentimental romance, which relies on a masking of sexual desires and explicit references to the body, that structures Joyce's description of Gerty's beauty and Bloom's mysterious good looks: 'The very heart of the girlwoman went out to him, her dreamhusband'.[6]

A sentimental discourse similar to the terms of this sentence structures the first half of the 'Nausicaa' episode; its second half is narrated in a style of harsh realism. The section of text that sealed the legal fate of *Ulysses* concludes the sentimental section of the episode, and acts as a bridge to the realism that follows:

> She would fain have cried to him chokingly, held out her snowy slender arms to him to come, to feel his lips laid on her white brow, the cry of a young girl's love, a little strangled cry, wrung from her, that cry that has rung through the ages. And then a rocket sprang and bang shot blind blank and O! then the Roman candle burst and it was like a sigh of O! and everyone cried O! O! in raptures and it gushed out of it a stream of rain gold hair threads and they shed and ah! they were all greeny dewy stars falling with golden, O so lovely! O so soft, sweet, soft.
>
> Then all melted away dewily in the grey air: all was silent.[7]

In the court room, Magistrate Corrigan stated that, despite the fact that the novel was hard to understand because of its experimental-ism, it was obvious to everyone that here Bloom 'went off in his pants'.[8] Joyce does play with the sexual undercurrents of the lan-guage: a Roman candle is a particular kind of firework, but it also references Bloom's alter ego, the Roman hero Ulysses. While the 'O's are partly the collective expressions of awe at the exploding fireworks Bloom's more personal candle might also be said to have burst. There are other embedded jokes here. Gerty's plea to Bloom that he 'come' can be read in a sexual way, and Bloom has, indeed, been firing 'blanks' in his relationship with his wife, Molly.

Yet, despite these jokes, the nature of what is obvious in this piece of prose seems less certain than Corrigan implied. There is no explicit reference to sex or masturbation. Obscenity, to some extent, resides in the juxtaposition of this paragraph with the prose style which follows it. The second half of the 'Nausicaa' episode includes references to Bloom's earlier decision not to masturbate in the bath and his illicit conversations and flirtations with prostitutes: 'Girl in Meath street that night. All the dirty things I made her say all wrong of course.'[9]

The juxtaposition highlights the difference between what realism expresses, the 'dirty things' Bloom describes, and religious or sentimental discourses, which rely on the repression of sexuality and the body. *Ulysses* was considered particularly shocking and offensive because Bloom masturbates in view of a seventeen-year-old virgin who is likened to the Virgin Mary. It was, in many respects a deliberate attempt on Joyce's part to transgress and ridicule Catholic beliefs, as well as a particular fictional style.

The exposure of the sexual repression embedded in sentimentalism and religion structures *Ulysses* as a whole, and was a significant feature of modernist writing generally. Lawrence, after *The Rainbow* was banned, went on to write the significantly more obscene book *Lady Chatterley's Lover*. It includes a sustained argument about the social dangers of covering up sex. Just after Connie Chatterley discovers the little hut where her gamekeeper Mellors works on his bird coops, she goes for a walk with Clifford in the woods. When Connie picks some flowers for Clifford he quotes from Keats, 'Thou still unravished bride of quietness'. She responds with displeasure:

> She was angry with him, turning everything into words. Violets were Juno's eyelids, and windflowers were unravished brides. How she hated words, always coming between her and life: they did the ravishing, if anything did: ready-made words and phrases, sucking all the life-sap out of living things.[10]

Connie's recognition of Clifford's verbalism represents an important break in their relationship. She attacks the way that words, here poetic words, block the human relationship to life. This recognition is the prelude to the consummation of her affair with Mellors. Immediately after this exchange, she visits Mellors' hut again, continuing to consider Clifford's words: 'Ravished! How ravished one could be without ever being touched. Ravished by dead words become obscene, and dead ideas become obsessions.'[11] Words are obscene because they are divorced from the actions or relations of lived experience. The connection between obscenity and dead language continues through the novel. When Connie is in Germany, she finds herself regretting her liaison with Mellors. 'She was weary, afraid, and felt a craving for utter respectability, even for the vulgar and deadening respectability of the Guthrie girls.'[12] Here, Connie has been hounded down by structures of respectability.

Both Joyce and Lawrence deliberately wrote novels which were likely to be considered obscene by the legal authorities. Their texts also question the validity of the legal definition of the obscene. These legal encounters and fictional impulses reveal the extent to which transgression and heresy are central to modernist writing. One could go so far as to suggest that the term modernism, in its more liberatory and futuristic guises, implies radical transgression, whether with regard to a literary break from the past or in the impulse to overstep religious and moral boundaries. Important models of the transgressive come by way of modernist writing and many key theorisations of transgression, by Surrealist writers such as André Breton and Georges Bataille are produced and disseminated in and around the texts of the late nineteenth and early twentieth century.

Modernist texts often stage the discursive prohibitions against which their transgressions take place. In *Lady Chatterley's Lover*, for instance, dirty words and sexual descriptions deliberately transgress a hypocritical moral–sentimental culture that wants to denigrate the natural impulses of the human body. The book offends both in its parts – the fucks and cunts of the language – and as a whole, by dramatising a moral battle over understandings of the human body and society. Joyce, in *Ulysses*, also depicts and subverts the moral codes and discursive practices of the Catholic Church.

Both Lawrence and Joyce, along with other writers in the period such as T. S. Eliot, Wyndham Lewis and Ezra Pound, take this protest further. They suggest that the religious or moral–sentimental beliefs that seek to control the body and the written word, actually enjoy and are grounded in the texture of the illicit. In *Lady Chatterley's Lover*, the prurient individuals who try to destroy Connie and Mellors enjoy their own shocked responses to the sexual relationship – a response that Lawrence depicts as a kind of pornography. As Lewis put it in *Time and Western Man* (1927): 'every licence where "sex" is concerned has been invested with the halo of an awful and thrilling lawlessness'.[13]

The trial of *Ulysses* mobilised the international avant-garde to agitate on Joyce's behalf. Some of these avant-garde writers attended the courtroom to hear the judgement. It also clarified, to some extent, the anti-institutional aspects of English-language modernism. From the early 1920s, modernist publishers gravitated away from England and America, and towards the Continent, particularly Paris. The French authorities were uninterested in prosecuting Paris-based publishers of English-language books. The editors of the *Little Review* ended up moving operations to Paris in the early 1920s, partly to find a more amenable publishing environment. New presses emerged. There was the Three Mountains Press which was set up by the American journalist William Bird in 1923 and published Ezra Pound, William Carlos Williams, Robert McAlmon and Ernest Hemingway. Nancy Cunard created the Hours Press, which followed on from the Three Mountains Press in 1927, and published Beckett's *Whoroscope* (1930) and poems by Laura Riding, George Moore and others. Robert McAlmon's Contact Editions brought out volumes by Bryher, H. D., Mina Loy, Hemingway, Djuna Barnes, Stein and Mary Butts. All of these writers were involved in censorship disputes, or engaged with the issue of censorship in their writing.

Images of censorship are frequent in modernist texts. Writers describe both fairly abstract images of the censor, as well as more concrete depictions of characters involved in the activity of censorship. Mina Loy, in her 1922 poem 'Apology of Genius' (1922), presents the image of an all-encompassing 'censor's scythe' hanging over the activities of artists. Ezra Pound bases his poem 'L'Homme Moyen Sensuel' (1917) on a fictional New York vice crusader called Radway. Aldous Huxley, in his 1928 novel *Point Counter Point*, describes a language that has 'become what a mysterious convention has decreed to be unprintable'.[14] Wyndham Lewis pictures the sexually curtailing power of imaginary and ubiquitous customs officials in *Snooty Baronet* (1932): 'the shadow of the Custom House Officer had never disturbed our contraband caresses, our illicit still of bubbling free-love'.[15]

Pound's historically informed character, Loy's sinister and faceless scythe and Lewis's psychologically disturbing shadow suggest the different kinds of images used to represent censorship. These literary snippets also reveal the interest writers had in using images of the censor to focus on questions of linguistic or bodily freedom. In Loy's poem, 'the Beautiful' is connected to an undomesticated natural landscape, what she calls 'raw caverns' and 'Chaos', and is opposed to the censor and its law. In Lewis's text, the individual liberties of 'bubbling free-love' are defined in opposition to the observations of government agents.[16] The desire to delve into the uncensored and 'raw' or 'bubbling' spaces of the obscene body and psyche becomes central to modernist and avant-garde writing in the 1910s, 1920s and 1930s.

The censorship of literature did not deter writers from writing about sex. On the contrary, prohibition seemed both to galvanise some writers to become more explicit about sex and to encourage other writers to push their explorations of obscenity beyond the naturalistic depiction of the sexualised body, into different areas of the body or the mind. The focus on excrement – Mina Loy's description of her 'Forebears excrement' in 'O Hell', for instance – disgust, or explorations of the obscene frontiers of the body, become significant features of literary texts in the 1920s and 1930s.

Nathanael West's *The Dream Life of Balso Snell* (1931), for example, is a playfully obscene book. It opens with its poet protagonist deciding to enter the Trojan horse. There are three openings, the mouth, the navel and the posterior opening of the alimentary canal: 'The mouth was beyond his reach, the navel proved a cul-de-sac, and so, forgetting his dignity, he approached the last'.[17] Balso's journey up the horse's anus is also an excursion through the history of literature. As West himself put it, 'the intestine of the horse is inhabited solely by authors in search of an audience.'[18]

The implication is that both the authors and their literary texts are infused with the particular smells and consistencies of their context. As Balso puts it, 'Art is a sublime excrement'.[19]

Two Paris-based American writers, Henry Miller and Anaïs Nin, created surrealistic and highly sexualised prose pieces. Miller's *Tropic of Cancer* (1934) and *Tropic of Capricorn* (1939) were influenced by Breton's ideas that the irrational elements of the unconscious, desire and chance encounters could unleash forms of literary and political freedom. Miller inverts the ideas connected to obscenity, and suggests that the obscene lies at the source of literature's effects. His text exuberantly explores textual erotic and physical obscenities, while questioning conventional understandings of the obscene. He declares that 'a man who is intent on creation always dives beneath, to the open wound, to the festering obscene horror', but also claims that there is something 'obscene about this spiritual racket which permits an idiot to sprinkle holy water over Big Berthas and dreadnoughts and high explosives.'[20] Miller uses the word obscene to denote both a physical source of creativity, which he tends to connect to a grotesquely and violently imagined female body, and to the moral hypocrisy of those who combine religion and militarism.

Perhaps the most sustained and fascinating literary exploration of the obscene, however, is Djuna Barnes's last novel, *Nightwood*, which involves a meditation on the conflict between French and American understandings of ethics and the body. *Nightwood* is an extraordinarily dark and ambitious text. T. S. Eliot wrote a preface to the book, in which he claimed that it has 'the beauty of phrasing, the brilliance of wit and characterization, and a quality of horror and doom very nearly related to that of Elizabethan tragedy'.[21] The doom Eliot sees in the book is partly a product of its historical moment, in which deracinated and marginalised individuals such as Jews and lesbians travelled across Europe to escape persecution. It combines descriptions of a cast of drifting and hedonistic characters in 1920s Paris, with a series of philosophical, witty and poetic meditations on the ethical vacuity or doom of their night-time lives. The characters include Felix Volkbein, described as a wandering Jew, who fabricates a wildly unlikely aristocratic heritage. There is Robin Vote, who, despite being virtually silent throughout the novel, is the key object of desire for the other characters. While Felix marries Robin, Nora Flood, an American drifter connected to the circus, falls in love with her, before losing her to Jenny Petherbridge, a hollow figure described both as a pecking bird and a 'squatter'. Then there is Dr O'Connor, whose words, which seek to explain this group of individuals to themselves, form the substance of much of the novel.

This cast of drifters are cut loose from structures of nation, citizenship, religion, politics and ethics. The text writes about their individual searches for some kind of significance to their lives, whether they look for this meaning in Paris churches, abandoned chapels, brothels, or each other. Their ethical nudity requires characters to search back through their bodies to find some kind of grounding or moral compass. However, the American, sanitised, approach to bodies blocks out this route to self-understanding. At one point in the novel, Dr O'Connor, Barnes's central character, is in conversation with American-born Nora. He says to her: 'The French have made a detour of filthiness – Oh. The good dirt! Whereas you are of a clean race, of a too eagerly washing people, and this leaves no road for you.' While the Frenchman 'can trace himself back by his sediment', the American 'separates the two for fear of indignities so that the mystery is cut in every cord'.[22] By being severed from the body's experiences the American, according to Dr O'Connor, cuts the cord that leads to truth.

Nightwood is partly about the clash between French and American ways of understanding the world. At one point in the novel Nora visits Dr O'Connor in his room, and is forced to encounter his 'filthiness'. She discovers a room 'so small that it was just possible to walk sideways up to the bed, it was as if being condemned to the grave the doctor had decided to occupy it with the utmost abandon'. Along with dirt and a weird array of cosmetics, there is a 'rusty pair of forceps', 'half a dozen instruments that she could not place', and a 'swill-pail' 'brimming with abominations'. Nora considers that there 'was something appallingly degraded about the room, like the rooms in brothels, which give even the most innocent a sensation of having been accomplice'.[23] The doctor's appearance, meanwhile, is also degraded. Dressed in a woman's nightgown he wears a golden wig and is 'heavily rouged', all of which makes Nora think of Red Riding Hood encountering the wolf in bed.

While this scene is partly about a clash of moral ideologies, it also raises questions about what the doctor's grave-like room might mean. The details – the forceps, the instruments, the swill-pail – are scattered objects without any redeemable meaning. They do not tell the reader about history, the contemporary world, or the doctor's interior life. Just as these are objects that cannot be placed as Nora puts it, so the lives of these characters do not fit, either into the nation state or into religious or mythical structures.

MODERNISM AND FEMINISM

In addition to developments in the novel form towards greater sexual explicitness, another reason for the conflict between litera-ture and the law connected to a new kind of feminism of sexual and psychic openness. Politically there had been significant changes in women's rights in Britain in the late nineteenth and early twentieth century. In 1919, after a long battle for suffrage, women over thirty won the right to vote and the Sex Disqualification (Removal) Act removed the bar preventing them from entering professions such as the law, medicine and the civil service. There were notable changes in women's jobs in the late nineteenth and early twentieth century. In particular, there was a shift away from employment in domestic service, and into the expanding service industries of shops and offices. The First World War altered employment gender divisions further, as women successfully took up industrial jobs left vacant by fighting men. Alongside suffragette agitators, other kinds of femi-nism were significant in the period. Campaigners Marie Stopes and Dora Russell, dismayed at the problems women with large families faced, fought hard to spread knowledge about birth control, and to introduce birth control clinics in Britain. Stopes opened the first family planning clinic in London in 1921 and Russell founded, with H. G. Wells and John Maynard Keynes, the Workers' Birth Control Group in 1924. There were similar developments in America. Margaret Sanger created a family planning and birth control clinic in New York in 1916, and founded the American

Birth Control League in 1921. These women had to fight against both the prejudices and laws of the wider culture. The distribution of birth control information was a crime under US obscenity laws. Sanger's clinic was raided nine days after it opened. There had also been a leap forward in women's access to public education. Many of the women writers discussed in this book attended university or art college. They also wrote openly about sex.

In critical accounts the recovery of women writers from the late 1970s significantly altered understandings of modernism. New editions of works by Mina Loy, H. D., Djuna Barnes, Dorothy Richardson and others were published and made available previously inaccessible writing.[24] A number of influential studies of individual writers sought to introduce marginalised women writers to a new generation of readers. There were also groundbreaking wider accounts of women's writing, such as Sandra Gilbert's and Susan Gubar's three volume *No Man's Land: The Place of the Woman Writer in the Twentieth Century* (1988–94). These different contributions to the question of modernism and gender shifted perceptions of the modernist literary landscape.[25] They altered the status and significance of previously marginalised or forgotten women writers, and changed interpretations of the ways in which writers, both male and female, wrote about sexuality and gender difference.

Novels and poems of the early twentieth century engage with and register these changes. Virginia Woolf, in her feminist essay *A Room of One's Own* (1929), suggests of her generation that 'no age can have been as self-conscious' about the 'sex question'. Woolf identifies the suffragettes as one cause of this self-consciousness: 'The Suffrage campaign was no doubt to blame. It must have roused in men an extraordinary desire for self-assertion'.[26] Both the political demands of the suffragette movement, and the tactics of violence and hunger strikes used to further the cause, did indeed have a significant impact on writing.

There was a vogue for suffragette novels in the Edwardian period. Many were modelled on and extended the narrative coordinates of *fin de siècle* 'new woman' fiction, which had documented the experiences of women struggling for financial and sexual independence. Olive Schreiner's *The Story of an African Farm* (1883) is an early account of a woman's feminism, religious scepticism, and free-thought which also includes the open depiction of premarital sex.[27] Other writers, such as George Gissing, Sarah Grand, Ella Hepworth Dixon and Thomas Hardy, tracked the struggles of women trying to attain financial and emotional independence in the face of patriarchal society.[28] Hardy's *Jude the Obscure* (1896) depicts the prohibitions on women's lives and the fatal costs of trying to escape them. Novels that attacked the immorality of the new woman were also fashionable. Eliza Lynn Linton's *The Rebel of the Family* (1880), for instance, is critical of the costs of female independence, and includes a literary portrait of the late-Victorian lesbian community in London, featuring a character called Bell Blount and her "little wife" Connie.

Suffragette novels of the 1900s adopted some of the themes and narrative structure of these new woman novels. Gertrude Colmore's *Suffragette Sally* (1911), Constance Elizabeth Maud's *No Surrender* (1912), as well as short stories such as Evelyn Sharp's 'The Women at the Gate' and W. L. Courtney's 'The Soul of a Suffragette', represent women's struggles with patriarchal power and involvement in the Women's Social and Political Union and suffragette groups. Autobiographical accounts of the struggle were also popular. Constance Lytton's *Prisons and Prisoners: The Stirring Testimony of a Suffragette*, Cicely Hamilton's *Life Errant* and Emmeline Pankhurst's *My Own Story* importantly aided the struggle for women's votes. A woman's revolt from patriarchal rule is a feature of H. G. Wells's *Ann Veronica* (1909), which relates the story of Ann's belligerent decision to leave home and become financially and sexually independent, a journey that involves a brief entrance into suffragette circles in London.

Sexually and financially independent female characters dominate fiction in the 1910s and 1920s. These characters have similarities with the new women figures of *fin de siècle* fiction, but their assertions of independence are often both more promiscuous and psychologically intimate and anxious. A number of writers produced epic historical novel sequences in which women's liberation, and its relationship to industrialisation, the First World War and political emancipation, was central. D. H. Lawrence's *The Rainbow* (1915) and *Women in Love* (1921) focus on the complexities of the new gender relations that were unleashed through women's sexual and financial liberation. *The Rainbow* documents the history of the Brangwen family through the nineteenth century and early 1900s. In particular it focuses on the way that nineteenth-century industrialisation and modernisation changed the role and status of women. Ursula Brangwen, the youngest of the female characters, studies science at university, becomes a schoolteacher, and gets involved in both a lesbian relationship and extramarital sex. *Women in Love* traces Ursula's subsequent development and relationship with Rupert Birkin, and also depicts Ursula's ultra-modern artist sister, Gudrun Brangwen, whose sexual and psychological independence involves shrugging off all attempts to control her.

Lewis Grassic Gibbon, in his modernist epic *A Scots Quair*, also represents the changing role of women through history. Comprising three novels, *Sunset Song* (1932), *Cloud Howe* (1933) and *Grey Granite* (1934), Gibbon's epic follows the life of female protagonist Chris Guthrie, as she travels from a small Scottish farming community to the town, and then to the political cut and thrust of the city. The first novel, *Sunset Song* (1932), creates a chilling description of Jean Guthrie, Chris Guthrie's mother, being ground down by a cycle of pregnancies before dying in childbirth. Chris is a complex character with both strong links to the land and the desire to look beyond this environment, with its sexual ignorance and violence, to the more emancipated sexual relations of the city.

This narrative structure, in which a central protagonist experiences the conflicts and liberation of moving from the country to the city, was an established one in nineteenth-century novels. In the hands of Lawrence and Gibbon this narrative trajectory and elements of 'new woman' fiction combined to stage the conflicts of modern gender roles. History is depicted in both the familial cycles of birth, desire, procreation and death, and as an overarching process of industrialisation and modernisation, a process which both liberates and imprisons. Lawrence and Gibbon acutely depict the conflicts of female liberation, seeing independent women as suffering forms of loss by conforming to the abrasive and egotistical isolation of modern subjectivity. For Lawrence, modern subjectivity is legalistic and political, a category divorced from the life cycles and bodily processes which are seen as the real basis of individual freedom.

Ford Madox Ford's post-war novel *Parade's End* (1924–8) also positions women's freedom in relation to the competing ideologies of modern political subject positions, particularly liberal ideals of legality and rights, and more direct kinds of action, although sexuality is almost farcically repressed under codes of matrimonial decency. Comprising four novels, *Some Do Not* (1924), *No More Parades* (1925) *A Man Could Stand Up* (1926) and *The Last Post* (1928), *Parade's End* begins in the immediate pre-war period and includes a scene in which the suffragette Valentine Wannop protests against male power on a golf course. Valentine Wannop's feminism is presented as both a historical marker and potential futuristic politics. These novels follow her love affair with Christopher Tietjens, who is a landed Tory civil servant described at a number of points in the novel as 'pure eighteenth century'. At one point in the novel Tietjens says to Valentine, 'You and I are standing at different angles and though we both look at the same thing we read different messages. Perhaps if we stood side by side we should see yet a third.'[29] The implication is that both the Tory Tietjens and the Futurist Valentine offer a vision opposed to the liberal consensus.

All three writers stage the conflicts between history and gender through techniques of interior monologue and narrative fragmentation. In Gibbon's text, Chris's shift from land to the city, from farming to education, is described in a language which registers these conflicts:

So that was Chris and her reading and schooling, two Chrissies there were that fought for her heart and tormented her. You hated the land and the coarse speak of the folk and the learning was brave and fine one day and the next you'd waken with the pewits crying across the hills, deep and deep, crying in the heart of you and the smell of the earth in your face, almost you'd cry for that, the beauty of it and the sweetness of the Scottish land and skies.[30]

The novel is grounded in a communal Scottish narrative voice which mediates descriptions of Chris' split self – the 'two Chrissies' of this description. Chris is both addressed in this paragraph and forms the substance of a writing which follows the rhythms of her language. This is a description of the semi-articulate desires and anxieties of a woman's striving for the liberation embodied in education. The conflicts of her relationship to a land and to folk both brutal and beautiful will be played out in the narrative. The fight in her is one that pits the desire for education and enlightenment against the pull of home. But the First World War, which intrudes on the narrative in 'Harvest', wakes up both Chris and her community, in a different sense. The war destroys the men who go to fight – Chris's husband, Ewan, sets off to fight as a young and blushing boy and returns home a hardened and bullying soldier – and decimates the community through death.

With the granting of the vote in 1918, interest in suffragette groups waned, for obvious reasons. Virginia Woolf's late novel *The Years* (1937) covers a broad historical period: the novel splits its action into different years across a time span running from 1880 to the present (the novel was published in 1937). Suffragette activity is located in 1911, when Rose, rebellious in youth, is nearly thrown in prison for throwing a brick for her politics.

H. D., in her novel *Bid Me To Live* (1960), also sees the suffragettes' action as a historical moment: she describes the 'valiant militant suffragette' Miss Ames, who is 'already a period-piece in 1914, in 1917 already pre-war'.[31] H. D.'s novel begins by capturing the fast-changing shifts in fashion and custom during the war: 'Oh, the times, oh the customs! Oh, indeed, the times! The customs! Their own, specifically, but part and parcel of the cosmic, comic, crucifying times of history.'[32] Miss Ames features as a signifier of these mutating 'times of history'; her historical moment, we are led to believe, has already passed.

H. D.'s novel shifts the focus of feminist action from a 'crucifying' history of political agitation to the conflicts of history as they are played out in her protagonist's emotional and psychic life. The 'sex question', then, in H. D.'s hands, is focused on the domestic and artistic relationships between men and women. H. D. describes the complexities of being a modern woman:

In 1913, the 'modern woman' had no special place on the map, and to be 'modern' in Mrs Carter's sense, after 1914, required some very special handling. 'I believe in intelligent

women having experience' was then a very, very thin line to
tow, a very, very frail wire to do a tight-rope act on.[33]

The novel is a *roman-à-clef* which focuses on the group of writers
and artists with whom the author associated during the war. In
life this group included her husband, Richard Aldington, D. H.
Lawrence, with whom she discussed her poems and had a brief flir-
tation, Frieda Lawrence, Lawrence's German wife, Bella Cohen,
with whom Aldington had an affair, and Cecil Gray, who fathered
H. D.'s daughter.

In H. D.'s novel, the 'tight-rope act' of modern femininity
involves a fraught negotiation of sexual and artistic desires. Julia's
fantasy of being a poet is in tension with her sexual identity. Rafe
Ashton, the character based on Richard Aldington, insists that
the ethereal, poetic Julia is asexual. The novel angrily ironises
this view, but captures the difficulty of synthesising female poetic
ambition and sexual experience, of walking along the 'frail wire' of
women's liberation in the cultural sphere.

In another part of the book she describes the experimental nature
of the extramarital sexual relations and artistic discussions of this
group of writers during the war: 'they were, separate elements in
a test-tube'. The image of the test tube captures the unpredictable, futuristic, and potentially explosive and destructive nature
of the relationships between individuals. But H. D. complicates
the image: 'It was herself who inherited New England thorough-
ness who was perhaps the most experimental, herself part of it, but
herself watching the mixture now poured into the test-tube, about
to bubble.'[34] Julia is described as both a key element in the test tube
and an observer of it.

H. D.'s poetry and prose often focus on an individual, or
merely a self, who is situated on this fragile boundary between
participation and observation, and some of the particular features
of her writing are a result of this endeavour. History, while being
represented quite forcefully in *Bid Me To Live*, is always filtered
through the lens of individual experience and involves a struggle
with perspective and language. Returning to the test tube image,
for instance, the elements that are part of the unpredictable chemi-
cal mix of history involve the war, the presence of independent and

sexually promiscuous women, the creation of experimental art and Freudian ideas about the mind. But, by bringing to life the difficulties of both living and representing history, the novel destabilises an idea of history as that which can be objectively told.

In the place of objective history, H. D. creates a text of overlapping memories in which psychic or linguistic echoes, rather than temporal order, serve to bind together experiences. If we return to the opening lines from the novel, with their highly performative description of times and history, it becomes clearer why H. D. constructs 'the cosmic, comic, crucifying times of history' through the acoustical connections between words. As she puts it, 'their words echoed, were not lost in the drawl of later sirens'.[35]

History, in H. D.'s writing, resides in echoes and memories, as well as an acute sense of the positioning of selfhood in writing. H. D.'s representation of modern femininity is a powerful one because she captures the complexities and anxieties, even the absurdities, of both occupying and observing this subject position. The language she employs – the tightrope act, the 'bubble' of the test tube – often revolve around fragile, unstable, borderline or ephemeral images. These acrobatic protagonists, one imagines, could easily lose their balance; or be pushed off the wire.

The idea that history resides in the fabric of language and memory, rather than in the documentation of events, and that writing the past requires a self-consciousness about how one situates oneself in an inherited language, is a significant one in modernist writing. Marcel Proust, James Joyce and Virginia Woolf recreate in writing the complex ways in which memory and history reside in found linguistic and associative echoes. The use of this style to capture women's experiences is a particularly significant feature of modernist writing.

Mina Loy, Djuna Barnes, Virginia Woolf, Katherine Mansfield, Dorothy Richardson, Gertrude Stein, Mary Butts and Jean Rhys all write, in different ways, about how women situate themselves in language. All of these writers satirise or ironise informing conceptions of femininity, whether these ideas relate to traditional notions of the female role or to the equally abstract notion of modern femininity. Returning to Woolf's discussion of the sex question in *A Room of One's Own*, for instance, she stages a set of

wider, more philosophical and less overtly political questions surrounding women's liberation: are men and women intrinsically
different to one another? Or are gender differences the product of
their life experiences? Is their relationship to language different?
Might there be a way of writing that is feminine? Might there be a
woman's sentence structured differently to a masculine sentence?
This essay, like H. D.'s novel, asks questions about what it means
to be a woman writer.

In asking these questions Woolf was participating in a wider
cultural debate about the relationship between gender difference and language, a debate in which she had been involved for
some time. In a review of Brimley Johnson's critical survey, *The
Women Novelists*, in 1918, Woolf suggested that George Eliot and
Charlotte Brontë adopted male pseudonyms 'in order to free their
own consciousness as they wrote from the tyranny of what was
expected from their sex', a claim for the freedom in unconsciousness that she was to foreground in her discussion of female writing
in *A Room of One's Own*.[36] Discussing a fictional modern writer
called Mary Carmichael, Woolf declares that she writes as a woman
who 'has forgotten that she is a woman'.[37] The idea that literary
freedom resides in escaping the confines of one's gendered position
is significant for a number of women modernists.

Mina Loy, in her 'Feminist Manifesto' (1914), demanded
that women prepare themselves for a 'devastating psychological
upheaval' and 'destroy in themselves, the desire to be loved', a
comment that gets to the heart of the complicated ways in which
women's freedom is tied to their relationships to men.[38] In a
number of early poems, she pictures the prison of conventional
femininity. In 'Virgins Plus Curtains Minus Dots' she describes
'Houses hold virgins / The door's on the chain'. Katherine
Mansfield's short stories also often focus on female characters
trapped inside social rules or conventions. In 'Prelude', both Aunt
Beryl and Linda are confined by their roles as spinster and wife.

The exciting texts by women modernists address the complex
task of depicting the psychic life of the liberated woman. There is
often an attempt to create pictures of female subjectivity through
the fraught sexual and emotional relationship with male lovers.
Loy, in 'Songs to Joannes', produces a number of arresting

images of female subjectivity through a relationship between a woman and her male lover. In Chapter 1, I briefly discussed the cubistic form and polyglot registers of Loy's 'Songs'. She wrote thirty-four of these Songs, the first four of which were published under the title 'Love Songs' in the New York journal *Others* in 1915. Along with the image of the 'Pig Cupid', which I have already discussed, she creates a number of others which traverse a history of literary, visual or biblical language and bodily or obscene images.

At the centre of this poem sequence is a female 'me' or 'I' who comes to life through images of birth or 'emergence' as Song XXVII puts it. Alongside a raw language of the procreative body, with references to 'spermatozoa' (IX) 'flesh from flesh' (XII), and 'infructuous [unfruitful] impulses' (II), there are also 'foetal buffoons' and 'Bird-like abortions' (IV). Through their love, meanwhile, they 'might have given birth to a butterfly' (III). The grotesque distortions of prenatal matter provide shocking images of semi-human flesh. By working to strip the human form of all cultural accoutrements, they suggestively point to the idea that new gender roles might involve some kind of primitive return. But, in the image of the butterfly, the new is also pictured positively, and the attempt to find a language to describe the love that is at its source is central to the poem sequence.

The unpredictable nature of their shared existence features in other poems. Song XVI has the lines:

> We might have lived together
> In the lights of the Arno
> Or gone apple stealing under the sea
> Or played
> Hide and seek in love and cob-webs
> And a lullaby on a tin-pan
> And talked till there were no more tongues[39]

The biblical connotations of stolen apples and talking in tongues constitute one kind of language of love. 'A lullaby on a tin-pan' both references Pan, the Greek god of rustic music, as well as the companion of the nymphs and the contemporary popular songs of

Tin Pan Alley, which was at the height of its influence in New York in the late 1910s and early 1920s. The poem's meaning is produced through the temporal and cultural dissonances of these combinations: a lullaby which synthesised Pan's lyre and a Tin Pan Alley song involves both a temporal and geographical imaginative leap and would, one imagines, produce cacophonous noise. Noise also features in the reference to talking in tongues: here, vocal noises gesture towards, but do not communicate, meaning. The poem concludes on this note: the lovers could have wasted their bodies away in talk, but still would not have known each other any better. Love is a series of noises or images, some lyrical and beautiful, others physically inchoate or obscene. But, the more general suggestion of the poem is that there is a gap separating knowledge and expression.

The poem states that love is a game of hide and seek, a line that implies that the voluptuousness, playfulness and slipperiness of love and poetic language are similar to one another. In this sense, these 'Songs' might be seen to perform, rather than simply describe, the modern love they reference. Love, in this reading, is contained in the poetic imagery and form that might express it. For Loy, love is imagined in fleeting images of energy and light. There is an insistent return to a language of energy and movement in these poems: the physical dimensions of love are in the 'impact of lighted bodies / Knocking sparks off each other' in XIV, or in the metaphorical fireflies bouncing 'off one another' in XIX. The imagery of momentary impact also captures something about the psychological transformations of love.

Colour is also a significant term in Loy's vocabulary, used as a way to indicate the momentary synthesis of ephemeral light effects. 'Song I' concludes with the image of experience as 'Coloured glass', while there is a 'cosmos / Of coloured voices' in IX and a 'colorless onion' peeled by the poet's lover in XI. At moments, the poem seems to gesture towards a more sincerely felt set of psychic and emotional registers. The poem has the lines:

> And I am burnt quite white
> In the climacteric
> Withdrawal of your sun

It is left open, however, whether these lines are a sincere description of loss, or an ironic take on the lover's claim to be the centre of the universe. Irony is never far away in Loy's writing, particularly when she depicts male egotism, and it is certainly present in these lines. But, the poem as a whole does revolve around images of synthesis and separation, energy and colour, the light-effects of which take place in the purview of the sun. The female self described in these poems is partly dependent on the energy source of the male, even while she undermines his authority.

If H. D. describes modern femininity as a tightrope act, Loy also pictures female selfhood as a precarious performance. Other writers, such as Mansfield and Woolf, depict femininity as masquerade. The formal freedoms of these Songs allow Loy to mine contemporary registers and traditional imagery, and to enjoy the dissonances of these juxtapositions. Her modern femininity seems to be located in this dissonance. In other texts Loy spells out more straightforwardly her sense that women cannot simply discard the history of sexual relations that have produced them; at the same time, this history has produced an energetic drive towards a different, more enlightened future.

SEXUALITY

Alongside the revolutionary developments in women's self-understanding, there were also significant shifts in the writing of sexuality, another feature of modernist writing which led to a confrontation with the law. Towards the end of the nineteenth century and beginning of the twentieth century a number of significant new scientific accounts of sexuality were published. One important area of debate focused on the question of homosexuality. While there had been a tendency to diagnose homosexuality as a form of degeneration in previous studies, these new accounts attempted to separate out sexuality from disease.[40] British psychologist Havelock Ellis, in his influential book *Studies in the Psychology of Sex* (1897), announced that the question of homosexuality is currently a 'psychological and medico–legal problem so full of interest that we need not fear to face it, so full of grave social actuality that we are bound to face it'.[41] He investigated different types within the broad division of 'simple inversion', which involves 'all those individuals who are sexually attracted only to their own sex' and 'psycho-sexual hermaphroditism', which describes 'those who are attracted to both sexes'.[42] Ellis departed from previous psychologists in documenting the experiences of women as well as men: 'It seems', he declared, 'probable that homosexuality is little, if at all, less common in women than in man', and yet, 'we know comparatively little of sexual inversion in woman'. Ellis described numerous case studies, and divided these cases into those whose sexuality is 'acquired' and those whose sexuality is 'congenital' but concludes that 'sexual inversion' is 'largely a congenital phenomenon'.[43,44]

Freud, in *The Interpretation of Dreams* (1900), extended and shifted Ellis's ideas by arguing that childhood sexuality was at the origin of adult sexual behaviour and identity. In *Three Essays on the Theory of Sexuality* (1905), by locating adult sexuality in childhood identifications and fantasies, Freud sought to move beyond the dichotomy of 'innate' and 'acquired' explanations of sexuality.[45] He argued for the importance of loosening 'the bond that exists in our thoughts between instinct and object', claiming that it 'seems probable that the sexual instinct is in the first instance independent of its object; nor is its origin likely to be due to its object's attractions'.[46] This statement is radical in its insistence that sexual instincts, born of a series of childhood experiences and identifications, can, in adulthood, attach themselves to men and/or women. For Freud, what society might regard as the sexual perversions hold the key to normal sexual life; there is no definite boundary separating perversion and normal sexuality.

The opening up for discussion of homosexuality by Ellis and Freud was significant for a number of writers, even while literary depictions of homosexual activity in Britain and America remained harshly policed. In 1913, E. M. Forster wrote, but did not attempt to publish, his novel *Maurice*, which documents Maurice's internal struggle to accept his own sexuality. While Forster creates a positive ending, the text brings to life the deeply repressive attitudes which controlled attitudes to homosexuality in the period, particularly in its reproduction and enforcement of a language of disease, dirt and obscenity.[47]

A number of other writers were directly influenced by the work of Havelock Ellis, and his ideas about the congenital nature of gay and lesbian identity. Bryher, H. D.'s lover, was a friend of Ellis's, and consulted him about her sexuality, as did Radclyffe Hall, whose book *The Well of Loneliness* documents the experience of a character who believes herself to be a man born in a woman's body. Both Ellis's and Freud's work created a philosophical and scientific context which facilitated, to some extent, the focus on homosexuality in modernist texts. In many of these texts, the ambiguous nature of sexuality is playful and undecided. Woolf for example depicts gay and lesbian figures in *Mrs Dalloway*, *Orlando* and *The Years* and Gertrude Stein writes of a female relationship in *The Autobiography of Alice B. Toklas*. Djuna Barnes, in *Nightwood* and *Ladies Almanack*, represents lesbian relationships and creates a playful and innovative language to capture these culturally suppressed desires.

As was discussed in Chapter 1, *Ladies Almanack* produces an extraordinarily lush language of lesbian desire. The book's twelve episodes focus on a range of characters. There is January's Patience Scalpel, loosely based on Mina Loy, who declares that 'I am of my Time my Time's best argument', but who also understands nothing of 'Women and their Ways'. Then there is Lady Buck-and-Balk and plain Tilly-Tweed-In-Blood, characterisations of Radclyffe Hall and her lover, Una Troubridge. At the centre of the text, however, is Dame Evangeline Musset, based on Natalie Barney, who is 'esteemed for her Slips of the Tongue', connections between bodily tongues and linguistic slips which inform the text as a whole.[48]

In addition to his discussion of sexuality, Freud's ideas about the unconscious spread quickly across Continental Europe and Britain. The Society for Psychical Research, and the London Psycho-Analytic Society (set up in 1913), which became the British Psycho-Analytical Society in 1919, were essential to the dissemination of Freud's ideas in Britain. Groundbreaking analysts and theorists such as Joan Riviere, James and Alix Strachey, Melanie Klein and Anna Freud were members of the British Psycho-Analytic Society in the 1920s who produced influential papers and new theories, particularly in the areas of female and child psychology.[49] Psychoanalysis also, significantly, attracted and influenced a number of Bloomsbury artists and writers.

Writers often mention the vogue of psychoanalytic thinking in post-war British culture. Richardson, in her 'Preface' to *Pilgrimage*, lists a number of historical shifts, one of which is 'post-War Freudianity'.[50] H. D. gives a more caustic description of this engagement, describing the 'new mode of the Bloomsbury intellectuals, with half-baked misapplied theories from Vienna'.[51] H. D.'s scepticism about the superficial response to Freud was a product of her own more sincere interest in Freud's ideas, as well as in Freud as a person. She was psychoanalysed by him during 1933–4 and documented her experiences in her book, *Tribute to Freud* (1956), in which she characterises herself as a chosen student of his semi-mythical new philosophy, and as a poet whose writing bears the imprint of his philosophy: her writing practice is 'my own intense, dynamic interest in the unfolding of the unconscious or the subconscious pattern'.[52] The narrative, rather than unfolding chronologically, plays with patterns or designs of image and word associations. As a text it reproduces the Freudian process and experience of uncovering hidden identifications and desires: 'Fragmentary ideas', she states in one part of the book, 'apparently unrelated, were often found to be part of a special layer or stratum of thought and memory, therefore to belong together; these were sometimes skilfully pieced together'.[53] The style of this text, as well as others such as *Bid Me To Live*, reveal Freud's influence on her writing. While a fellow analysand J. J. van der Leeuw wants to learn psychoanalysis at the feet of the master in order to apply psychoanalytic principles to the aim of 'international co-operation and understanding', H. D. describes herself as a different sort of disciple, poetic and intuitively insightful.[54] As with many of H. D.'s texts, however, the power dynamic initially presented to the reader, in which Freud is a masterful, almost God-like figure, is, at times, undercut in the subsequent narrative. As a whole, the book seeks to balance the psychological truths of poetry against Freud's scientific insights.

While psychoanalytic ideas infiltrate H. D.'s writing, and psychoanalytic terms such as 'the unconscious' and 'subconscious' appear in poems and texts by Loy and Butts, the explicit discussion of Freud's ideas by modernist writers was often hostile or satirical. Woolf, despite suffering from psychological illness throughout her life, refused to be psychoanalysed. Writing of *To the Lighthouse* she said, 'I suppose that I did for myself what psycho-analysts do for their patients. I expressed some very long felt and deeply felt emotion. And in expressing it I explained it and laid it to rest.'[55] Woolf sees literature and psychoanalysis as aiming at the same thing – the uncovering of an intense emotional memory – but certainly does not accord privilege to the scientific approach.

In *Finnegans Wake* Joyce produces an irreverent description of the violations of psychoanalytic discourse:

> Be who, farther potential? and so wider but we grisly old Sykos who have done our unsmiling bit on 'alices, when they were yung and easily freudened, in the penumbra of the pro-curing room and what oracular comepression we have had apply to them![56]

There are linguistic echoes of the word psychoanalysis in the phrase 'unsmiling bit on 'alices', repression in 'oracular comepression', of Jung in 'yung' and of Freud in 'freudened'. The analytic room becomes a 'procuring room' in Joyce's text. Joyce draws an analogy between biological and Catholic fathers, and describes both as old psychos in their relation to young girls. But the old psychos are also the psychoanalysts; all of these men do their 'unsmiling bit' on young girls. The thing that is being 'done' to these girls is partly the mapping of drives and desire with a scientific vocabulary. Joyce continues: 'can be suggestive of under the pudendascope and, finally, what a neurasthene nympholept, endocrine-pineal typus, of inverted parentage with a prepossessing drauma present in her past and a priapic urge for congress with agnates and cognates'.[57] Joyce humorously lists classificatory terms such as neurasthenia and inverts, as well as the creation of a new word 'pudendascope' to capture the synthesis of scientific instruments and dissection. The sinister psychological fascination with the female body involves the 'oracular' obsessions of both 'old Sykos' and a psychoanalytic discourse.

This is a funny satire of psychoanalysis because it taps into the

gendered nature of Freud's new science, which took female hyster-
ics as its first case studies and extended this gender power imbal-
ance through claims about penis envy and the Oedipus complex, or
the 'eatupus complex' as Joyce refers to it a bit later in the text.[58]
Joyce's satire pinpoints one of the key reasons for artistic scepticism about psychoanalysis: the idea that Freud's ideas reduced the
sexual instincts, repressed memories and emotions to a sterile scientific language. Other writers attacked Freud on similar grounds,
suggesting that the sciences of psychology and psychoanalysis
could obscure, rather than reveal, the irrational elements of the
self.

D. H. Lawrence, in an extended essay entitled *Psychoanalysis
and the Unconscious*, also criticised what he saw as the Freudian
attempt to master the unconscious by rationalising it. Instead he
identifies what he terms a 'pristine unconscious', specifically dislo-
cating this entity from the mind and repositioning it in the body:
'it is not a shadow cast from the mind. It is the spontaneous life-
motive in every organism'. Further, he argues that writing can only
capture this ever-changing life force by recreating an experience in
language: 'It cannot be conceived, it can only be experienced, in
every single instance'.[59] Robert Graves, in a humorous book about
the joys of swearing published in 1927, suggests that in the place
of old forms of discursive authority such as religion, the world has
created 'newer semi-religious institutions', one of which is psychoanalysis: he identifies the modern interest in 'superstitious objects
such as pipes, primroses, black–shirts, and blood–stained banners',
and 'the intentional use of Freudian symbols as objurgatory material'.[60] Mina Loy was also alert to the contradictions in modern
forms of social intervention. In 'Hot Cross Bum' she ridicules the
language of psychiatry and sociology. Addressing the figure of the
homeless bums of New York in the poem, she describes the bum
shouting out '"It's not my fault"', which is a 'truth psychiatry /
weighs courteously'.[61]

The distinction is important because there is a shared modernist interest in what Freud called the unconscious elements of the
psyche, but writers found different ways of capturing this elusive
element. For Lawrence and H. D., as for Woolf and Joyce, novels
and poems were best placed to explore the linguistic texture of the

unconscious parts of the self. A number of writers identified the private or unconscious self with the raw aesthetic energy of the obscene, a literary development that heightened the conflict between literature and the law.

SUMMARY OF KEY POINTS

- Modernism was often in conflict with the law.
- A number of modernist texts were censored for obscenity. The conflict between literature and the law in the early twentieth century was a product of historical shifts in the novel form towards more realistic portrayals of sex, and the tightening of restrictions on literary expression.
- Modernist texts were also considered controversial in their representation of women's rights and sexual impulses. A number of modernist writers explored the emotional and psychological consequences of female sexuality.
- Modernist texts also engaged with shifts in the understanding of homosexuality and the unconscious, both of which Freud discussed. While the modernist response to psychoanalysis was often sceptical, the writing of the unconscious produced formal and thematic innovations.

NOTES

1. Wyndham Lewis, 'Cantleman's Spring Mate', in Margaret Anderson (ed.), *Little Review Anthology* (New York: Hermitage House, 1953), p. 143.
2. Djuna Barnes, *Ryder* (Normal: Dalkey Archive Press, [1928] 1990).
3. Quoted in Morris L. Ernst and William Seagle, *To the Pure . . . A Study of Obscenity and the Censor* (London: Jonathan Cape, 1929), p. 130. For a full discussion of the debates surrounding the act see M. J. D. Roberts, 'Morals, Art and the Law: The Passing of the Obscene Publications Act of 1857', *Victorian Studies*, 28.4 (1985), 606–29, and David Saunders,

'Victorian Obscenity Law: Negative Censorship or Positive Administration?' in Paul Hyland and Neil Semmels (eds), *Writing and Censorship in Britain* (London: Routledge, 1992), pp. 155–70.

4. Law Reports, 3 QBD, 1867–8, 371.

5. Émile Zola, 'Naturalism on Stage', in Vassiliki Kolocotroni, Jane A. Goldman and Olga Taxidou (eds), *Modernsism: An Anthology of Sources and Documents* (Edinburgh: Edinburgh University Press, 1998), pp. 172–3.

6. Maria Cummins, *The Lamplighter* (London: T. Nelson and Sons, 1854).

7. James Joyce, *Ulysses: The Corrected Text*, ed. Hans Walter Gabler with Wolfhard Steppe and Claus Melchior (London: Bodley Head, 1986), p. 293.

8. Joyce, *Ulysses*, p. 300.

9. See Paul Vanderham, *James Joyce and Censorship: The Trials of 'Ulysses'* (Basingstoke: Macmillan, 1998), 51.

10. Vanderham, *James Joyce and Censorship*, p. 353.

11. D. H. Lawrence, *Lady Chatterley's Lover* (Harmondsworth: Penguin Books, [1928] 1973), p. 96.

12. Lawrence, *Lady Chatterley's Lover*, p. 97.

13. Lawrence, *Lady Chatterley's Lover*, p. 276.

14. Wyndham Lewis, *Time and Western Man* (Santa Rosa: Black Sparrow Press, [1927] 1993), p. 17.

15. Aldous Huxley, *Point Counter Point* (London: Harper Collins, [1928] 1994), p. 21.

16. Wyndham Lewis, *Snooty Baronet* (Santa Barbara: Black Sparrow Press, [1932] 1984), p. 104.

17. Mina Loy, 'Apology of Genius', in *The Lost Lunar Baedeker*, ed. Roger L. Conover (Manchester: Carcanet, 1996), p. 78.

18. Nathanael West, *A Cool Million and The Dream Life of Balso Snell: Two Novels by Nathanael West* (New York: Farrar, Straus and Giroux, 2006), p. 3.

19. Nathanael West, *Novels and Other Writings* (New York: Library of America, 1997), p. 398.

20. West, *The Dream Life of Balso Snell*, p. 8.

21. Henry Miller, *Tropic of Cancer* (London: Harper Perennial, 2005), p. 251, p. 276.

22. T. S. Eliot, 'Preface', in Djuna Barnes, *Nightwood* (London: Faber and Faber, [1936] 1990), p. 7.

23. Barnes, *Nightwood*, p. 123, p. 124.

24. Barnes, *Nightwood*, p. 115, p. 116.

25. New editions were published during the late 1970s and 1980s. See Dorothy Richardson, *Pilgrimage* (London: Virago, 1979); Mina Loy, *The Last Lunar Baedeker*, ed. Roger Conover (Manchester: Carcanet, 1982); and Mina Loy, *The Lost Lunar Baedeker*, ed. Roger Conover (Manchester: Carcanet, 1996); H. D., *Collected Poems, 1912–1944*, ed. Louis L. Martz (New York: New Directions, 1983). A number of important and influential anthologies were also published around this time, particularly Bonnie Kime Scott (ed.), *The Gender of Modernism: A Critical Anthology* (Bloomington: Indiana University Press, 1990) and Jane Dowson (ed.), *Women's Writing of the 1930s* (London: Routledge, 1995).

26. Sandra Gilbert and Susan Gubar, *No Man's Land: The Place of the Woman Writer in the Twentieth Century*, vols 1, 2 and 3 (New Haven: Yale University Press, 1988, 1989, 1994). For more recent criticism on modernism and women's writing see Maren Tova Linett (ed.), *The Cambridge Companion to Modernist Women Writers* (Cambridge: Cambridge University Press, 2010).

27. Virginia Woolf, *A Room of One's Own and Three Guineas* (Harmondsworth: Penguin Books, 1993), p. 89.

28. Published under a pseudonym, it was a controversial bestseller.

29. George Gissing, *The Odd Women* (1893), follows the lives of three sisters who are forced to earn their own money after their father dies and leaves them in poverty. Sarah Grand's bestseller *The Heavenly Twins* (1893) was a controversial account of the dangers of sexual ignorance and the failure of marriage. Ella Hepworth Dixon's *The Story of a Modern Woman* (1894) focuses on a woman who is forced to make money by writing fiction after the death of her father.

30. Ford Madox Ford, *Parade's End* (Harmondsworth: Penguin Books, [1924–8] 1982), p. 234.

31. Lewis Grassic Gibbon, *A Scots Quair* (London: Penguin Books, [1932–4] 1986), p. 37.

32. H. D., *Bid Me To Live* (London: Virago, [written 1927; first published 1960] 1983), p. 9.
33. H. D., *Bid Me To Live*, p. 7.
34. H. D., *Bid Me To Live*, p. 97.
35. H. D., *Bid Me To Live*, p. 88.
36. H. D., *Bid Me To Live*, p. 7.
37. Virginia Woolf, *Collected Essays*, vol. 2 (London: Hogarth Press, 1966), p. 315.
38. Woolf, *A Room of One's Own*, p. 84.
39. Mina Loy, 'Feminist Manifesto', in Loy, *The Lost Lunar Baedeker*, p. 153, p. 155.
40. Loy, *The Lost Lunar Baedeker*, p. 59.
41. R. von Krafft-Ebing, for example, in *Psychopathia Sexualis* (1877), described and classified a large number of homosexual case studies under headings such as inversion, hermaphroditism and masochism.
42. Havelock Ellis, *Studies in the Psychology of Sex* (New York: Random House, 1936), p. 35.
43. Ellis, *Studies in the Psychology of Sex*, p. 42.
44. Ellis, *Studies in the Psychology of Sex*, p. 78, p. 79, p. 129.
45. Sigmund Freud, *On Sexuality*, in *The Pelican Freud Library*, ed. Angela Richards, vol. 7 (Harmondsworth: Penguin Books, 1984), p. 51.
46. Freud, *On Sexuality*, pp. 59–60.
47. E. M. Forster, *Maurice* (London: Penguin Books, [1971] 2005).
48. Djuna Barnes, *Ladies Almanack* (Manchester: Carcanet, [1928] 2006), p. 11, p. 9.
49. There was a particular focus, in the translation of Freud's works into British intellectual life, on the analysis of child psychology and the understanding of female sexuality and identity.
50. Dorothy Richardson, 'Preface', *Pilgrimage*, p. 12.
51. H. D., *Bid Me to Live*, p. 148.
52. H. D., *Tribute to Freud* (Oxford: Carcanet, [1956] 1971), p. 13.
53. H. D., *Tribute to Freud*, pp. 20–1.
54. H. D., *Tribute to Freud*, p. 12.
55. Virginia Woolf, 'A Sketch of the Past', in Virginia Woolf,

Moments of Being, ed. Jeanne Schulkind, introduced and revised by Hermione Lee (London: Pimlico, 2002), p. 94.

56. James Joyce, *Finnegans Wake* (London: Faber and Faber, [1939] 1975), p. 115.

57. Joyce, *Finnegans Wake*, p. 115.

58. Joyce, *Finnegans Wake*, p. 128.

59. D. H. Lawrence, *Psychoanalysis and the Unconscious; and Fantasia of the Unconscious*, ed. Bruce Steele (Cambridge: Cambridge University Press, 2004), p. 50, p. 24, p. 35, p. 41.

60. Robert Graves, *Lars Porsena, or, the Future of Swearing and Improper Language* (London: Kegan Paul, 1927), p. 49.

61. Mina Loy, 'Hot Cross Bum', in Loy, *The Lost Lunar Baedeker*, p. 190.

CHAPTER 4

Modernism and Mass culture

In the introduction to this book I described some of the specific features of the new mass media of the early twentieth century: an expanding mass-distribution newspaper network and readership, cheap mass-produced novels, the cinema and the radio. While modernist writers had complicated relationships to each of these things, they also engaged with the literary impact of mass culture, a term that synthesises these different cultural forms and implies that a capitalist logic of commercial exploitation holds them together. The term, and what it implies, has served a dual purpose. Claims about modernism as a collective artistic endeavour have often been grounded in arguments about its separation from mass cultural entertainment. But this argument has proved controversial in responses both to modernist writing, and its self-definitions. Where does the difference reside? Who decides that one kind of novel is written and consumed for entertainment, and another kind of novel explores truth and beauty and forms part of a privileged literary tradition? For many readers and critics, the very idea of art as something distinct from mass or popular culture involves a problematic distaste for popular writing. The Marxist cultural critic Antonio Gramsci argued that it relies on the imposition of the values of a dominant and privileged class and denigrates the expressive resistance of subordinate groups. Theodor Adorno, in contrast, while also working within a Marxist tradition, claimed that modernist art, in its difficulty and dissonance, resists the absolute capitalist domination of the cultural sphere.

Adorno wrote about a wide range of subjects in his lifetime, including philosophy, musicology, social theory, literature and art. One of his boldest arguments was that radio, cinema and leisure time had become forms of 'administered life'. The books, films and music of Western cultures were organised as a 'culture industry' designed to confirm capitalist structures and values. Adorno argued, however, that some cultural products could not be accommodated by the culture industry, notably the autonomous art work which, as he put it, 'has renounced consumption'.[1] This renunciation rests on the idea that some art works have a 'truth-content' independent of commodified understandings of value. This truth can only be experienced through an attention to the particular features of individual art works or pieces of writing. Adorno's interpretation of individual texts, therefore, involves the close attention both to their language and form, and to what they assume art to be.

Adorno's theory of the culture industry and art has been controversial. Some critics have accused him of élitism in his approach because they argue that he has decided in advance whether certain cultural products are art. He thereby fails to attend to the particular features of film or jazz, for instance, while assuming that modernist music or 'difficult' poetry are worth dissecting and understanding. In addition, much recent historical work on modernism has argued that the relationship between writers and mass culture is much more complicated than Adorno allows. An attention to the history of modernist publishing, for instance, reveals a complex picture of modernist collusion with, and manipulation of, the publishing industry. Or, an understanding of the history of cinema creates a more complicated picture of the different kinds of films being produced at the time and the divergent responses to it.

Others, however, have found Adorno's theory important and invaluable for an understanding of the political value and radical critical potential of modernist formal experimentation and 'difficulty'. His aesthetic theory helps us to understand both the attempt by writers to expose the social and economic power of new media, and the claims made by modernist writers for artistic autonomy and value.

MODERNIST AUTHORITY

The modernist literary immersion in new media constitutes one of its most exciting elements. Writers influenced by the European avant-garde movements of Futurism, Dadaism, expressionism and Surrealism sought to capture the speed, unpredictability and innovations of new media and popular culture such as the cinema, jazz and radio. This energy fuelled both the formal experimentation of modernist texts, and provided new vocabularies and metaphors for the modern. Antonin Artaud declared that 'the great public looks to the movies, the music hall, or the circuses for violent satisfactions, whose intentions do not deceive them'.[2] Marinetti describes a 'wireless imagination' in his manifesto *Zang Tumb Tuuum* (1912–14), using new technology to create a metaphor of rapid imaginative speed. Jazz was also a central resource for images of the modern. The Polish Futurist writer Anatol Stern combines sound, physical energy and innovation in his description of 'the jazz-band / of discoveries / shimmy of relativity'.[3]

Anglo-American writers who adopted and extended the language of the European avant-garde recreated this connection of new technology and energy. In her essay 'Modern Poetry', Mina Loy argues that American jazz is 'the collective spirit of the modern world', a spirit she uses in her image of a 'jazz-band sunset' in 'Mexican Desert' (1921) and in 'The Widow's Jazz' (1927), which creates both racially inflected images of white flesh quaking to 'the negro soul' and ideas of jazzy language as an 'unerring Esperanto / of the earth'.[4] Joyce creates new words, such as 'readiooscillating epiepistle' and keep your 'ear on the movietone', to put into writing the rippling oral excitement of radio and film.[5] Loy sees the international 'Esperanto' of jazz as the fertile ground of new writing.

Other Anglo-American responses to mass cultural forms or new kinds of popular expression were much more overtly hostile. Eliot, Pound, Lewis, Lawrence and Laura Riding explicitly defined the difficulty of their experimental writing against the values and easily consumed products of mass-produced and market-oriented novels and films, and tended to figure contemporary popular forms, such as the jazz of Loy's sunset, as symbols of racially defined chaos.

Wyndham Lewis aggressively attacks popular writers, cinematic stereotypes, journalism and jazz, but he also makes these objects of his attack the substance of his writing. As his character Tarr puts it in his novel of that name: 'I gaze on squalor and idiocy, and the more I see it, the more I like it'. Far from being a 'pure' art which occupies an abstract place outside modern media, his writing might be said to bury its 'face in it', as Tarr puts it.[6] In another description, Lewis's journal *Blast* diagnoses and ridicules the 'stupidity' of humanity but also seeks to appeal to the 'fundamental and popular instincts in every class and description of people'.[7]

Lewis refers to jazz, meanwhile, in ways which are racially inflected, or, by assuming racial inferiority, racist. He concludes *The Apes of God* with a description of jazz sounds coming through the window of Lady Fredigonde's house as part of an image of England's social and economic collapse during the general strike of 1926. Zagreus hears from the street a 'sentimental jazzing one-time stutter – gutter-thunder', street noises that prompt Archie Margolin to sway 'with elf-like nigger-bottom-wagging'.[8]

Lewis produces another racially inflected reference to jazz, whose coordinates are more complicated. During Lord Osmund's party, there is a description of a 'sumptuous staircase', with 'gilded' and artistically decorated stairs. Zagreus mounts the staircase in a way which recalls Swann's ascent of the luxurious staircase of Saint-Euverte's mansion in Marcel Proust's *In Search of Lost Time*.[9] The staircase in Proust's novel is emblematic of recognisable class distinctions, distinctions which are specifically held together by Swann's mental perspective in which footmen are similar to the great works of Renaissance art. The cultural artefacts on Lewis's staircase, in contrast, herald the collapse of stable class distinctions:

Above the squat gilded stairs (hastily enriched with bogus gold-leaf upon the period balustrade) brooded a pantheon of Verrio. It had been executed with a jazz agility by an American negro-designer, who was very cheap because he was black. A dull and thick-limbed peasant-goddess – or goddess of the dull potato-patch Demos – by Maillol – squatted half-way up – then a barbarous ice-cream-tinted panel by an East-End confiserie-cubist was a few steps from the dull daughter of Demos.[10]

Verrio's artistic brocade is a sham as it has actually been created by an unnamed 'negro-designer'. Maillol's sculpture, meanwhile, sits next to another unnamed panel, this time Cubist in design. The staircase, the paragraph implies, claims for itself a cultural democratisation and inclusivity, with its mix of contemporary and traditional art. However, the gesture, like the Verrio, is a fake. The driving force behind the make-up of the staircase is the aristocratic exploitation of racially and class-defined subjects. Lewis's writing represents both divergent kinds of contemporary art, and the financial terms of its production.

Complexities of tone also inform Pound's reference to jazz in *The Cantos*:

> Another day, between walls of a sham Mycenian,
> 'Toc' sphinxes, sham-Memphis columns,
> And beneath the jazz a cortex, a stiffness or stillness,
>   Shell of the older house.
> Brown-yellow wood, and the no colour plaster,
> Dry professorial talk . . .
>   now stilling the ill beat music,
> House expulsed by this house.[11]

Pound exploits the different meanings of the word jazz, which refers both to a style of music and is a slang word signifying energy and excitement. Mycenian civilisation, the sphinxes and the Memphis columns are all described as counterfeit structures (the word 'toc' is French slang for sham or ugly), and are opposed to the life and energy of contemporary music. These distinct elements are likened to thought. The brain's cortex is similar to a 'shell' of an older house, images which pick up on lines from the preceding stanza which refer to dry and empty words, 'a shell of speech'. The 'dry professorial talk' and the stiff cortex require the energy of the 'ill beat music', the 'life' that we are told 'goes on' in a subsequent stanza.[12] Jazz is opposed to dry professorial authority, but Pound implies he requires both elements in his epic modern poem.

Eliot also refers to jazz in *The Waste Land*. After a lush description of a woman sitting, as Shakespeare's Cleopatra does, on her 'burnished throne', Eliot refers to a popular American jazz song called 'that Shakespeherian Rag', whose lines about 'elegance and intelligence' are both quoted and ironised. The poem juxtaposes scattered elements of modern life with references to an established tradition of cultural and religious knowledge. It asks us to recognise the gap separating past and present, elegant verse and inelegant jazz, intelligent writing and its opposite.

Pound's judgemental words, 'sham' and 'ill beat', mediate the reader's response to jazz on the level of individual words. Eliot's ironies assume that the 'Shakespeherian Rag' will be neither elegant nor intelligent, and that his reader will recognise the irony. Lewis's 'sham' jazz, meanwhile, joins a list of other pseudo-artistic works paid for by a declining and barbaric class élite. These references to jazz both incorporate its energies and seek to control it.

This judgemental immersion in popular cultural forms is both one of the defining features of Pound's, Eliot's and Lewis's modernism, and has been one of its most controversial features. From where does the judgement come? What kind of authority allows Tarr – or Lewis – to name the idiocy of others and pass judgement upon them? Or why do Eliot and Pound assume that jazz is a sham or inelegant? And how can these approaches possibly claim to appeal to the popular instincts in people? At its worst, this self-selective élitism is grounded in, and is part of, the anti-Semitism, racism and misogyny which is a significant feature of Lewis's writing, and of texts by Pound, Eliot, Lawrence and others.

In its more enlightened form, however, this opposition of art and popular culture forms part of a critique of the capitalist domination of cultural values. In his 1920 poem *Hugh Selwyn Mauberley* Ezra Pound describes a writer called Mr Nixon. After giving financial details about royalties and reviewers, Mr Nixon advises the hopeful young poet to 'give up verse, my boy, / There's nothing in it'.[13] While Mr Nixon's 'nothing' is defined numerically by the absolute domination of financial value, the poem insists that poetry has non-commercial value. These contested understandings of value are part of what Pound saw as an antagonistic battle between literature and commercial fiction, culture as it should be and as it is. The critique of established cultural values also helps us to read Lewis's appeal to the 'popular instincts in every class' in *Blast*. It involves a demand that the link between cultural authority and British class hierarchies be dislodged.

In modernist texts there is often a strain between the incorporation of the energies of new media, and the judgemental imposition of timeless notions of artistic form. This conflict, which is arguably a social and historical one, lies at the heart of Anglo–American modernist writing. It is at the centre both of its most remarkable achievements and its most troubling gestures.

CINEMA

One of the most significant new technologies to emerge in the early twentieth century was that of the cinema. Virginia Woolf, in a 1926 essay on 'Cinema', argues that while people say that 'we are at the fag-end of civilization, that everything has been said already, and that it is too late to be ambitious', they have forgotten one new phenomenon: 'these philosophers', she declares, 'have presumably forgotten the movies'.[14]

The origins of cinema lie in the experiments with various photographic and film technologies in the 1890s, but the exhibition of the first projected film to a paying public by the Lumière brothers in 1895 is a useful historical marker. Technological developments moved quickly, with small cinema theatres or booths opening across America and Europe through the 1890s and 1900s and rapid advances in filming, perspective and cutting techniques. By the time that world war broke out in 1914, film as both a narrative and documentary medium was well established. Innovators attempted to marry sound to film from early on, but had to settle for silent film with accompanying sound effects until the mid 1920s. Synchronised sound was properly introduced in the Vitaphone system in 1926. By the end of 1929 Hollywood was completely dominated by the 'talkies'.

Alongside the exploitation of film for mass audiences, whose commercial and political potential was immediately realised, there was a significant strand of avant-garde film-making, both in the experimental wing of the fledgling Soviet film industry and among Surrealist artists. Eisenstein's film theory of montage, as well as films such as *Strike* (1924), *Battleship Potemkin* (1925) and *October* (1927), influenced both the commercial and artistic elements of film production. In Paris, meanwhile, Surrealist films such as Man Ray's *Return to Reason* (1923), Germaine Dulac's (with a screenplay by Antonin Artaud) *La Coquille et le Clergyman* (1928) and Luis Buñuel and Salvador Dalí's *Un Chien Andalou* (1929) and *L'Age d'Or* (193) created a new language of cinematic art.

Both strands of avant-garde film-making had an impact on avant-garde British film and film theory. Kenneth Macpherson collaborated with Bryher and H. D. to create the film journal *Close Up* in 1927. They also made a number of films, of which only *Borderline* (1930), starring Paul Robeson, Eslanda Robeson, H. D. and Bryher, survives. *Borderline* uses Eisenstein's montage techniques to create a psychologically fraught representation of anxious inter-racial relationships. The combination of psychoanalysis, Russian film theory and experimentalism were central to the essays published in *Close Up*. This was a journal specifically devoted to cinema as an art form, independent of commercial interests. Dorothy Richardson wrote a regular column for the journal, and H. D. contributed a number of essays about silent film.

The cultural impact of cinema as a new technology, as well as a novel cultural language of film images and techniques, was, as Woolf suggests, epoch-changing, and had a significant influence on literature and art. In Chapter 2 I briefly mentioned that Wyndham Lewis, at the beginning of *Tarr*, references the American cinema. In the 1918 version of *Tarr* Lewis writes the following:

> Inconceivably generous and naïve faces haunt the Knackfus Quarter. = We are not however in a Selim and Vitagraph camp (though 'guns' tap rhythmically the buttocks). = Art is being studied. = Art is the smell of oil paint, Henri Murger's 'Vie de Bohème,' corduroy trousers, the operatic Italian model. But the poetry, above all, of linseed oil and turpentine.[15]

The 'Selim' camp seems to be a mistake: it should surely be 'Selig' and thereby a reference to the Selig Polyscope Company which was the first permanent movie studio in California. This would connect it with the American Vitagraph, one of the most significant of the American studios by 1907. Both film companies were renowned for their Westerns. When Lewis came to republish *Tarr* in 1928, he revised the text substantially. There are a few revealing alterations to this passage: Knackfus becomes Vitelotte Quarter and 'a Selim and Vitagraph camp' becomes 'Hollywood camp of pseudo-cowpunchers'. In the 1928 text, Lewis also inserts a new sentence: 'Art is being studied. – But " art" is not anything serious or exclusive: it is the smell of oil paint'. In a subsequent paragraph, Lewis also changes 'a Vitagraph group or two drinking and playing billiards' to 'a Middle West group or two, drinking and playing billiards.[16] In terms of the changes to the 1928 text, references to the two separate and specific American film companies become the more generic 'Hollywood', and the connection between Hollywood and Westerns is much more explicit. The movies are presented as an established and coordinated industry in the revised version. The substitution of 'Middle West' for 'Vitagraph', meanwhile, removes the cinematic reference and replaces it with nationality. The changes reveal something about the historical shifts in the American cinema industry, which had become more integrated and professionalised by 1928. While the earlier text references fragmented film companies, fragmentation is replaced with a synthesised industry in the later text.

In both versions of *Tarr* the movies are used in an opposition between the cinema industry and art. Yet the text introduces this opposition, only to destabilise it. The individuals studying the Art of oil paint and corduroy trousers turn out to be as naïve and superficial as the 'pseudo' products of the Hollywood cinema, a point emphasised by the insertion of the new sentence about seriousness and exclusivity in the 1928 text. Both groups are as 'disheartening and admonitory' as wax dummies.

Lewis's novel stages a series of debates about what art is, and also inserts third person commentary focused on this question. These definitions often reiterate the opposition laid out in this opening paragraph between 'pseudo' and modernist art. It is significant that the movies are fore-grounded in the idea of the pseudo. While the 1918 text is less explicit, both versions rely on an idea of simulation: the artists who are studying art are performing a role. They are as divorced from genuine artists as the Hollywood 'cowpunchers' are from real cowboys.

Lewis's writing often attends to the absurdities and social consequences of this difference between reality and simulation. In some respects, the reference to the movies at the beginning of *Tarr* is simply a way of illustrating the superficiality of German, American and British art tourists. At another level, one could read Lewis's wider interest in the performativity of selfhood as partly a response to the new mass media of film. The terms of this extend into the texture of his language. The effects of this paragraph are to place quotation marks around the words 'art' and 'poetry': 'Art is being studied', 'Art is the smell of oil paint', poetry is 'linseed oil and turpentine'. Lewis satirises these words in their superficial disconnection from the real. As Andrzej Gasiorek points out, however, Lewis's writing does not present a stable linguistic place outside the simulated language of cliché: 'It is in the ambiguous space that opens up when the stale language of cliché and stereotype is seen through but is still in force that Lewis finds his material.[17] Lewis's writing is, in itself, a kind of posture. It seems to dwell in a pre-existing counterfeit language of art in which individuals ape poverty and artistic passion. Yet, in reality, Lewis creates the particular blend of this fake language, in which economics, fashion, national stereotyping and aesthetics combine and inform each other.

In Lewis's later novels *The Apes of God* (1930) and *The Revenge for Love* (1937) cinematic imagery is also central, but its terms of reference shift. He now uses the idea of film to capture the workings of the mind and the strengthened power of Hollywood. In *The Apes of God* Lewis creates a semi-conscious interior monologue which relies on the idea of film. Lady Fredigonde closes her eyes and fantasises about a museum full of lace-caps:

> The day and night cinema that exists immediately within was encouraged to operate. The brain on its own initiative from its projector was flashing lace-caps upon the screen. All her collection was idly called forth, in startling close-ups, for her inspection.[18]

Here the brain is pictured as both a space and a mechanism: it has a screen, a projector and the ability to manipulate close-up techniques. Lady Fredigonde, as an entity separate from her mind's cinema, is still in control; she encourages her cinema to start projecting, she calls forth her collection of images, however idly. But the boundary between her agency and her mental cinema is fragile.

Alongside the personal psychic cinemas in individual heads, Lewis depicts the shared filmic signs that mediate the relationships between people. In the middle of Lord Osmund's Lenten party

> Dan could not *see* the narrowing of the eyes to feline film-star-slits, nor clenching of cow-boy fists, but the modern cinema was upon a sudden all about him: the dropping of the voice at the unmasking of the villain, when the name was uttered and 'Harry Caldicott' stood revealed, came straight out of the Dime-days and the popular photoplay.[19]

Modern cinema exists as a system of collectively recognised signs: the narrowed eyes and clenched fists of Hollywood vamps and cowboys, as well as the modulations of voice and gestures. Cinematic illusions, in this sentence, have created a shared cultural and financial logic that is independent of the experience of watching any one particular film. The logic that holds this illusionary structure together is one that is similar to what Adorno meant when he wrote about a 'culture industry' in the mid-1940s. The logic both supersedes the particulars of individual films and extends its power into other cultural spheres. Lewis suggests that art and artists are part of the same structure. Artists are 'pseudo-artists' who ape the imaginary activities of genuine artists. Like God, art is something abstract, ubiquitous and illusory in *The Apes of God*. It turns out that the supposed origin of these artistic endeavours – the artistic 'God' of the novel's title – is, himself, also a forgery.

The film industry was a fast-moving one, and Lewis's later novel, *The Revenge for Love*, picks up on changes in the Hollywood movie industry in the 1930s. The novel focuses on a number of different characters in the heightened political atmosphere of the 1930s. At its heart, however, are the apolitical couple Victor

Stamp and Margot, who get duped by communist fighters in the Spanish civil war. Victor Stamp is a poverty-stricken and rather unimpressive Australian artist who, at one point in the novel, is forced to paint forged Van Gogh pictures in order to make some money. Throughout the novel, he is likened to a Hollywood hero: 'he smiled his Clark Gable smile – one side of his face all sardonic half-mirth, the scalp muscles ploughing up the forehead to make it all go careworn, so as to embitter the onesided smile down below still more'.[20]

Lewis's extraordinary description of a smile, part of a life-long interest in the fine line between grimacing and amused facial expressions, exploits the dominance and ubiquity of the Hollywood star system, which ensures that a Clark Gable smile is both internationally recognisable and physically transmittable. The Hollywood star system, in which actors were vigorously promoted by the studios, became a significant feature of cinema after the shift to talkies in the late 1920s. By the mid 1930s, after starring in both gangster films such as *A Free Soul* (1931) and steamy romances such as *Red Dust* (1931), Gable was MGM's most important male star. Lewis both manipulates the power of Clark Gable's image, and attends in some detail to the specific movements of the facial features. The result is to present a kind of physiological conflict in which cinematic identifications do not fully map the physical gestures that they spawn.

Lewis was not alone in wanting to identify the relationship between Hollywood as an industry exploiting economics and illusion. The connection of cinema and itinerant fantasies of instant wealth is a feature of much writing in this period. Christopher Isherwood, in his autobiographical novel *Goodbye to Berlin*, evokes the infiltration of fantasies of cinematic celebrity culture on everyday life: 'We talked continually about wealth, fame, huge contracts for Sally, record-breaking sales for the novels I should one day write'.[21]

In a 1921 poem called 'Perlun', Mina Loy, like Lewis before her, uses the movies as a key signifier of an international cultural logic dominated by post-war monetary values. The poem focuses on a character called Perlun, who is both a 'pert blond spirit' and a 'vivacious knick-knack tipped with gold'. Perlun, whose national origins are uncertain, is free to put the world to the 'test of intuition', but his choices are constrained by the harsh logic of finance. Attempting to live 'from other hands to mouth', Perlun makes money by clasping various individuals in his arms:

> Holding in immaculate arms
>   the syphilitic sailor
>   on his avoided death bunk
>   or the movie vamp
>   among the muffled shadows of the shrubberies –
> Picking lemons in Los Angeles   broke[22]

The luminous moon that is partly contained in the 'lun' of Perlun's name captures an image of international wandering that is both glamorous and financially precarious. Perlun presents his beautiful body to a world composed of diseased sailors, movie vamps, boxers, flappers and millionaires. These faceless character types are connected in the creation of an imaginary post-war world composed of individuals seeking money and freedom. Hollywood is by no means accidental to the logic that might be seen to hold these types together. This is a world in which one can sell one's beauty both to sailors and to the film industry, a world which functions on the precarious boundary between prostitution and glamour. Not only are the movies one route to financial freedom, their illusionary substance creates a particular idea of wealth: the 'knick-knack' gold of Perlun's body.

As in Lewis's writing, cinema culture influences both the language and form of Loy's poem. She wittily evokes Perlun's chosen status as a commodity to be bought and sold in a human marketplace. This objectifying logic informs the language of the poem, which relies on the fact that individuals can be reduced to character stereotypes and that these types will be recognisable. The power of this illusionary realm, what Lewis Grassic Gibbon in an essay on cinema called 'free and undefiled illusion', infiltrates the language of poetry.[23]

While Lewis and Loy were interested in the psychic effects of movie culture, a number of other modernist writers tried to engage with the artistic potential of the medium. Woolf, H. D.

and Richardson became interested in the mid to late 1920s, in the artistic possibilities of silent cinema. In 'The Cinema' (1926) Woolf is critical of contemporary films, accusing them of creating bad adaptations of literary classics and of being technologically sophisticated but conceptually sterile. She does, however, make a number of tentative statements about the radical possibilities of film as an art form. The essay is interesting, not only for what it says about cinema, but also for what art is assumed to be.

Woolf is interested in film's ability to bring to life distanced, or dead, places and people: 'We behold them as they are when we are not there. We see life as it is when we have no part in it.'[24] Because film is disconnected from the spectator, it creates a concentrated and heightened form of reality. She also argues that film has the potential to bring to life hidden psychological dimensions. She imagines a new cinematic language in which filmed objects or shapes are able to capture emotions which have never been expressed before: 'the cinema has within its grasp innumerable symbols for emotions that have so far failed to find expression'. In another sentence she describes these hidden emotions as a kind of language: 'Is there, we ask, some secret language which we feel and see, but never speak, and, if so, could this be made visible to the eye?'[25]

In trying to flesh out what this secret language might look like she makes two, rather divergent, claims. Relying on the terminology of the visual arts, she suggests that cinematic language will be divorced from realism: 'Something abstract, something which moves with controlled and conscious art'. At another point, however, she undercuts this idea of the non-mimetic abstraction of cinematic art by describing film as a product of being in the city. She pictures 'violent changes of emotion produced by their collision', 'contrasts' that are 'flashed before us', and the annihilation of the distance created by time and geography. She locates the source of this style in experience in the 'chaos of the streets . . . when some momentary assembly of colour, sound, movement, suggests that here is a scene waiting a new art to be transfixed'.[26] Woolf's essay implies that art is oriented psychologically. Such a definition chimes with her novels which create new languages of the self within tightly controlled narratives. Her claim that the imagistic collisions and dissonant juxtapositions of cinematic language are essentially urban is also interesting. Woolf's argument encourages us to ask a retrospective question about these connections: do modernist representations of the city contain within them a third element: that of the cinematic?

Certainly, in their ability to splice together images of different geographies and time zones, modernist texts such as *The Waste Land* and *Ulysses* can be seen, and have been read, in relation to cinematic techniques. The clearest example of this kind of writing is that of Joyce's *Finnegans Wake* which, as we saw in Chapter 2, refers to fantasy film studios and a 'landescape' present tense.[27] He creates a cinematic language by connecting panoramic views of landscape, the Hollywood star system and some of the key movie genres, such as Westerns and detective stories.

Laura Marcus has also made a compelling case for reading *To the Lighthouse* (1927) as a cinematographic novel, not with regard to its geographical and temporal juxtapositions, but in relation to her focus on a kind of 'ghostly realism'.[28] This is to pick up on Woolf's first claim about film in her cinema essay: its ability to allow us to 'behold' people and things 'as they are when we are not there'.[29] Marcus concentrates in particular on the middle section of the novel, called 'Time Passes', in which the play of light resembles the light effects of silent film. Through a historical account she shows how Woolf's use of parentheses in brackets to document significant events such as childbirth, marriage and death function like film inter-titles, and the prose is like a 'dream-space, drawing upon the profound conceptual connections between dreams and cinema'. Not only is there an image of a curtain parting to reveal distinct images, as though in a cinema, but the 'world in "Time Passes" is given over to light'.[30]

Woolf's writing in 'Time Passes' is centrally focused on objects and energies which, as she put it in her 'Cinema' essay, are 'more real' because they are both dislocated from the present and are an inanimate representation of the past. After a description of the objects in the house that have been left behind, she describes reflected light effects which both bear the recent imprint of life and movement and are dislocated from human life, as in a film. Once the looking-glass had held a world hollowed out in which a figure turned, a hand flashed, the door opened, in came children rushing and tumbling; and went out again. Now, day after day, light turned, like a flower reflected in water, its clear image on the wall opposite.[31]

Rather than the turning figure and the flashing hand, movement resides in the play of reflected light and dark on the wall. The description relies on a contrast between the now of light imagery and the past of human activity, a contrast which suggests the loss of human presence. Loss is central to the novel in a number of respects, but the ghostly cinematic aspects of the description above contrast with other moments in the book when a character or an object are visualised as 'the thing itself'. The novel ends, for instance, with Lily Briscoe suddenly turning to her canvas and realising 'There it was – her picture'.[32]

Dorothy Richardson and H. D. also discussed whether film might produce an imagistic language of the psyche. Richardson had a regular column called 'Continuous Performance' in the film journal *Close Up* in which she discussed film techniques, such as slow motion, the use of film captions and film music. She was particularly interested in women's responses to film, and was an advocate of the expressive dimensions of silent film, as opposed to the talkies.

H. D. was also involved in the *Close Up* circle. She wrote eleven essays for the journal between 1927 and 1929, three of which were titled 'The Cinema and the Classics', and a separate essay-pamphlet on the film *Borderline* published by the Mercury Press (1930). Like Woolf and Richardson, H. D. was interested in cinema as a 'living art', distinguishing this from the 'commercial' side, which she likened to a 'Juggernaut crushing out mind and perception in one vast orgy of the senses'.[33]

She took up a particular line on modern film which reveals much about her understanding of art. She argued that, in the beauty of individual actors and actresses, cinema had the potential to mediate and disseminate images which are at once modern and classical. H. D. was interested in the film actress Greta Garbo, whom she excitedly remembers first seeing in a cinema in Switzerland. Garbo is an embodiment of a timeless beauty, a modern example of the beauty of Helen of Troy, or the 'frescoes of Simone Martini and the etchings of Albrecht Dürer'. Her beauty has 'something of a quality that I can't for the life of me label otherwise than classic'.[34] The challenge for modern cinema, according to H. D., is to harness this classic beauty, rather than destroy it. She is worried that Hollywood has tried to obliterate Garbo's natural beauty by making her into a movie type, a 'vamp'. Like Lewis and Loy she is wary of the Hollywood 'juggernaut' which subsumes individuals under a system of 'types'. Instead, she claims that the movies should exploit a neoclassical ideal of unchanging beauty. Garbo's beauty must be allowed to speak for itself within the medium of film.

The idea that the cinema should exploit neoclassical forms of beauty is central to a number of poems H. D. wrote about film, most notably 'Projector' and 'Projector II', both of which were published in *Close Up*. In these poems Imagist techniques of linguistic concision and incantation herald the artistic dimension of projected light. The two poems view film through a Greek lens, contrasting Greek Apollo, god of light, prophecy and poetry, with the new power of projected cinematic light. In 'Projector', 'Light takes new attribute', a new element which both illuminates and arranges fragmented forms:

> to reassemble
> and to readjust
> all severing
> and differing of thought,
> all strife and strident bickering

Cinema has the power to bring together and organise the fragmented thoughts of the audience, a power which depends on the screen projection of beautiful light effects:

> waves sparkle and delight
> the weary eyes
> that never saw the sun fall in the sea
> nor the bright Pleiads rise.[35]

H. D. presents a picture of the estrangement, strife and weariness of contemporary life, and of filmed images as lifting individuals into an imaginary world of beautiful illusion. She captures the immense power of projected light to reshape the imagination. In 'Projector II' she describes 'souls upon the screen / live lives that might have been / live lives that ever are'.[36] The poem evokes the play of light on a screen and how these effects create new forms in a timeless dimension. As in Woolf's writing, the reality of film is ghostly:

shadow folk
and ghost-beast
we speak of shadow-speech
we tread a shadow-rock,
we lie along ghost-grass
in ghost shade
of the hillock[37]

While on one level H. D. describes film as a distraction from everyday life, she is also interested in the ways in which the spectator identifies with ghostly cinematic images. This identification is also explored in her description of going to the movies in *Bid Me To Live*. As in 'Projector' and 'Projector II', cinema is described as a mass medium, this time in the context of the First World War:

Below her, below them, were the thousands; it seemed that all the soldiers in the world, symbolically packed into this theatre. There was music, too near, pouring at them from an organ, playing the usual sentimental ditties and the voices of the thousand thousands of all the soldiers in the world were joining to swell this chorus.[38]

The soldiers exist in a dual time scale. This is a realistic description of a cinema full of soldiers during the First World War. It is also, however, a scene which has been lifted away from realism and become futuristic and surreal: the thousands upon thousands of soldiers – all the soldiers in the world – packed into the cinema below her. H. D.'s protagonist, Julia, identifies with this massed cinematic audience of soldiers who, in turn, collectively identify with the moving image:

> The car swept on. She was dragged forward with the car . . . The car would swerve, would turn, it swerved, it turned, they swerved, they turned with it, it was dashing to destruction along the edge of a narrow cliff, they were dashing with it.[39]

Julia and the soldiers are carried forwards in time with the car, which plunges headlong into death and destruction. The experience of watching the car's movement towards death is likened to an artistic process of tragic theatrical catharsis, in which the observation of screen death purges the emotions: 'a thousand doomed, the dead were watching destruction, Oedipus or Orestes in a slim car, dashing to destruction'.[40] But the cathartic process is complicated through a powerful description of the soldiers sitting in the cinema as futuristic ghosts: 'The smoke from the thousand cigarettes was incense, breathed by ghosts-to-be, toward Beauty'. The chapter concludes by referring to these soldiers as 'angels, surging on toward their destruction'.[41]

Despite the fact that Garbo did not begin appearing in films until the mid 1920s, H. D., in this description of a cinema during the First World War, writes about a beautiful screen actress emerging onto the screen: 'a goddess-woman stepped forward. She released from the screen the first (to Julia) intimation of screen-beauty'. Like Woolf, H. D. sees this screen image as ghostly, using the word to capture the temporal and spatial dislocations of film: 'Here was Beauty, a ghost but Beauty'. The inherent ghostliness of filmed bodies merges with the more literal and chilling 'ghosts-to-be' of the soldiers.

Woolf's and H. D.'s focus on the temporal dislocations of the film medium, in which absent bodies are able to come to life again, was particularly productive for their literary engagements with cinema. I want to conclude this section on modernism and cinema with one final, rather different, use of film as a metaphor for modern experience, one which fuses psychic trauma with surrealistic imagery. In this description, cinema is viewed from the position of an alienated subject.

One of the important discursive strands in Jean Rhys's novel *Good Morning, Midnight* (1939) is the danger of sentimental language, a sentimentalism that is produced through popular ballads and the movies. Rhys was born in Dominica in 1890, the daughter of a Welsh doctor and a white Creole mother. She travelled to England in the 1900s, and then settled in Paris, where she began to write in the 1920s. She was encouraged to publish by Ford Madox Ford, who brought out her work in his journal the *transatlantic review* and with whom she had an affair. Her first collection of stories, called *The Left Bank*, was published in 1927, with her first novel, *Quartet* (1928), appearing soon afterwards. Other novels include *After Leaving Mr Mackenzie* (1930), *Voyage in the Dark* (1934) and *Good Morning, Midnight* (1939). After dropping out of sight for many years, Rhys suddenly published her most successful novel, *Wide Sargasso Sea*, in 1966, a novel which won her the Royal Society of Literature Award.

Early in *Good Morning, Midnight* one character is described as 'vaguely like the man who always took the spy-parts in German films some years ago'.[42] Recalling an interchange with a member of her family, the protagonist, Sasha, considers:

> They think in terms of a sentimental ballad. And that's what terrifies you about them. It isn't their cruelty, it isn't even their shrewdness – it's their extraordinary naiveté. Everything in their whole bloody world is a cliché. Everything is born out of a cliché, rests on a cliché, survives by a cliché. And they believe in the clichés – there's no hope.[43]

As the novel progresses, it becomes clear that the real danger both of films and clichéd language is their power to penetrate Sasha's psychic and emotional life. Towards the end of the novel, she is seduced by a gigolo who ends up attacking her. Before she allows him to come to her room she warns herself against the power of an internalised cinematic sentimentalism: 'My film-mind . . . ("For god's sake watch out for your film-mind . . .")'.[44] Her film-mind synthesises sentimental cliché, static images from her past, and the idealistic elements of her psyche. At the end of the novel, the dangerous sentimentalism of ballad and cinema produces a surreal description of hallucinatory knowledge which is presented as another 'damned voice in my head':

> Venus is dead; Apollo is dead; even Jesus is dead
>   All that is left in the world is an enormous machine, made of white steel. It has innumerable flexible arms, made of steel. Long, thin arms. At the end of each arm is an eye, the eyelashes stiff with mascara. When I look more closely I see that only some of the arms have these eyes – others have lights. The arms that carry the eyes and the arms that carry the lights are all extraordinarily flexible and very beautiful. But the grey sky, which is the background, terrifies me . . . And the arms wave to an accompaniment of music and song.[45]

This is an extraordinary description of a surreal cinematic machine whose eyes and lights combine surveillance, spectacle and a distorted beauty. The machine takes the place of mythic and religious knowledge. Rather than Venus or Jesus, there is simply an enormous stage or screen. Persecutory eyes, disconnected from character or agency, dominate the novel as a whole. Here, their disconnection is highlighted and exaggerated, as is their ability to observe and illuminate, so that they become a remarkable symbol of the society of spectacle Rhys describes. Words in this novel partake of this idea of mechanised surveillance. The clichéd language of her family is both cruel and naïve, personal and generalised. The words fail to recognise Sasha's individual predicament, glancing over her as though as though she is an inert object. Like the arms with eyes, clichéd words have become separated from the individuals who speak them.

Despite the radical differences in the approaches to film by the writers discussed above, there are shared aspects to their responses. The movie industry is seen as a mass medium which forms part of a society of spectacle and performance which controls the body and the mind. Rhys's 'film-mind' is much more threatening and destructive than Lady Fredigonde's internal cinema in *The Apes of God*, but both writers powerfully register the impact of the movie industry on the individual imagination. Woolf and H. D. also seek to capture the relationship between film and mind, although they view this relationship in a more positive light. All writers use the cinematic to define art. Woolf and H. D. ask whether film can be an art form, and thereby assume that art is something specific – psychological nuance and revelation on the part of Woolf and classical beauty in the case of H. D. Lewis incorporates the detailed particulars of the cinema as mass cultural medium, and, through satire, seeks to control these particulars. Loy sees movie imagery as part of her collage of found modern character types. The artistry of Rhys's writing is located in her own surrealistic image-making – her creation, for instance, of a fantastical picture of a cinematic surveillance machine which reveals much about modern forms of estrangement.

POPULAR FICTION AND JOURNALISM

Leopold Bloom, in Joyce's *Ulysses*, after going to the toilet in 'Calypso', wipes his backside with a popular magazine called *Tit-Bits*, which includes a story by a writer called Mr Philip Beaufoy. This casually disdainful gesture seemingly signals the disposable and transitory nature of popular fiction, but the action is complicated when the author of the story reappears to Bloom in 'Circe'. Here, written in the hallucinatory style of the episode, Mr Philip Beaufoy rises up to accuse Bloom: 'No born gentleman would stoop to such particularly loathsome conduct'.[46] It turns out that Beaufoy is annoyed with Bloom for plagiarising, rather than soiling, his words. Bloom, an avid reader of popular fiction and pornography, is in no position to dismiss the sentimentalism of Beaufoy's prose. Popular fiction features centrally in the self-definitions of modernist writers, but the nature of these statements are as ambivalent as Joyce's depiction of Bloom's responses.

The publishing industry evolved rapidly during the late nineteenth and early twentieth centuries. The creation of universal education for five to twelve year olds in the Education Act of 1870, and the concomitant rise in literacy, had created new kinds of mass readerships. Publishers worked both to target books and magazines to these new readerships and to make them affordable. New magazines, aimed at the teenage market, sprang up in the 1890s, and new ventures, such as the Little Leather Library', started in America in 1916, made classic novels available to a world audience.

The category of popular fiction as it is figured in modernist writing incorporates a wide range of different kinds of writing. Arnold Bennett, the hugely successful middlebrow writer of realistic fiction, is central, not only to one of the most famous essays on modernist style, Woolf's 'Modern Fiction', but also pops up, barely disguised, in a number of modernist poems and novels. He makes an appearance as Mr Nixon in Pound's *Hugh Selwyn Mauberley*, and as the character Shodbutt in Wyndham Lewis's novel *The Roaring Queen*. In both cases he is used to exemplify the practices of writing solely for money and the corrupt system of patronage in the British literary world. Lewis writes: 'Could not he, Shodbutt, with a single blast, transform *any* Butterboy whatever for that matter into a more famous "genius" than they could ever concoct, with *all* their international puffs?'[47] Alongside the references to Bennett, modernist writers take regular swipes at sentimental or pornographic fiction, either directly or through parody. These gestures involved the construction of a generic category of sentimental poetry and fiction, such as the style which mediates Gerty's voice in *Ulysseys* discussed in the previous chapter.

Journalism and newspapers were also routinely attacked by modernist writers on the grounds of their censorious attitudes to experimental writing. In his poem 'Salutation the Third', Pound derides the 'smugness of *The Times*' and imagines worms 'wriggling in their vitals' because of their objections to 'newness' and 'free speech'.[48] As we have seen, episode seven of *Ulysses* is set in a newspaper office and newspapers are figured as both focal points for the flow and dissemination of metropolitan knowledge, and as vehicles for 'windy', vacuous language. The newspaper is 'tossed' aside by the group, which includes Ned Lambert, Professor MacHugh and Simon Dedalus. But the commercial significance of this mocked 'high falutin' rubbish is identified: 'All very fine to jeer at it now in cold print but it goes down like hot cakes that stuff'.[49] Woolf describes one journalist as 'self conscious, conscious only of nothing', who rises up to sip the blood of a poet.[50] Eliot, meanwhile, in 'Tradition and the Individual Talent' (1919), warns readers against listening to the 'confused cries of the newspaper critics and the susurrus of popular repetition that follows'.[51]

Alongside these attacks on the journalistic powers of censorship, control and parasitism, modernist writers also created more metaphorical images of the journalistic as a kind of writing style, or position in language. It is here, in many ways, that journalism becomes important, not only to the linguistic substance of poems and novels, but also to some key definitions of the artistic dimensions of modernism.

One of the most concerted efforts to define poetry against journalism was produced by American-born Laura Riding, who was a prolific poet and essayist in the mid to late 1920s and the 1930s, before she renounced writing in 1941. Riding was born in New York of Jewish and socialist parents. Her first poems were published in a journal called *The Fugitive* (1922–5), which was the official organ of a group of poets called the Fugitives. The group included John Crowe Ransom, Allen Tate, Merril Moore, Donald Davison and Robert Penn Warren, and was influential in developing and popularising the textual analysis techniques of new criticism which came to dominate the study of English literature in the early twentieth century. Riding travelled to London in 1926, where she met the English poet and novelist Robert Graves. She lived with him in London and Deya, Majorca, until 1939, and published numerous books of criticism, poetry and fiction. She returned to America in 1939 where she met and married Schuyler B. Jackson. After the publication of her *Collected Poems* in 1938 and two critical books in 1939, she renounced poetry. Instead, from 1948 she devoted her life to creating, with her new husband, a book called *Rational Meaning: A New Foundation for the Definition of Words*, which was published posthumously in 1997.

Riding's work was a remarkably committed attempt to marry a poetry of semantic precision with ethics, an ethics defined partly against journalistic language. Her co-authored *Survey of Modernist Poetry* (1927), which I discussed in the Introduction, was a significant intervention and defence of the difficulty of modernist poetry. In 1970 she published *Selected Poems: In Five Sets* with a preface in which she explained that she had given up poetry because it distorts, rather than captures, linguistic meaning. In the opening to *Rational Meaning*, Riding, along with her co-author Schuyler Jackson, argued that language is 'the human mind's organ of rationality' and that its ordering of thought expresses what 'we call truth'.[52] The book has a moral aim: 'that there is need of a total refreshment of the knowledge of language . . . for the reinvigoration of the intellectual processes of modern consciousness'.[53]

The attention to fresh language to map modern consciousness was also a feature of her poetry. In *A Survey of Modernist Poetry* Riding and Graves criticise earlier modernist poets such as Pound, H. D. and Eliot for being subservient to the 'external factors of history and economics'. Poetry, rather than wedding itself to the journalistic values of history, should embrace its ethical foundations: the task is to 'separate false modernism, or faith in history, from genuine modernism, or faith in the immediate, the *new* doings of poems (or poets or poetry) as not necessarily derived from history'.[54]

Journalism is a useful shorthand for this enslavement to historical significance. Her poems contain a number of images of debased journalistic language. Newspapers are described as the 'corrupt oxygen of time' in a poem whose title signals its own focus on a historical moment: 'In Nineteen Twenty-Seven'.[55] The idea that journalism is both physically and morally asphyxiating recurs in other poems, essays and novels. In a novel which Riding wrote under the pseudonym Barbara Rich, called *No Decency Left* (1932), she depicts a journalist called Scandals. Barbara, the main protagonist of the novel, says to Scandals: 'You admit that you write very utter bilge', and Scandals replies:

I do. We journalists are the most abject prostitutes of the pen.
That's stolen from Dostoevsky.
Probably. I steal everything.[56]

The synthesis of sensuality, corrupt morals and linguistic theft represented by journalists and journalistic language is situated in opposition to a poetic language whose ethical knowledge is distinct from these properties. In her 'Introduction' to her 1938 *Collected Poems* she argues that poetry 'presents *itself* as the definition' of the special concerns of poetry, an attempt to make poetry itself the foundation for its ethical meaning.[57]

This attempt to ground poetry in linguistic meaning structures Riding's poetry generally, and energises her poems. In one of her best poems, 'Come, Words, Away', she separates words from the sensual properties of voice:

> Come, words, away from mouths,
> Away from tongues in mouths
> And reckless hearts in tongues
> And mouths in cautious heads
> Come, words, away to where
> The meaning is not thickened
> With the voice's fretting substance[58]

Words made dense by the physical and emotional taint of voices are counterposed to the mute dimensions of words. In some senses, Riding wants to cancel out the aesthetic, playful and individualistic dimensions of voice. She is hostile to the ability of beautiful singing voices to transport and distract listeners from the meaning of words, to the way that voices carry the imprint of their speakers, or to forms of eloquence which privilege linguistic playfulness and rhetoric over sincere meaning. There is also the desire to silence the ubiquitous chatter of modern communication systems. She writes of the overused aspects of language: 'Memory of man-flesh over-fondled / With words like over-gentle hands'.[59]

Her silent words, however, do not reside in writing, as opposed to speech. Instead, the poem, addressing words, seeks to 'fly you home from where / Like stealthy angels you made off once / On errands of uncertain mercy'. This linguistic home is variously imagined. It is a primal human and linguistic encounter in which recognition and communication are central; that of the 'marvelling on man by man'. It is also words divorced from human sound: 'the silent half of language' and the 'utter telling / In truth's first soundlessness'.[60] The poem founds a myth of linguistic birth and fall, one in which angelic signs winged their away from their origins. Poetry, the poem implies, is the only thing that can hold words to account: 'I am the conscience of you'.[61]

There is an extraordinary modernist linguistic utopianism in

Riding's writing, which tries to found a myth, and write the ethical truth of language. But this utopianism is coupled with a damning critique of the debased ethical substance of contemporary culture, what she describes as the 'mouldered mouths writhe to outspeak us' at the conclusion to 'Come, Words, Away'.

Riding attempts to create and ground an ethical poetic language outside the sensual properties of words, and the ubiquitous voices and noises of modern communication systems. The attempt to remove the body from words represents a fascinating counterpart to the embodiment of vocal rhythms and slang in modernist writing from *The Waste Land* to *Ulysses*. From Riding's perspective, techniques such as Joyce's or Richardson's interior monologues, or Eliot's fragments of contemporary history, are dangerously immersed in the present. Ethical language, in this argument, sits outside the mutable fashions of the zeitgeist.

Riding renounced poetry in 1938 because she claimed that it was unable to perform the ethical task she had hoped for it. There is a symbolic neatness to the gesture. It incorporates a range of ways in which Riding's utopian claims for modernist poetry might be seen to fail. She attempts to connect poetry to ethics, and to banish history, technology and the body from poetic language. The terms of this withdrawal from history reveal much about the relationship between modernism and mass culture. While Riding seeks to find a poetic register outside the modern moment, Mina Loy expresses a radically different view. For her, modern poetry is all about embracing that moment. In her essay 'Modern Poetry', for instance, she claims that modern poetry has come from America because of its enviable location as a place of a 'thousand languages'. It has thereby created an 'English enriched and variegated with the grammatical structure and voice-inflection of many races, in novel alloy with the fundamental time-is-money idiom of the United States, discovered by the newspaper cartoonists'.[62] Loy identifies poetry as modern in so far as it is able to recreate and exploit the internationalism of this vocal 'novel alloy'. The other writers discussed in this chapter locate the modernism of their writing in a balancing act between new technologies and form. Some, such as H. D. and Eliot, see modern media as requiring neoclassical or literary forms to make them meaningful. Others, such as Lewis and

Rhys, by exposing the social and psychic power of new media, seek a place for art outside it.

SUMMARY OF KEY POINTS

- Modernism is often defined in opposition to mass culture. At the same time, however, modernist texts exploit mass culture as metaphors of modernity.
- Through a close look at one aspect of mass culture, the cinema, different approaches are evident. While some writers considered the artistic potential of the new medium, others saw it as a potent form of commodified culture.
- The poetry of Laura Riding is an attempt to find an ethical position independent from mass cultural forms.

NOTES

1. Theodor Adorno, 'On the Fetish Character of Music and the Regression of Listening', in Theodor Adorno, *The Culture Industry* (London: Routledge, 1991), p. 31.
2. Antonin Artaud, *The Theatre and Its Double*, trans. Victor Corti (1938; London: Calder, [1938] 1993).
3. Quoted in Jerome Rothenberg and Pierre Joris (eds), *Poems for the Millennium*, vol. 1 (Berkeley: University of California Press, 1995), p. 254.
4. Mina Loy, 'Modern Poetry' and 'The Widow's Jazz', in Mina Loy, *The Lost Lunar Baedeker*, ed. Roger Conover (Manchester: Carcanet, 1996), p. 157, p. 95.
5. James Joyce, *Finnegans Wake* (London: Faber and Faber, [1939] 1988), p. 108, p. 62.
6. Wyndham Lewis, *Tarr: The 1918 Version* (Santa Rosa: Black Sparrow Press, [1918] 1996), p. 26, p. 27.
7. Wyndham Lewis, *Blast 1* (London: Thames and Hudson, 2008), p. 7.
8. Wyndham Lewis, *The Apes of God* (Harmondsworth: Penguin Books, [1930] 1965), p. 649, p. 650.

9. Marcel Proust, *In Search of Lost Time*, vol. 1, trans. C. K. Scott Moncrief and Terence Kilmartin (London: Vintage, 1992), pp. 390–3.
10. Lewis, *The Apes of God*, p. 505.
11. Ezra Pound, *The Cantos* (London: Faber and Faber, 1986), p. 26.
12. Pound, *The Cantos*, p. 27.
13. Ezra Pound, 'Hugh Selwyn Mauberley', in Ezra Pound, *Selected Poems: 1908–1969* (London: Faber and Faber, 1977), p. 103.
14. Virginia Woolf, 'The Cinema', (1926), in Virginia Woolf, *Collected Essays*, vol. 2 (London: Hogarth Press, 1966), p. 268.
15. Lewis, *Tarr*, p. 21.
16. See Wyndham Lewis, *Tarr* (Harmondsworth: Penguin Books, 1982). This is the 1928 edition of the book.
17. Andrzej Gasiorek, *Wyndham Lewis and Modernism*, Writers and their Work, ed. Isobel Armstrong (Devon: Northcote House, 2004), p. 9.
18. Lewis, *The Apes of God*, p. 23.
19. Lewis, *The Apes of God*, p. 490.
20. Wyndham Lewis, *The Revenge for Love* (Harmondsworth: Penguin Books, [1937] 1982), p. 90.
21. Christopher Isherwood, *Goodbye to Berlin* (St Albans: Panther Books, [1939] 1977), p. 52.
22. Mina Loy, 'Perlun', in Loy, *The Lost Lunar Baedeker*, p. 75.
23. Lewis Grassic Gibbon, 'A Novelist Looks at the Cinema', in Lewis Grassic Gibbon, *Smeddum: A Lewis Grassic Gibbon Anthology*, ed. Valentina Bold (Edinburgh: Canongate, 2001), p. 742.
24. Virginia Woolf, 'The Cinema', in Woolf, *Collected Essays*, p. 269.
25. Virginia Woolf, 'The Cinema', in Woolf, *Collected Essays*, pp. 270–1.
26. Virginia Woolf, 'The Cinema', in Woolf, *Collected Essays*, p, 271, p. 272.
27. Joyce, *Finnegans Wake*, p. 53.
28. Laura Marcus, *The Tenth Muse: Writing about Cinema in the*

Modernist Period (Oxford: Oxford University Press, 2007), p. 151.

29. Virginia Woolf, 'The Cinema', in Woolf, *Collected Essays*, p. 269.
30. Marcus, *The Tenth Muse*, p. 146, p. 148.
31. Virginia Woolf, *To the Lighthouse* (Oxford: Oxford University Press, [1927] 2000), p. 176.
32. Woolf, *To the Lighthouse*, p. 281.
33. H. D., 'The Cinema and The Classics', in James Donald, Anne Friedberg and Laura Marcus (eds), *Close Up, 1927–1933: Cinema and Modernism* (London: Cassell, 1998), p. 105.
34. H. D., 'The Cinema and The Classics', in Donald et al., *Close Up*, p. 108, pp. 107–8.
35. H. D., 'Projector', in *H. D.: Collected Poems, 1912–1944* (Manchester: Carcanet, 1983), p. 352.
36. H. D., 'Projector', in *H. D.: Collected Poems*, p. 358.
37. H. D., 'Projector', in *H. D.: Collected Poems*, pp. 353–4.
38. H. D., *Bid Me To Live* (London: Virago, [1960] 1983), pp. 122–3.
39. H. D., *Bid Me To Live*, p. 123.
40. H. D., *Bid Me To Live*, p. 123.
41. H. D., *Bid Me To Live*, p. 124, p. 125, p. 126.
42. Jean Rhys, *Good Morning, Midnight* (Harmondsworth: Penguin Books, [1939] 2000), p. 40.
43. Rhys, *Good Morning, Midnight*, p. 36.
44. Rhys, *Good Morning, Midnight*, p. 147.
45. Rhys, *Good Morning, Midnight*, p. 156, p. 157.
46. James Joyce, *Ulysses: The Corrected Text*, ed. Hans Walter Gabler with Wolfhard Steppe and Claus Melchior (London: Bodley Head, 1986), p. 347.
47. Wyndham Lewis, *The Roaring Queen*, ed. and intro. Walter Allen (London: Secker and Warburg, 1973), p. 82.
48. Ezra Pound, 'Salutation the Third', in Wyndham Lewis, *Blast 1* (Santa Barbara: Black Sparrow Press, 2009), p. 45.
49. Joyce, *Ulysses*, p. 104.
50. Virginia Woolf, 'Fantasy upon a gentleman who converted his impressions of a private house into cash', reproduced in

Appendix B of Quentin Bell, *Virginia Woolf: A Biography*, vol. 2 (London: Hogarth Press, 1972), pp. 253–4.

51. T. S. Eliot, 'Tradition and the Individual Talent', in T. S. Eliot, *Selected Essays*, 3rd edn (London: Faber and Faber, [1951] 1986), p. 17.

52. Laura (Riding) Jackson, with Schuyler B. Jackson, *Rational Meaning: A New Foundation for the Definition of Words and Supplementary Essays* (Charlottesville: University of Virginia Press, 1997), p. 39.

53. Riding, *Rational Meaning*, p. 41.

54. Laura Riding and Robert Graves, *A Survey of Modernist Poetry* (New York: Haskell House Publishers, 1928), p. 158.

55. Laura (Riding) Jackson, *The Poems of Laura Riding: A New Edition of the 1938 Collection* (Manchester: Carcanet, 1991), p. 122.

56. Riding published the novel under a pseudonym: see Barbara Rich, *No Decency Left* (London: Jonathan Cape, 1932), p. 115.

57. Riding, *Collected Poems*, p. 1.

58. Riding, *Collected Poems*, p. 134.

59. Riding, *Collected Poems*, p. 136.

60. Riding, *Collected Poems*, p. 134, p. 136.

61. Riding, *Collected Poems*, p. 136.

62. Mina Loy, 'Modern Poetry', in Loy, *The Lost Lunar Baedeker*, p. 158.

CHAPTER 5

Modernism and Politics

During and immediately after the First World War, the polarised political landscape which would dominate Europe and Russia for the next two decades began to take shape. The communist Russian revolution of October 1917 destroyed the autocratic power of the Tsar and led to the creation of Lenin's Bolshevik-run Soviet Union. Revolutionary socialist activity threatened to spread across eastern Europe. The political systems of Germany and Hungary were briefly replaced with Soviet-style republics during 1918–19. Alongside the revolutionary emergence of Marxist communism, another new political ideology and system rose up in the 1920s. Benito Mussolini marched on Rome in 1922 and ousted the Liberal prime minister. His National Fascist Party was created out of disaffection with the socialist movement with which he had earlier identified. Rather than a proletariat revolution, he advocated a revolutionary nationalism led by a revolutionary élite. Between 1925 and 1927 he dismantled the democratic system he had inherited, removing constitutional restraints on his power and creating a totalitarian police state. He outlawed all other political parties and abolished parliamentary elections in 1928. Mussolini carefully manipulated the new mass media of the press, radio and cinema to create an image of fascism as the new political doctrine of the twentieth century, one that could productively replace liberal democracy. Hitler's rise to power in Germany in 1933, and creation of a single-party dictatorship involving an ideology of pan-Germanism, anti-Semitism, and anti-communism shadowed cultural activity in the 1930s until the outbreak of war in 1939. The ideological conflict between socialists and fascists became a military battle in Spain in 1936 when a group of right-wing generals organised a coup which challenged the power of the democratically elected Spanish Republic. Under the leadership of General Franco, and with the financial support of Nazi Germany and Mussolini's Kingdom of Italy, the fascist rebels won the war in 1939.

The political polarisation of Europe in the 1910s, 1920s and 1930s split the arts. Some Anglo-American writers were either active members of the International Communist Party, or broadly sympathetic to Marxist ideas, such as W. H. Auden, Stephen Spender, Christopher Isherwood, Nancy Cunard and Hugh MacDiarmid. Others, such as E. M. Forster, Virginia Woolf, James Joyce, Mina Loy, H. D. and George Orwell, can be broadly defined as democratic socialist or liberal in political persuasion. A number of these writers produced significant essays defending democratic and liberal ideals in the 1930s when such beliefs were seen to be radically threatened. Ezra Pound flirted with Marxist ideas in the 1920s before becoming an active supporter of the Italian fascists and broadcasting on their behalf in the late 1930s and early 1940s. As a result in 1945 he was imprisoned by the US authorities for treason. Wyndham Lewis was a political maverick. He wrote a broadly sympathetic book called *Hitler*, published in 1931 before Hitler took control of Germany, which argued that Hitler was a man of peace threatened by communist agitators. He later retracted these views in *The Hitler Cult* (1939). But in his scathing attacks on the British left and persistent anti-Semitism, he was politically isolated and despised by anti-fascists in the 1930s. W. B. Yeats, D. H. Lawrence and Laura Riding flirted with fascist ideas in the 1920s and 1930s, but were too individualistic to sign up to political parties. Ford Madox Ford and T. S. Eliot are best described as political conservatives.

The politics of modernism, particularly the identification by a number of prominent writers with fascist ideas, has been one of its most controversial and complicated features. This is not simply because fascism is a heinous and discredited politics and ideology. It is also the case that there seems to be a central contradiction in the relationship between the creation of radical writing and the identi-fication with authoritarian politics. When Eliot's *The Waste Land* was first published, a number of readers equated its experimental form with socialism and revolution. Yet Eliot was a conservative political thinker, and tended to want to order and control, rather than unleash, revolutionary energies. How was it that Eliot, and other writers such as Pound, Yeats, Lewis and Lawrence, could marry authoritarian or conservative politics and radical aesthetics?

In the twentieth and twenty-first century reception of mod-ernist writing, critics and readers have struggled to understand the anti-liberal politics of modernist writers. Lionel Trilling, an influential liberal literary and cultural historian of the 1940s and 1950s, argued that the best European novels and poems of the early twentieth century

> [have] been written by men who are indifferent to, or even hostile to, the tradition of democratic liberalism as we know it. Yeats and Eliot, Proust and Joyce, Lawrence and Gide – these men do not seem to confirm us in the social and political ideals which we hold.[1]

Trilling both identifies a genealogy of modernist writers, and suggests that there is a fundamental political gulf between their modernism and a post-Second World War political liberal consen-sus. This sense of estrangement has continued to trouble readers. How is it possible that so many modernist writers can have either embraced authoritarian political ideas or actually identified with fascism? Should a literary sensibility be tied to humane values? Is it possible or right to ignore these facts and read the texts of Pound, Lewis and Yeats as divorced from the history of their production?

One answer to these questions lies in an understanding of the reasons for the hostility to the liberal consensus described by Trilling. In the early twentieth century, British liberalism was in crisis. While the meaning of the terms liberalism and democracy are historically specific and complicated, they can generally be defined as involving an extensive suffrage, free and fair elections, a constitution which limits the authority of government, and an independent judiciary. Nineteenth-century British liberalism had been replaced by a more mass democratic state after the war, which included a degree of gender and class equality, the emergence of the modern day Labour Party as a significant feature of domestic politics, and important shifts in British power over its colonies. At the historical moment when key features of the mass democratic state were put in place, however, commentators and writers betrayed deep anxieties about the future of liberal capitalist democracy. Looking back in 1939, W. H. Auden put it like this: 'The most obvious social fact of the last forty years is the failure of liberal capitalist democracy'. Auden argued that liberal ideals such as freedom of speech, equality, the right to vote and to a fair trial have been enshrined in law. But these legal rights are meaningless, he claims, in the context of the stark economic inequalities that structure British society. As a result, liberal capitalist society is 'the most impersonal, the most mechanical and the most unequal civilisation the world has ever seen', a 'civilisation torn apart by the opposing emotions born of economic injustice'.[2] The sense of political failure articulated by Auden, and the identification of economic inequality as the cause of this failure, was a significant feature in the political proposals and identifications of modernist writers. The critique of the impersonal and unequal liberal society described by Auden came from both left and right, from men and women, in the 1920s and 1930s.

Despite the nature of the political views espoused by some modernist writers, a number of important critics have argued that the modernist engagement with politics is one of its abiding strengths. Not because their fascism is excusable; but because the attempt to marry politics and art embodies the historical conflicts of Western liberal societies. Anglo-American critics such as Raymond Williams, in his essays on modernism and politics (1989), Fredric Jameson, in his book on Wyndham Lewis (1979), and Michael North, in his work on Yeats, Eliot and Pound (1991), have argued that modernism is, by definition, political.[3] North insists that, in their failed attempts to resolve political and economic contradictions in their poetry, Yeats, Eliot and Pound were faithful 'to the real conflicts of our century', that politics is a 'disruptive force in the formal organization of their works'.[4] This is helpful because it allows us to step back and ask different questions of the politics of these texts. North reads the politics of modernist poems with regard to the way they stage historical contradictions and issues. Another significant question is why writers were so actively politicised in this period. Why did Pound, for example, think that poetry could somehow resolve the economic contradictions of the age? How was it that Laura Riding could sincerely propose that in the light of the manifest failures of male political systems in Europe, women writers should seize control? Perhaps the most remarkable thing about modernist writers is what seems, from a contemporary perspective, their extraordinary cultural and political hubris.

This brings us to the second key reason for the seemingly odd synthesis of authoritarian politics and radical aesthetics in modernist texts. Many modernist writers believed that literature was as important as philosophy or scientific research in the development and enlightenment of Western civilisation. It is important to understand the cultural and social importance these writers placed on literature and art, and the extent to which they believed that literature was undervalued and even persecuted by the American and British liberal democratic societies. This combination of self-importance and cultural embattlement produced some remarkably arrogant claims for the significance of poems and novels. But this cultural positioning was also crucial for the experimental sincerity and tenacity with which writers pursued their projects. Despite the bemusement of readers and the interventions of the censor, writers including Joyce, Lawrence and Pound extended rather than retreated from literary experimentation and sexual explicitness in the 1920s and 1930s. The story of modernism is entailed in the individuality and boldness of their writing projects, and their personal stubbornness in pursuing them.

REVOLUTION AND ECONOMICS

The word 'avant-garde' was originally a military term, and European avant-garde groups proudly declared their anarchistic or Marxist revolutionary credentials as though they were going into battle. In various ways, the Futurists, Dadaists and Surrealists exploited a Marxist vocabulary in their use images of revolution, crowd power and lawlessness. Marx argued that the working classes, who through their labour produced the real material wealth of societies, would inevitably realise their power through a proletarian or communist revolution. Marx asked, however, why it was that the working classes had so far failed to overturn existing class relations. He developed theories both of ideology and the commodity form in order to account for these existing class relations. On the one hand ideas, such as religious beliefs, educational practices or art and culture, falsify the nature of material and economic reality, and work to maintain unequal class relations. On the other hand, in his theory of the commodity, Marx claimed that false consciousness resides in the individual's relationship to objects. He argued that the commodity is an object presented for exchange in the capitalist market place. Its value depends on masking both its use-value and the structure of social and economic relationships which produce it. It also relies on the capitalist system, which encourages individuals to fetishise (or identify with and overvalue) its illusionary exchange value. The commodity structure, and the individual's relationship to it, creates the false-consciousness which maintains the status quo.

Avant-garde groups attempted to jolt their readers out of their ideological assumptions about art and religion, and to dislocate their fetishised relationships to commodities. Marinetti's Futurists were energised by the anarchistic desire to capture the excitement and energy of uncontrollable urban crowds, institutional destruction and a Futuristic politics which radically questioned the status quo. The Dadaists embraced forms of psychic and bodily freedom outside existing political vocabularies, and attempted to challenge the power of commodified structures by unleashing the artistic dimensions of objects. The Surrealists more explicitly tied their revolutionary artistic energy to a Marxist ideology. Walter Benjamin argued that the Surrealists 'are the first to liquidate the sclerotic liberal-moral-humanistic ideal of freedom', because they are convinced that freedom must be enjoyed in its fullness without 'pragmatic calculation'.[5] The Surrealist writing of the unconscious aimed to unlock those aspects of the self outside economic rationality, the capitalist state, the commodity-form and the law.

In its early stages, Anglo-American modernism, with its origins in avant-garde activity, also embraced the language of revolution and class overthrow. Lewis exhorts a revolutionary and classless art movement in *Blast*, claiming that 'great artists in England are always revolutionary' and that *Blast* will 'not appeal to any particular class, but to the fundamental and popular instincts in every class and description of people'.[6] He even hopes to convert the monarch to Vorticism: 'A VORTICIST KING! WHY NOT?'[7] As well as claiming that art is inherently revolutionary, Lewis also partially quotes from Marx by suggesting that England is the rightful home of revolutionary activity, claiming that 'revolt' is its 'normal state'.[8] *Blast*'s appeal, Lewis declares, is to 'THE INDIVIDUAL', who, as soon as he or she 'realizes himself as an artist', ceases to belong to a particular class or historical period. Not only is the artist removed from class hierarchies, the art disseminated in *Blast* is also positioned outside economic categories: 'Popular art does not mean the art of the poor people, as it is usually supposed to. It means the art of the individuals.'[9] Lewis, by proposing that the relationship between art and the reader or spectator can be unmediated by class, economics or history, suggests the radical political dimensions of art.

Alongside the connection between avant-garde writing and revolution, other modernists connected art to politics. Mina Loy, in her 'Feminist Manifesto' (1914), employs the language of class and revolution to criticise liberal definitions of women's freedom. She urged women to overthrow their subordinate position: 'NO scratching on the surface of the rubbish heap of tradition, will bring about <u>Reform</u>, the only method is <u>Absolute Demolition</u>'.[10] She insisted that women's gender dependency was class based: 'Men & women are enemies, with the enmity of the exploited for the parasite, the parasite for the exploited'.[11] Unlike Lewis's individualistic art revolutionaries, women are forced to think collectively in seeking to overthrow their subordinate position.

While some early avant-garde writers embraced the language of revolution and class overthrow, later modernist texts often figure revolutionary activity as one part of a power dynamic. T. S. Eliot in *The Waste Land* both depicts revolutionary groups, and positions them as threatening: he describes anonymous and mindless 'hooded hordes swarming' over Eastern mountains in 'What the

Thunder Said'. As a domestic corollary to these wandering groups, Eliot also focuses on the sinister features of mindless urban crowds in *The Waste Land*. There are the crowds 'walking round in a ring' and the crowds who flow 'over London Bridge', in 'The Burial of the Dead', and both images raise questions about the status of religious authority and order.

The idea that there were similarities between the behavioural features of urban and revolutionary crowds was a significant feature of political debate in the period. Crowds were seen as lacking cohesion and as being potentially susceptible to new kinds of political or ethical authority. For this reason, they were seen as a potent image of the political and social anxieties of the period. Fascist, Marxist and democratic leaders considered carefully how best to exert political power in face of the crowd or the masses. In Chapter 2 I briefly discussed the sociological and psychological theories of Gustave Le Bon, who described the irrational and unconscious nature of crowd behaviour in his influential book *The Crowd: A Study of the Popular Mind* (1896). Wilfred Trotter, in essays on the 'herd instinct' and his book *Instincts of Herd in Peace and War* (1916), popularised Le Bon's ideas for an English audience. The crowd theories of Le Bon and Trotter documented the physical and psychic activities of groups. They also, however, produced theories of modernity and politics. Le Bon argued that the crowd is a modern political phenomenon which forms part of the loosening of old group ties such as religious worship. He argued that in the place of religion, the crowd requires the power of a strong leader or image to make it cohere. Freud responded critically to Le Bon's theories in *Group Psychology and the Analysis of the Ego* (1921), and opposed the idea that a strong leader can exercise a 'hypnotic' effect on 'an individual in the group'.[12] Instead, Freud claimed that 'in a group the individual is brought under conditions which allow him to throw off the repressions of his unconscious instinctual impulses'. The idea that the group weakens the power of repression is very different to Le Bon's claim that individuals 'become obliterated in a group'.[13]

Despite these differences of opinion, the idea that urban crowds acted unconsciously and irrationally and that they wielded an unpredictable political agency entered the modernist artistic imagination. In the 1920s and 1930s, Mussolini features in modernist texts, often as a political impresario adept at manipulating crowds by way of the mass media. Lewis Grassic Gibbon, in an essay on cinema, jokes about the ubiquitous cinematic image of Mussolini: 'a speech by Signor Mussolini, simian and swarthy (why has Hollywood never offered him adequate inducements to understudy King Kong)'.[14] Wyndham Lewis also ridicules Mussolini by connecting him to a popular culture stereotype. In *The Apes of God* Dan talks to a blackshirt: 'this ironfisted altruist – dressed, [Dan] timidly and tentatively reflected, as Signor Mussolini, the Italian potentate in the political Dime Novel of Modern Rome – that boy-scout Caesar'.[15] Lewis, typically, satirises through the creation of mixed cultural and political references. The power of ancient Italian heritage is undermined by the modernity and childishness of the Boy Scout movement. Mussolini's political attempt to modernise Rome, meanwhile, is ridiculed by being seen as conforming to the pre-established narrative conventions and teleology of a dime novel. But both Gibbon and Lewis highlight a political connection between Hollywood and fascism, seeing Mussolini's manipulation of the spectacle of power as similar to popular cultural representations of raw physical strength.

Lewis's depiction of Mussolini as a 'boy-scout Caesar' forms part of his wider meditation on revolutionary politics in *The Apes of God*. The novel concludes with a depiction of the British general strike. The strike was seen as the historical moment of possible communist revolution in Britain. It was called by the Trades Union Congress (TUC) in an attempt to persuade the government to prevent wage reduction for coal miners and lasted for nine days in May 1926. The scale of the strike surprised everyone, with between 1.5 and 1.75 million people stopping work. A number of writers engaged with the strike, either positively, as in the case of Hugh MacDiarmid in his poem 'A Drunk Man Looks at a Thistle', or negatively, as in Evelyn Waugh's *Brideshead Revisited* (1945).

The Apes of God explicitly pins its narrative to this revolutionary historical moment. The final chapter of the novel is called 'The Strike' and the novel more generally traces the different political forces working to fragment and change English society in the 1920s. It describes social and class breakdown, characters who express democratic, fascist, communist and aristocratic ideological perspectives, and stages questions about leadership and power with regard to revolutionary crowds. The opening chapter of the novel focuses on Lady Fredigonde, who uses her class privilege autocratically to boss and bully her staff. Hers is a deathly, disintegrating body, whose breathless state symbolises a dying class. As she hobbles around her decaying mansion, she is traumatised by the mechanical and modern sounds outside her window. The impact of the 'current of machines' portends class breakdown: 'the window before her shook with the weight of the super-traffic'.[16] As well as the impending dangers of modernisation, she is also threatened by her own unconscious anxieties and fantasies. The novel manipulates interior monologue to capture an anxious fantasy of communist revolution. Dreaming that she is in a museum devoted to the memory of herself, she imagines Bolshevik children:

> [At] a word from the spectacled Red Scout-Master . . . *little jumping Bolsheviks smash the glasses of the show-cases. A thunder of small fists breaks out, like a crash of kettle-drums.* Death-the-drummer! *With idiot-yawp, civilized and whitmanic, they distribute the expensive headwear swiftly, passing from hand to hand.*[17]

Lewis's depiction of Lady Fredigonde's unconscious child Bolsheviks, described as 'robot-youth, in double file', suggests the imaginative power of revolutionary threat among the British aristocracy in the 1920s. Here the scoutmaster is a 'Red', but there are structural connections between the later Mussolini-like 'boy-scout Caesar' and this socialist leader. In both cases, revolutionary activity is depicted as necessary, mindless and infantilised and the power of the scout leader is exaggerated, a dynamic which conforms to Le Bon's theory of the power of charismatic leaders.

These fantasised young revolutionaries at the beginning of the book will come to life to some extent in its closing pages, although Lewis refrains from creating an actual picture of the striking workers. Instead his description of the strike begins with Dan, his central protagonist, wandering, uncomprehending, through eerily empty London streets. Throughout the novel Dan has been represented as an unknowing embodiment of the new mass democracy. In contrast to Lady Fredigonde's frail, lifeless body, Dan is a youthful simpleton whose body has an unconscious physical strength. He is referred to as drunken, brutish and uncontrollable. The novel also meditates on who might control and contain this physical strength. The élitist, fascistic and sinister Zagreus tells him:

> You are not asked to regard yourself as a pigmy: on the other hand it is expected of you to contrive to give the impression of *being no-bigger-than-anybody-else*. Woe to you if you don't! If you do not acquire this simple democratic habit of make-believe, there is no place for you in contemporary life.[18]

Democracy is described by Zagreus as a false ideology, in which the individual must ensure that he or she looks the same as everybody else, despite obvious differences in size. The strike, by implication, has shattered this make-believe democracy and allowed the working classes to unleash their power. Despite the revolutionary potential of this moment, Lewis chooses to represent it negatively, as absence. The most arresting description of the strike comes through third person narration:

> It was a grand and breathless calm in the rich neighbourhoods and at last peace had fallen (for the first time since the death of the Nineteenth-Century Middleclass Elizabeth, Victoria) upon all that private-thoroughfare where the mansion of the proud Folletts reared its victorian battlements to the May-sky – all was dead and pleasant. But it was a death of life – the throbbing circulation of incessant machines, in thunderous rotation, in the arteries of London was stopped.[19]

The calm of privileged London invites a historical flashback to a time before cars started to dominate the landscape of the city. This pre-modern Victorian era of middle-class capitalism – the Follet's mansion is a product of Victorian wealth – is momentarily dead. The 'breathless' nature of this calm has altered significance in the light of the 'death of life' referred to in the next sentence. Lack of breath can also imply lack of life. A London bereft of modern machines and productivity is a moribund city. If liberal democracy, as both a nineteenth-century and contemporary ideology, is on its last legs, the strike is also responsible for killing London life. The novel concludes with an image of a political vacuum within the context of revolutionary activity. While the strikers rage and swarm in some other part of London, Zagreus seals an unholy alliance with newly widowed Lady Fredigonde:

> Their lips met, and the love-light softened the old discoloured corneous surface of the fredigondian eyeball, once a lacteous blue . . . In the street outside there was a frenzied rattle. *Death the Drummer!* That was his fierce opening castanette! Immediately the mechanistic rattle penetrated to the inmost recesses of these embraces . . . The dove-light changed to the red-rose of battle . . . And in the gutter the crazy instruments at last struck up their sentimental jazzing one-time stutter – gutter-thunder.[20]

The novel begins and ends with Lady Fredigonde being tormented by the noises, a mixture of cars and jazz music, outside her window. While both sounds have been momentarily silenced during the strike, they are figured as part of an unstoppable and chaotic modernisation that neither Lady Fredigonde, nor any other character in the novel, can control.

Despite the fact that Lewis's depiction of the strike is ambivalent, the text does, as North suggests in his reading of Eliot's and Pound's poetry, reveal much about the political conflicts of the period. On the level of content, Lewis describes the competing political ideologies of the period in the context of a fading image of liberal England. Stylistically, the novel also embodies political and historical conflicts. The novel includes a variety of different stylistic devices, including interior monologue, the forensic description of bodies and ideological satire. The novel pins itself and its characters to a revolutionary historical moment. But revolutionary groups are pictured in the little Bolshevik children who smash apart Lady Fredigonde's unconscious, rather than as a concrete physical reality. The narrative, by infantilising the strikers, locates political agency in the possible political leaders – the scout leaders – who might step into the vacuum left open by the strike at the end of the novel. Revolutionary action, if it is to be represented as having any kind of power, would require a collective register which Lewis's narrative works against. The novel is both situated in history and creates a history that is personalised by being filtered through characters, all of whose politics are satirised.

Lewis's focus on the political vacuum at the heart of British society was a shared concern among writers in this period, although other writers saw this absence as ethical, rather than political. Eliot believed that the decline of religious faith had created a moral vacuum which produced individual isolation and social fragmentation. After being confirmed in the Church of England in 1927, he declared himself to be a 'classicist in literature, royalist in politics, and Anglo-catholic in religion'.[21] Eliot's identification with monarchical and religious authority was fuelled by the central claim that cultural power had dispersed into the hands of middle-class journalists and readers. In *The Use of Poetry and the Use of Criticism* (1933) Eliot complained about social power being 'in the hands of a class so democratised that whilst still a class it represents itself to be the whole nation'.[22] This critique of the power of the middle classes led Eliot to imagine other groups who might wield authority more responsibly. In *The Idea of a Christian Society* (1939) he imagined the benefits of a future Christian state run by a community of Christians.

Eliot's critique of both political democracy and the destructive power of middle-class, 'democratic', opinion was a feature of many books and essays by modernist writers. For Ezra Pound, the absence at the heart of the system was political, rather than religious. Like Eliot, Pound was vitriolic on the subject of middle-class cultural power, whose values he said were conservative, moralistic and hostile to art. He argued insistently that cultural power be handed to artists and intellectuals, whose perspicacity would help legislators to understand and control the challenges of early twentieth-century politics.

Lewis's description of democracy as an ideology which forces everyone to look and speak exactly the same was also a shared complaint among modernist writers. Lewis frequently attacked democracy as a system which worked to silence independent expression. In 1918 he argued that after the First World War 'and the "democratisation" of all countries, no man will ever say what he means, yes, seldomer even than at present'.[23] In *Time And Western Man* (1927) and *Men Without Art* (1934) he reiterated the claim that international democracy threatened to curtail individual freedom.

Liberal democracy was routinely criticised by modernist writers for being a system that promoted individualism but which created uniformity of personality. For some writers, the desire to break away from poetic repetition and monotony, as described in Chapter 1, had a distinct politics to it as well. One of the features of the modern city described by Ford in *The Soul of London* is its expression of a new democratic spirit, but this spirit is seen in a negative rather than positive light: it is a 'gigantic pantheon of the dead level of democracy'. D. H. Lawrence, in his novel *Kangaroo*, expresses something similar: 'And there went the long street, like a child's drawing, the little square bungalows dot-dot-dot, close together and yet apart, like modern democracy, each one fenced round with a square rail fence'.[24] It is striking that 'modern democracy' could be used in a simile to clarify the repetitive urban architecture of an Australian suburb. The point of the image is to create a picture of human isolation within dreary suburban uniformity. What does the bungalow represent if, despite being just the same as all the other bungalows on the street, its individuality is located in the boundaries which fence it off from other houses?

Lawrence's image is powerful because it pinpoints the way that this model of individuality is located in a singleness demarcated by boundaries. For Lawrence, these boundaries are legalistic and economic, part of a liberal-capitalist system which promotes legal equality and rights at the expense of other kinds of freedom. All of Lawrence's novels, as well as many of his short stories and essays, are concerned to dismantle these legalistic forms of understanding. Words such as equality, democracy and rights are dissected and attacked. In *The Rainbow* Ursula states '"I hate equality on a money basis"'.[25] Lawrence's mantra was that the capitalist logic which governs society has worked to debase concepts such as equality and value. '"Only the greedy and ugly people come to the top in a democracy"', announces Ursula Brangwen in *Women in Love*.[26] In the novel more generally Lawrence stages political conflicts through polarised debates between characters. Rupert Birkin, in dispute with Hermione, states: '"We are all abstractly and mathematically equal, if you like . . . But spiritually, there is pure difference and neither equality nor inequality counts. It is upon these two bits of knowledge that you must found a state. Your democracy is an absolute lie".'[27] Birkin's description of the 'pure difference' between individuals, forms part of his argument that society should allow these differences to flourish. As the novel develops, he tries to live out these principles by ditching his job, and escaping the repressive mechanisms of the British state by travelling with Ursula to the Continent.

The ideas put forward by Lawrence's characters, such as Rupert Birkin and Ursula Brangwen, formed part of a wider political debate about democracy in the 1900s and 1910s. One important intellectual resource for Lawrence's critique of democracy was the philosophy of Friedrich Nietzsche. Along with Marx's ideas, Nietzsche's philosophy had a profound impact on the political understanding of modernist writers. Nietzsche's works, such as *Thus Spoke Zarathustra* (1883–4) and *The Case of Wagner* (1888), began to be translated into English in 1896. Other English translations followed, with *On The Genealogy of Morals* (1887), *Beyond Good and Evil* (1886) and *The Birth of Tragedy* (1872) being published in English-language editions in 1899, 1907 and 1909 respectively. The London-based journals *The New Age* and *The Freewoman* (later *The New Freewoman* and *The Egoist*) were 'Nietzsche' journals in the 1900s and early 1910s.

In *Hugh Selwyn Mauberley*, Pound describes Mauberley 'amid the neo-Nietzschean clatter', suggesting the ubiquity of Nietzsche's ideas in the 1910s.[28] Lewis conjures up a similar image in his 1915 'Preface' to *Tarr*: 'In Europe Nietzsche's gospel of desperation, the beyond-law-man, etc., has deeply influenced the Paris apache, the Italian Futurist "litterateur," the Russian revolutionary.' Lewis captures Nietzsche's impact on both political activists and artists, and suggests the ideological similarities in their activities. He also, typically, indicates that Nietzsche's ideas, by being disseminated too widely, have turned back on themselves:

'Nietzsche's books', he states, 'have made "aristocrats" of people who would otherwise have been only mild snobs or meddlesome prigs', 'they have made an Over-man of every vulgarly energetic grocer in Europe'.[29]

Lewis satirises the popularisation of Nietzsche's ideas, both by referring to categories such as 'beyond-law' and the 'Over-man', and by suggesting that his philosophy has allowed small-minded élitists to claim for themselves a superiority over others. The categories of 'beyond-law' and 'over-man' are referred to in *Thus Spoke Zarathustra*, Nietzsche's most popularised and playful text: 'I teach you the Superman', Nietzsche writes, an idea which asks his readers to create 'something beyond themselves' other than God or God's attendant humane concepts such as reason, virtue, justice and pity.[30] Nietzsche famously announced that God is dead, but also argued that an unacknowledged Christian morality lived on in modern social and political systems. He insisted that late nineteenth-century liberal democracies relied on a hidden and repressive logic, in which legalistic categories such as rights, equality and individual freedom masked the inequalities and uniformities of liberal society. He also claimed that the genuine artist, or the 'sovereign individual' as he called him, is that singular person who is able to stand outside the repetitions of modernity and modern life and impose his or her will or authority on it.

Pound and Lewis jokingly refer to Nietzsche as a fashionable philosopher whose ideas are elegantly exchanged in privileged literary salons. But as well as being a popular philosopher, Nietzsche's arguments about democracy, politics and art also had a clear impact on the writing of a number of modernist writers. Birkin's description of the 'pure difference' between individuals has important similarities with Nietzsche's ideas of individualism. Lawrence's virulent critique of the repressive mechanisms and ideologies of modern democracy also bear the traces of Nietzsche's philosophy. Returning to the sentence from Lawrence's *Kangaroo*, the redundant individuality of the bungalow which demarcates its singleness by means of its property borders is energised by an idea of a genuine spiritual or intellectual individuality informed by ideas of will, independence and sensuality. Lawrence's interest in sex and sexuality forms part of his attempt to imagine a bodily form of individual freedom outside the politicised and legal definitions of the self.

Lawrence's lament about a system which rewards the 'greedy people' was central to the politics of a number of writers. Auden's 1939 description of the failure of liberal democracy also focused on the way that it promoted legal equality while creating economic inequality. Scepticism about the stability of the money system was also an important feature of post-war political debate. After the war many writers and commentators started to argue seriously that the cause of the war had been financial, and that the inflationary instabilities of the post-war period had further destabilised political and national stability. Rather than the nation state, writers argued that it was a group of financial speculators who controlled international events.

Mina Loy pinpointed the way that international economic interests controlled modern democracies in her political pamphlet of 1921, 'International Psycho-Democracy'. She criticised the fact that 'Modern social existence is a form of psychic activity based on *Ideas* promoted by the self-conscious minority of *Power*'. These ideas are disseminated by way of the '*Dummy Public* originated by the Press, financed by the Capitalist'.[31] Loy's Dadaist aesthetic infiltrates her perspective on modern democracy. She is attuned to the way in which power is asserted and produced in the international, rather than national, arena. She also highlights the means with which resistance to power might be mobilised beyond the boundaries of the nation state. In her pamphlet, for instance, she invites people to invest their 'consciousness' in her 'Idea-Market' and to 'make the world' their 'Salon'.[32] Loy's critique of the economic interests controlling the dissemination of information was central to a number of modernist texts. Ezra Pound, for instance, became convinced in the early 1920s that the money system was at the heart of the social and political problems of the period. Despite the fact that the 1920s were a decade of unprecedented wealth and growth, in which Americans, in particular, were encouraged to borrow money to invest in the stock market, the Wall Street crash of 1929, and subsequent falls during the next three years, radically devalued socks and shares and arguably produced the economic depression of the 1930s. The crash created renewed intellectual interest in the instabilities of the money system in the 1930s.

Pound's politics were partly a product of his anxieties and frustrations about the hidden and self-destructive economic forces which controlled nation states. In the period immediately following the end of the First World War, an economist called C. H. Douglas published a new theory of monetary order called *Economic Democracy*. It was to have a huge impact on Pound's writing, as it seemed to offer a revelatory new understanding of the causes of the war. According to Douglas, the overproduction of goods by nation states encourages them to discover new markets abroad. Imperialism leads to war. Criticising this economic system by which financiers hold power over nation states, Douglas argued for alternative forms of economic organisation, most notably a system of social credit.

Pound had begun *The Cantos* some years before reading Douglas's work. However, he now altered them to accord with his new understanding of politics and culture. He also wrote a new poem, *Hugh Selwyn Mauberley* (1920). From this point on, the word 'usury' came to dominate Pound's writing. Pound employed the word by extending its more established meaning as the charging of interest on loans to designate the systematic financial speculation of money lenders. For Pound, financial speculation is firmly opposed to use-value, which includes the entrepreneurial activities of men who build railways or the non-monetary but progressive energies of those who create art. *Hugh Selwyn Mauberley*, for instance, assigns blame for the war on usurers. Those who fought return

> home to old lies and new infamy;
> usury age-old and age-thick
> and liars in public places.[33]

These lines suggest that just as usury trades on the fictional value of paper money, so public falsehoods violate the stable meaning of words. The connection between language and money was to be an important and fertile one for Pound. He had been fascinated by the idea that a fixed linguistic system produced a knowable ethics from the early 1910s. In both *Hugh Selwyn Mauberley* and *The Cantos* the social importance of stable words is clearly connected to economics. The civilisation that was defended during the war was already 'botched', comprising a 'few thousand battered books'. The dubious financial dealings of capitalist usurers created both the war and a bungled civilisation, in which economically success-ful writers 'butter reviewers' and 'accept opinion'.[34] The poem wittily describes a variety of semi-fictional writers who attempt to elude this harsh economic logic: there is the 'Unpaid, uncel-ebrated' stylist and Mauberley himself, who vainly tries to resist 'current exacerbations'.[35]

The idea that poetry might have value outside economic defini-tions was central to his writing. He defended poetry by claiming that stable language was socially important in essays of the 1920s and 1930s, and this idea was at the heart of his politics. In an essay on *Ulysses* of 1922 he claimed that 'We are governed by words, the laws are graven in words, and literature is the sole means of keeping these words living and accurate'.[36] Pound would revisit the idea that literature keeps the language of law precise in a number of subsequent essays, including *How to Read* (1928), 'The Teacher's Mission' (1934) and 'Date Line' (1934). In *How to Read*, in the middle of a meditation on why one should read or write books, Pound argues that literary writing preserves the language of the law:

> the individual cannot think and communicate his thought, the governor and legislator cannot act effectively or frame his laws, without words, and the solidity and validity of these words is in the care of the damned and despised *literati*. When their work goes rotten – by that I do not mean when they express indecorous thoughts – but when their very medium, the very essence of their work, the application of word to thing goes rotten, i.e. becomes slushy and inexact, or excessive or bloated, the whole machinery of social and of individual thought and order goes to pot.[37]

Pound pictures a precarious nation state in which functioning gov-ernment is close to anarchy. Not only will the law be unworkable if words become imprecise, but individuals will be unable to think or communicate. He accords extraordinary power to the writer who maintains the meaning of legal and political language.

Pound's theory of language and the law is important for understanding his poetic voice as it developed during the 1920s and 1930s, and for his attempt to marry poetry and politics. Since the days of the first Imagist anthologies, he had argued the case for a precise rendering of external objects in poetry. In *Hugh Selwyn Mauberley*, he extends the significance of this linguistic precision to include the representation of history. The poem traces a recent history of poetry, wittily referring to the aesthetic impulses and lives of poets ranging from Swinburne to Wilfred Owen. Through rhythmical and linguistic echoes and partial quotations the poem recreates the idioms of different writers. Owen's 'Dulce et Decorum Est', for instance, is half quoted:

> Died some, pro patria,
>   Non 'dulce' non 'et décor' . . .[38]

Pound is careful to preserve the life and tone of Owen's poetic voice so that Owen's words become the means with which the poem represents the language of suffering and war.

Pound argued that the past is contained in language wrought at moments of historical crisis. In *The Cantos* he would resurrect a huge range of similarly potent phrases or poetic lines which capture key moments of historical crisis in the history of enlightenment. This project would lead him to refer across a vast range of historical documents and different cultures. Pound's political affiliations, however, were to shift in the 1930s. During the period he moved from writing supportively of the American Communist Party and making analogies between fascism and Bolshevism to becoming a wholehearted advocate of Mussolini's Fascist Party. Between 1939 and his imprisonment at Pisa in 1945, he stopped writing poetry and instead devoted his time to broadcasting and journalism. In *Jefferson and/or Mussolini* his main object of attack was the American liberal capitalist system. Cantos LXXII–LXXIII, written in the late 1930s and published in 1940, as well as two Italian language Cantos, published in 1944, attempt directly to write a poetry which voices an authoritarian and anti-Semitic politics of the state. Canto LII is typical of the hectoring tone of this sequence:

> Thus we lived on through sanctions, through Stalin
>   Litvinov, gold brokers made profit
> rocked the exchange against gold
> Before which entrefaites remarked Johnnie Adams (the elder)
> IGNORANCE, sheer ignorance ov the natr ov money
>   sheer ignorance of credit and circulation.
> Remarked Ben: better keep out the jews[39]

The sequence, known as the 'Adams Cantos', was based on two main textual sources, de Mailla's *Histoire générale de la Chine* and *The Life and Works of John Adams*. Chinese history and language, as well as the ideas of Adams, offer resources for Pound's fascist politics. The poem splices together these texts with contemporary individuals and events. Stalin, Mussolini, who is often referred to as 'Ben' in *The Cantos*, and Litvinov, who was People's Commissar for foreign affairs before being replaced by Stalin in 1939, partly because of his Jewish ancestry, all feature here. The writing tries dogmatically to enlighten the collective 'IGNORANCE' about the nature of money, credit and circulation. Subsequent Cantos in this sequence refer straightforwardly to political actions connected to Mussolini, such as opening 'the granaries' and a 'charter of labour'.[40] The political certainty of these Cantos means that they are bleached of the open-ended, ambiguous, playful or ironic linguistic and lyrical features which had been such a central part of *Hugh Selwyn Mauberley* and the earlier Cantos.

This sequence was a final, and failed, attempt to connect poetry to a fascist politics. Soon after this, Pound was imprisoned at Pisa and 'Ben' had been killed by Italian partisans. Pound's 'Pisan Cantos' document his experiences in jail, and, for some readers, represent a return to the less dogmatic writing of his earlier Cantos. They being with a reference to the 'enormous tragedy of the dream' and reintroduce the open-ended, lyrical and exploratory nature of the first Thirty Cantos.[41] Other critics have read them as far less contrite. Peter Nicholls interprets these opening lines of Canto LXXIV as holding fast to his fascist beliefs:

> Thus Ben and la Clara *a Milano*
>   By the heels at Milano
> That maggots shd/eat the dead bullock
> DIGONOS, Δίγονος, but the twice crucified[42]

Mussolini and his lover Clara Petacci were shot dead by communist partisans in 1945; their bodies were then taken to the Piazzale Loreto in Milan and hung upside down and photographed. Here, Ben (Mussolini) and Clara are deified by being 'twice crucified'. A later line, 'To build the city of Dioce whose terraces are the colour of stars', suggests a visionary, transcendent city which, Nicholls argues, could be interpreted as a version of the fascist state.[43] The 'enormous tragedy of the dream', then, can be seen as Pound's comment on the death of Mussolini: the tragic end of the fascist idea of the dream state.

In addition to the difficulty of reading the Adams Cantos in the light of their beliefs, there are also other, wider questions that they raise: can poetry bear the weight of direct political statement? Or should poetry be more playful and open-ended? Is it possible to write worthwhile political poetry, perhaps if it is tied to a different, more enlightened politics? What is wrong with this sequence of Cantos: is it their political perspective, or the attempt to marry poetry and politics in the first place?

WAR

These are important questions for understanding the relationship between modernism and politics. They were central to discussions about literature in the mid to late 1930s. In 1937 Louis Aragon, W. H. Auden, Nancy Cunard, Stephen Spender and Tristan Tzara, among others, issued a pamphlet called *Authors Take Sides* under the auspices of the *Left Review*. It asked the 'Writers and Poets of England, Scotland, Ireland and Wales' to take sides on 'the struggle in Spain', stating that the 'equivocal attitude, the Ivory

Tower, the paradoxical, the ironic detachment, will no longer do'. 'Are you for, or against, the legal Government and the People of Republican Spain. Are you for, or against, Franco and Fascism?'[44] Not only does the pamphlet reveal the way that politics dominated cultural activity in the 1930s, it also suggests a set of significant aesthetic oppositions. The ironies and poetic ambiguities typical of Eliot's poetry are here explicitly debunked in favour of a literature that is explicit about its political affiliations, and politically committed writing is also opposed to playful and equivocal writing.

Theirs was one among a number of home-grown political pamphlets issued and circulated in the late 1930s in response to the civil war in Spain, Hitler's rise to power in Germany and the Hitler–Stalin pact. Many of these statements were idiosyncratic. One of the strangest contributions was produced by Laura Riding, who argued that women had the answers to the political polarisation of Europe. In 1937, she sent 'A Personal Letter, With a Request for a Reply' to writers, artists, poets and what she called 'private women'. The completed book, a 529 page tome called *The World and Ourselves*, was published in 1938, and included letters from American housewives alongside prominent feminists and writers such as Christina Stead and Naomi Mitchison. The book concludes with Riding's fourteen-point conclusion and twenty-seven 'Resolutions'. Number eleven states: 'The moral stability of the world depends on the framing of a new moral Law from the point of view of women.'[45]

Artists and writers felt a need to intervene, partly because the British government were reluctant, and militarily unprepared to get involved in the Spanish war. Writers and artists, on the other hand, believed that the fate of Western civilisation was at stake. A number of writers, including George Orwell, Ernest Hemingway and W. H. Auden, travelled to Spain to either fight or write on behalf of the Republican Popular Front, and documented their experiences in essays, novels and poems. Essays in the *New Statesman*, Orwell's *Homage to Catalonia* (1938), Hemingway's *For Whom the Bell Tolls* (1940) and Auden's poems, including the famous 'Spain 1937', respond to the conflict between communists and fascists in Spain.

Both Auden and Orwell belong to a later generation than that of Eliot and Pound, a generation that reached intellectual maturity in the 1920s after both the Russian revolution and Mussolini's rise to power. Many of the writers of this later generation held strong anti-fascist political views. 'Spain 1937' repeats a number of phrases, such as 'to-day the struggle', to identify the political demands of the historical moment:

> 'What's your proposal? To build the Just City? I will.
> I agree. Or is it the suicide pact, the romantic
>   Death? Very well, I accept, for
> I am your choice, your decision: yes, I am Spain.'[46]

Auden declares that the poem ties its historical fate to that of Spain's. The implication is that art cannot maintain a position outside this history, and the poet is unable to shirk their choices and responsibilities.

Some of the writers involved in the connection of literature to politics would later retract their earlier positions. Auden, for one, revoked his earlier Marxism and later discarded 'Spain 1937' from his *Collected Works*. In some respects, this only highlights the fraught cultural conditions of the period. It was hard to escape politics in the mid to late 1930s. There was certainly no hiding place for those living in Germany, Spain or France. Writers, as during and after the First World War, were on the move again. Jewish intellectuals fled Germany and Spain to escape persecution.

The demands in the late 1930s that writers take sides on the political conflict in Spain, however, also produced its own reaction among writers and artists who began to ask whether literature could bear the weight of this political responsibility. One of the clearest and most forceful essays on this issue was George Orwell's 'Inside the Whale' (1940), which specifically directs literature away from politics. The essay retracts some of his earlier arguments about the political responsibilities of the writer, and argues instead that literature should divorce itself from politics. By so doing the essay interestingly points the way towards a post-war Anglo-American literary consensus.

The ostensible subject matter of Orwell's essay is the difference between Henry Miller's novel *Tropic of Cancer* (1935) and the politically committed writing of the British left, such as that of 'Auden and Spender and the rest of them' in the 1930s.[47] Miller's story of a drunken, sexually promiscuous and impoverished writer living in a Paris composed of drifters, prostitutes and would-be writers seems an unlikely book to champion in the dark days of the late 1930s. Orwell defends Miller's novel, not for its subject matter, but for its imaginative freedom, and uses his essay to pose some general and significant questions about the relationship between literature and politics. To what extent should writers involve themselves in politics? Is it possible to write a good political novel or poem? Or does literature depend on a kind of imaginative freedom divorced from fixed political agendas? In effect, does literature rely on a liberal culture? Is the creation of literature possible within a totalitarian political system? Reversing the statement of the *Authors Take Sides* pamphlet that writers tie their writing to a political position, Orwell suggests that literary writing is distinct from this; literature, for Orwell, is inherently equivocal, paradoxical and playful.

Orwell asks these large questions by means of a careful argument. In the context of the unfolding political events in Europe, he asks how could a novel 'about American dead-beats cadging drinks in the Latin Quarter' be of any interest? A novelist, he suggests, who 'simply disregards the major political events of the moment is generally either a footler or a plain idiot'. Miller's *Tropic of Cancer*, according to Orwell, accepts the world as it is. But what Miller is accepting in the 1930s is 'concentration camps, rubber truncheons, Hitler, Stalin' among other things.[48] Is this acceptable? The tying of literature to politics, however, has its own problems. Orwell vividly pictures the new orthodoxies of writers such as Auden who identify with the British left, suggesting the difficulties of identifying with a Communist Party which supports Stalin, particularly in the light of Stalin's changing foreign policy in the 1930s, and the oppressiveness of the cultural atmosphere of British anti-fascism in this period. The books about the Spanish civil war are notable for their 'shocking dullness and badness'. This is partly because they are written from the point of view of 'cocksure partisans telling you what to think'.[49]

It is for this reason that Orwell argues that 'the literary history of the thirties seems to justify the opinion that a writer does well to keep out of politics'. This is because 'any writer who accepts or partially accepts the discipline of a political party is sooner or later faced with the alternative: toe the line, or shut up'. It is from this basis that Orwell makes his fundamental claim that without bourgeois 'liberty' the creative powers wither away'.[50] Orwell champions *Tropic of Cancer* precisely because Miller's writing is apolitical, amoral and passive.

Orwell's essay is a defence of 'the liberal–Christian culture' in face of the 'destruction of liberalism' in the late 1930s and during Second World War.[51] It is also grounded in a definition of literature and freedom that is essentially opposed to Pound's. Pound creates poetry which incorporates and transforms the political forces of the time, and which thereby assumes that literature is a positive embodiment of political ideas. In contrast, Orwell articulates Miller's authorial rights negatively, as the writer's right to be free of constraint.

Orwell's argument points forward and connects to the liberal literary perspective of Trilling described at the beginning of this chapter, that there is an essential connection between literature and liberalism. The essay is helpful because it clearly articulates a set of basic presuppositions about what literature can hope to encompass, the kind of political system required to allow it to flourish, and the desire that writers relinquish their claims politically to transform the world.

The defence of negatively defined liberal values would inform a number of literary responses to the Second World War. The threat to life and freedom during the war, particularly during the Blitz of 1940, shifted the parameters of arguments about modernism and politics.[52] There are a number of extraordinarily powerful texts which depict the Blitz, including Eliot's *Four Quartets*, H. D.'s *Trilogy* and Elizabeth Bowen's *The Heat of the Day* (1949). These texts were less concerned with interpreting and directing political ideology and more interested in figuring politics as an externalised and unmanageable violence which threatens to destroy both the private sphere and the individual. All three texts, in different ways, dissociate politics and the individual.

Virginia Woolf, who committed suicide in 1941, depicted the way that violence would come from the skies in the war. In *Between The Acts* (1941) she pinpoints the trauma of this aerial violation of domestic boundaries, and draws powerful analogies between architectural and psychic violations. She had been preoccupied by these connections through the late 1930s. In *The Years* (1937) she evokes the invasive power of politics on psychic life. Peggy considers 'But how can one be "happy"? she asked herself, in a world bursting with misery. On every placard at every street corner was Death; or worse – tyranny; brutality; torture; the fall of civilization; the end of freedom.'[53] The international threats to civilisation and freedom infiltrate the emotional life of characters to the extent that the boundary separating politics and individualism disintegrates.

In *Three Guineas* she argued more forcefully that the frontier separating political and private life has been destroyed. She controversially also claimed that the threat to freedom was not simply connected to the political situations in Germany, Italy and Spain, but also to the patriarchal domestic and professional structures in British life:

> There, in those quotations (advocating that men take jobs that women are currently doing for the good of society) is the egg of the very same worm that we know under other names in other countries. There we have in embryo the creature, Dictator as we call him when he is Italian or German, who believes that he has the right whether given by God, Nature, sex or race is immaterial, to dictate to other human beings how they shall live; what they shall do.[54]

Woolf's feminist argument about the erosion of liberal values identifies the fascistic elements within British society.

Eliot and H. D., in *Four Quartets* and *Trilogy* respectively, also engaged with the violent psychic consequences of the Blitz. In *Four Quartets* Eliot attempts to reconcile the particular historical events of the Second World War with a religious scheme or 'destiny', which was Eliot's preferred term at this time. At stake in this poem is a larger question: can poetry provide a kind of knowledge or meaning that persists through violence? The poem raises questions about whether poetry can harness a religious vocabulary to make immediate historical reality meaningful. The difficulties of knowledge and communication which featured in 'The Love Song of J. Alfred Prufrock' and *The Waste Land* are more explicitly religious questions in *Four Quartets*:

> Words strain,
> Crack and sometimes break, under the burden,
> Under the tension, slip, slide and perish,
> Decay with imprecision, will not stay in place,
> Will not stay still.[55]

While the external world breaks apart, words also crack and strain. 'The Dry Salvages' and 'Little Gidding' create powerful images of trauma amidst violence: 'There is no end of it, the voiceless wailing'.[56]

H. D. in *Trilogy* also creates images in which aerial invasions are connected to psychic violations. The poem is composed of three parts, *The Walls Do Not Fall* (1944), *Tribute to the Angels* (1945) and *The Flowering of the Rod* (1946). Its opening section produces a powerful description of the architectural scars of falling bombs:

> ruin everywhere, yet as the fallen roof
> leaves the sealed room
> open to the air[57]

The poem considers what might persist through the architectural and psychic destruction of war. One image of survival is of fire. H. D. describes the effects of 'Apocryphal fire' melting the flesh of London, and then resituates the image of fire to represent a redemptive image of inter-generational knowledge as a flame:

> yet the frame held:
> we passed the flame: we wonder
> what saved us? what for?[58]

The 'us' refers to poets or writers in this stanza, as well as in *The Flowering of the Rod* generally. The poem asks whether poetry can have any significance in the context of war. The flame imagery is carried forward, with a description of poets as 'companions / of the flame' in section thirteen.[59] But, in the context of 'ruin everywhere', the flame which might persist and hold things together is horribly fragile: 'the rare intangible thread / that binds all humanity'.[60]

Alongside the idea of the precarious task of passing on a flame or poetic tradition, the poem creates other ideas of redemptive beauty or value. These ideas are embodied in a number of images of self-generation. In the section four, H. D. addresses the role and significance of the poet and poetry in the context of the 'invasion of the limitless, / ocean-weight; infinite water'.[61] This image of invasion connects infinity or limitlessness to violence and power. In the context of this enormous ocean-weight, poets are likened to small seashells or worms. The imagery of scale serves to separate the individual entity or poet from the ocean or historical context in which they find themselves. There is no attempt to interpret this immense and invasive power; its scope is figured as beyond the purview of the individual and of language.

Poetic power is instead located in the abilities of self-preservation and self-generation. The seashell is able to 'beget, self-out-of-self, / selfless, / that pearl-of-great-price'. In another section an 'industrious worm' is pictured spinning her 'own shroud'.[62] These self-generating seashells or worms are potent images of individual isolation. The poem's own 'pearl' of value and industry resides in the poet's linguistic expertise and spiritual insight: 'if you do not understand what words say, / how can you expect to pass judgement / on what words conceal?'[63] By analogy, *Trilogy* creates a defence of poetic language. The poet's words might seem insignificant and useless in comparison to the violence of the Second World War, but without linguistic expertise and individual freedom, how can people make sense of the political forces controlling their lives?

Orwell's negative defence of authorial freedom, and novels and poems by Woolf, H. D. and others, connect modernism to a liberal politics in a way that is opposed to that of Pound or Lewis. Orwell's invitation to read the politics of modernism differently has also been important for the recent recovery and interest in a different genealogy of 1930s and 1940s texts, whose politics can be read only tangentially. Djuna Barnes's *Nightwood* (1936) Jean Rhys's *Good Morning, Midnight* (1939), Samuel Beckett's *Murphy* (1938), Henry Green's *Party Going* (1939), Patrick Hamilton's *Hangover*

Square (1941) and Elizabeth Bowen's *The Death of the Heart* (1938) are all novels which explore dispossession and individual trauma, but without tying themselves to a political ideology.

Orwell's two basic claims, that the literary writer be free from political constraint and that the writer steer clear of politics, define the author in a specific way. They offer a starting-point for understanding one kind of critical perspective that dominated literary criticism after the Second World War. It connects to the cultural and historical point of view exemplified by Trilling's criticism, in which the writer should not claim the cultural authority to direct the political views of his or her readers.

A different critical tradition, which would be labelled the 'New Criticism', would enthusiastically embrace this definition of literature and see literary value residing in the playful textual qualities of irony, linguistic or imagistic innovation. The principles of critical analysis exemplified by the New Criticism ignored the social and political context in which texts had been produced, and instead focused attention on the formal and linguistic qualities of poems and prose, treating these texts as semi-autonomous entities. The importance and centrality of New Critical methods and literary presuppositions would dominate Anglo-American literary criticism in the immediate post-war period.

However, as Trilling pointed out, the politics of modernism could not so easily be wished away. His bemusement and frustration at the anti-liberal politics of the modernist texts he most admired attest to the fundamental involvement of modernism with politics. The critical movement away from New Criticism in the 1970s and 1980s involved a new kind of attention to the historical and political contexts of modernism. These readings sought to expose and understand this politics, seeing the literary involvement in fascist politics part of the wider disaster of political totalitarianism in the early twentieth century.

SUMMARY OF KEY POINTS

- The political polarisation of Europe in the 1910s, 1920s and 1930s split the arts.

- Early avant-garde groups adopted revolutionary political language to describe their artistic activities.
- There was a widespread critique of liberal democracy among English-language modernist writers.
- Marx and Nietzsche had an important impact on modernist political claims.
- Writers were encouraged to be more overtly political in the 1930s and to connect their work to political parties and ideologies. The most extreme version of this connection of politics and poetry was the work of Ezra Pound. His support of Italian fascism and anti-Semitism has been one of modernism's most controversial features.
- In the late 1930s and during the Second World War there was a reaction against the connection of literature and politics. Writers argued that literature should be free of politics.
- A number of powerful poems and novels were written about the Second World War which shied away from direct political statement.

NOTES

1. Lionel Trilling, *The Liberal Imagination: Essays on Literature and Society* (Harmondsworth: Penguin Books, 1970), p. 299.
2. W. H. Auden, 'The Public v. the Late Mr. William Butler Yeats', in W. H. Auden, *The English Auden*, ed. Edward Mendelson (London: Faber and Faber, 1977), pp. 392–3.
3. Raymond Williams, *The Politics of Modernism: Against the New Conformists*, ed. Tony Pinkney (London: Verso, 1996); Fredric Jameson, *Fables of Aggression: Wyndham Lewis, The Modernist as Fascist* (London: University of California Press, 1979); Michael North, *The Political Aesthetic of Yeats, Eliot and Pound* (Cambridge: Cambridge University Press, 1991).
4. North, *The Political Aesthetic of Yeats*, p. vii.
5. Walter Benjamin, 'Surrealism', *One Way Street and Other Writings*, trans. Edmund Jephcott and Kingsley Shorter (London: Verso, 1985), p. 236.

6. Wyndham Lewis, *Blast 1* (Santa Barbara: Black Sparrow Press, 2009), p. 7.
7. Lewis, *Blast 1*, p. 8.
8. Lewis, *Blast 1*, p. 42.
9. Lewis, *Blast 1*, p. 7.
10. Mina Loy, 'Feminist Manifesto', in Mina Loy, *The Lost Lunar Baedeker*, ed. Roger Conover (Manchester: Carcanet, 1996), p. 153.
11. Mina Loy, 'Feminist Manifesto', in Loy, *The Lost Lunar Baedeker*, p. 154.
12. Sigmund Freud, *Civilization, Society and Religion: Group Psychology, Civilization and Its Discontents and Other works*, trans. James Strachey (Harmondsworth: Penguin Books, 1985), p. 100.
13. Freud, *Civilization, Society and Religion*, p. 101, p. 103.
14. Lewis Grassic Gibbon, 'A Novelist Looks at the Cinema', In Lewis Grassic Gibbon, *Smeddum: A Lewis Grassic Gibbon Anthology*, ed. Valentina Bold (Edinburgh: Canongate, 2001), p. 740.
15. Wyndham Lewis, *The Apes of God* (Harmondsworth: Penguin Books, [1930] 1965), p. 491.
16. Lewis, *The Apes of God*, p. 30.
17. Lewis, *The Apes of God*, pp. 24–5.
18. Lewis, *The Apes of God*, p. 634.
19. Lewis, *The Apes of God*, p. 643.
20. Lewis, *The Apes of God*, p. 649.
21. T. S. Eliot, *For Lancelot Andrewes* (Garden City: Doubleday Doran, 1929), p. vii.
22. T. S. Eliot, *The Use of Poetry and the Use of Criticism* (London: Faber and Faber, 1933), p. 22.
23. Wyndham Lewis, 'Imaginary Letters', *Little Review*, 4.12 (1918), p. 52.
24. D. H. Lawrence, *Kangaroo* (Cambridge: Cambridge University Press, [1923] 1994), p. 11.
25. D. H. Lawrence, *The Rainbow*, ed. John Worthen (Harmondsworth: Penguin Books, [1915] 1989), p. 512.
26. Lawrence, *The Rainbow*, p. 115.
27. Lawrence, *The Rainbow*, p. 115.

28. Ezra Pound, *Selected Poems: 1908–1969* (London: Faber and Faber, 1977), p. 109.
29. Wyndham Lewis, *Tarr: The 1918 Version* (Santa Barbara: Black Sparrow Press, [1918] 1996), p. 13.
30. Friedrich Nietzsche, *Thus Spoke Zarathustra* (Harmondsworth: Penguin Books, 1969), p. 41.
31. Mina Loy, 'International Psycho-Democracy', in Mina Loy, *The Last Lunar Baedeker*, ed. Roger Conover (Manchester: Carcanet, 1982), p. 278.
32. Loy, *Last Lunar Baedeker*, p. 277, p. 276.
33. Ezra Pound, 'Hugh Selwyn Mauberley', in Pound, *Selected Poems*, p. 100.
34. Pound, *Selected Poems*, p. 101, p. 103, p. 104.
35. Pound, *Selected Poems*, p. 104, p. 109.
36. Ezra Pound, 'Ulysses (1922)', in Ezra Pound, *Literary Essays of Ezra Pound*, ed. T. S. Eliot (London: Faber and Faber, 1954), p. 409.
37. Ezra Pound, *How to Read* (London: Desmond Harmsworth, 1931), p. 21.
38. Pound, *Selected Poems*, p. 100.
39. Ezra Pound, *The Cantos* (London: Faber and Faber, 1986), p. 257.
40. Pound, *The Cantos*, p. 279, p. 287.
41. Pound, *The Cantos*, p. 439.
42. Pound, *The Cantos*, p. 439.
43. Pound, *The Cantos*, p. 439.
44. *Authors Take Sides on the Spanish Civil War* (London: Left Review, 1937).
45. Laura Riding, *The World and Ourselves* (London: Chatto and Windus, 1938), p. 478.
46. W. H. Auden, *The English Auden: Poems, Essays and Dramatic Writings, 1927–1939*, ed. Edward Mendelson (London: Faber and Faber, 1986), p. 211.
47. George Orwell, *Inside the Whale and Other Essays* (Harmondsworth: Penguin Books, 2001), p. 48.
48. Orwell, *Inside the Whale*, p. 10, p. 17.
49. Orwell, *Inside the Whale*, p. 18.
50. Orwell, *Inside the Whale*, p. 39.

51. Orwell, *Inside the Whale*, p. 47, p. 48.

52. From 7 September to 2 November 1940 London was bombed every night, and in 1944 there were thirteen significant attacks between January and March. The Blitz destroyed approximately three and a half million homes.

53. Virginia Woolf, *The Years* (Oxford: Oxford University Press, 1992), p. 369.

54. Virginia Woolf, *A Room of One's Own and Three Guineas* (Harmondsworth: Penguin Books, 1993), p. 175.

55. T. S. Eliot, 'Four Quartets', in T. S. Eliot, *Complete Poems and Plays* (London: Faber and Faber, 1969), p. 175.

56. T. S. Eliot, 'Four Quartets', in Eliot, *Complete Poems and Plays*, p. 186.

57. H. D., *Trilogy* (Manchester: Carcanet, [1944–6] 1973), p. 3.

58. H. D., *Trilogy*, p. 4.

59. H. D., *Trilogy*, p. 21.

60. H. D., *Trilogy*, p. 24.

61. H. D., *Trilogy*, p. 9.

62. H. D., *Trilogy*, p. 12.

63. H. D., *Trilogy*, p. 14.

Conclusion

English-language modernism continues to excite and provoke its readers. For some, the writing that was produced in the early twentieth century represents a high point in the history of Western culture. The period is seen as one when writers felt emboldened to break apart the conventions, transgress the rules, unleash futuristic political visions and the uncharted elements of the psyche. But the literary legacy of modernism has been complex. Poems and novels by Eliot, Joyce, Pound and Lewis still have the power to transform their readers' experience of language. But these texts also sometimes anger their new readers, who are either irritated by their difficulties and obscurities or shocked by their racist, anti-Semitic, homophobic and misogynistic elements.

Stylistically, too, the fallout from modernism has been complicated. Some techniques, such as interior monologue, poetic fragmentation and parataxis, and the playful manipulation of typography, became part of the available repertoire of narrative and poetic form. A significant number of contemporary British and American poets locate their literary origins in the radical experimentation of Stein, Pound and William Carlos Williams, such as the Language poets in America or those British writers associated with the poetry of J. H. Prynne. Mid to late twentieth- and twenty-first-century fiction by Samuel Beckett, Vladimir Nabokov, Thomas Pynchon, Kazuo Ishiguro and Jennifer Egan clearly indicate their debts to modernist writers, particularly Franz

Kafka, Marcel Proust, Virginia Woolf and James Joyce. The cultural status of Woolf and Joyce is also undisputed. Woolf is famous enough to have had a Hollywood film made about her, and the annual international Bloomsday festival in Dublin attracts large numbers of people to the city to celebrate Joyce's life and work.

While the rhythms and parameters of modernist texts are a live issue for some contemporary writers, modernism has had a very different, but extraordinarily robust, recent life in the area of literary criticism. Debates about postmodernism have receded from view, but the discussion of modernism has become ever more extensive. The increased attention to modernism, however, has served to fragment it as an idea, and a brief survey of recent discussions of the term reveal a series of stark differences of opinion. In the last ten years, much of the most important academic research in the study of modernism has involved the uncovering of unfamiliar cultural and political histories, and a new focus on modernism in a global context. The sheer number of new anthologies of modernist writing, scholarly books on modernism, introductions to modernism, edited collections on modernism and websites of modernist texts and journals is breathtaking.

New books build on previous debates and questions, and reveal shifts in orientation. The changing parameters of modernist anthologies are particularly revealing. Bonnie Kime Scott's *The Gender of Modernism* (1990) introduced a wide range of previously neglected women writers to a new generation of readers. Kolocotroni, Goldman and Taxidou's *Modernism: An Anthology of Documents and Sources* (1998) situated avant-garde proclamations and literary essays next to extracts from philosophical, sociological, scientific and political works, and thereby highlighted the interdisciplinary focus of modernist criticism. Lawrence Rainey's edited *Modernism: An Anthology* (2005) includes extracts from key modernist texts with extensive editorial notes which help to resurrect an increasingly distanced history. The principle of historical contextualisation which animates Rainey's anthology also informs much recent criticism. New collections of essays, such as *The Oxford Handbook of Modernisms* (2010), exemplify this historicising spirit, with discussions of modernist texts in relation to the contexts of new media, the metropolis and transnational contexts.[1]

In addition, however, to modernism as a historical field of study, it has also had a significant life in more mainstream publishing in the last ten years or so. A number of books have been published on the subject by prominent cultural and literary historians. The influential visual art critic T. J. Clark announced his intentions in the title of his book, *Farewell to an Idea: Episodes from a History of Modernism* (1999).[2] Clark tried to imagine a future archaeologist looking at a handful of modernist paintings separated from their history, language and environment. What would they see? What would they experience? Clark's was a fond farewell to the modernist idea in the visual arts. But the combination of sadness and diagnosis in Clark's book heralded a wider shift in critical sensibility. A similar impulse sits at the heart of Gabriel Josipovici's *What Ever Happened to Modernism?* (2010).[3] His book is both a defence of an idea of modernism, and a frustrated declaration of its strange disappearance. Modernism, in these accounts, is over; but what has risen in its wake is a depressing new realism and cultural conformism.

Other books reiterate the claim that modernism is in the past, but are happy to situate it at a distance. Peter Gay's book *Modernism: The Lure of Heresy, From Baudelaire to Beckett and Beyond* (2007) is a cultural historian's history of modernism as a global and intercultural artistic outpouring.[4] This is an inclusive and wide-ranging account of modernism as a seismic shift in the arts. It incorporates the visual arts, writing, music, dance, architecture, design, drama and the movies.

A different current in recent books has been to question the radical claims made for the cultural significance of modernism. A collective modernism of experiment, transgression and revolution never really happened, according to these accounts. Chris Baldick, in *The Modern Movement* (2004), argues that modernism is best described as a 'minority current' within a wider literary culture.[5] Rather than a significant shift in sensibility, he sees a continuity of literary realism in the writing read by most people in the early twentieth century. Alexandra Harris's *Romantic Moderns: English Writers, Artists and the Imagination from Virginia Woolf to John Piper* (2010), meanwhile, highlights the Romantic and nostalgic elements within English modernism, and thereby revises accounts of modernism's break from the past.[6]

While Baldick and Harris question the historical reality of a significantly innovative modernism, a different critical tradition argues that a radical modernism of experiment is a live issue, both for some contemporary writers and for literary critics. In Peter Middleton's and Nicky Marsh's edited collection *Teaching Modernist Poetry* (2010), for instance, poets and critics write about the ongoing legacy of modernism. The editors employ the category of 'late modernism' to indicate that modernism continues to energise new writing. Arguing against the historicising impulse of much recent modernist criticism, they seek to challenge the boundaries separating past from present, and 'critical reading and creative writing'.[7]

A look at the different books published in the last ten years or so, then, might lead to confusion: modernism as a meaningful collective form of cultural revolution never really happened; modernism was a seismic shift in sensibility that dominated many forms of culture in different countries in a specific and increasingly distanced historical period; modernism was an extraordinarily exciting and important artistic and literary impulse whose hopes have died in a new cultural conformism; modernism was an outburst of literary innovation which continues to animate the most ambitious contemporary writers. While some readers see modernism as an idea or aesthetic impulse, others see it as comprising a number of material texts defined by their position in history.

The differences in perspective attest to the ongoing currency of modernism. Why, one might ask, is this still important? Why are we still so fascinated by modernism and its legacies? Is it too extreme to suggest that there is a desire by some writers either to kill off modernism once and for all, or to defend and resurrect it? And why would either of these gestures be necessary? Given the energy with which both of these endeavours are pursued, it is worth pausing and asking what is at stake in contemporary uses of the modernist 'idea' that critics and readers bat back and forth in books and reviews?

When Josipovici, in *What Ever Happened to Modernism?*, accused contemporary writers such as Martin Amis and Ian McEwan of a lamentable retreat from the modernist idea, Philip Hensher was keen to defend the modernism of these same contemporary writers.

It seemed that what was at stake for these contemporary critics and writers was something rather different than an historical idea; that they were really trying to say something about literary value. This question is of interest because theories of postmodernism are generally keen to dismantle claims for permanent literary value. The use of modernism to discuss the value of contemporary novelists perhaps attests to a twofold desire both to return to questions of literary value and to appeal to a set of texts whose values are assumed. Is it an overstatement to say that in European modernism, works by Kafka, Proust, Joyce, Mann, Pound, Eliot and Woolf are seen to have a literary quality which is now established and undisputed? So that when Hensher defends the modernism of Adam Thirlwell he is also emphasising that Thirlwell's work belongs to a valued literary tradition which includes Proust.

However, if modernist texts have become not just part of a tradition, but the founding texts of a tradition of modern writing, then what is left of their modernism? Their modernism, far from being one of transgression and iconoclasm, is instead a benchmark of contemporary literary value, or a set of strategies writers seek to emulate. Is it significant that here, modernist writers foresaw and diagnosed the ways in which their innovations would become accommodated by future generations? From early on, Ezra Pound, T. E. Hulme and T. S. Eliot thought hard about where their work fitted in a literary canon or tradition, with Eliot famously suggesting that the significance of a modern poet or artist involves 'the appreciation of his relation to the dead poets and artist'.[8] Gertrude Stein saw this relationship more humorously and dialectically:

> Those who are creating the modern composition authentically are naturally only of importance when they are dead because by that time the modern composition having become past is classified and the description of it is classical. That is the reason why the creator of the new composition in the arts is an outlaw until he is a classic, there is hardly a moment in between.[9]

This is a wonderfully prophetic description of how innovative or 'outlaw' modernists would become accommodated through time.

It also brilliantly philosophises about how such writers *could* only become classic once their innovations were no longer disruptive and challenging.

Such questions may seem rather distant from those that trouble research-based accounts of modernism, which tend to want to subvert and complicate any easy assumptions about literary traditions and values. But, in some respects, they are not so far apart. Here, too, modernism as a set of textual strategies which disrupt conventional ways of seeing or reading might be said to have disappeared, to leave a number of texts defined by their position in history. The question of value is perhaps also not so far away in these studies. Rainey's anthology includes both those writers who were at the modernist centre from early on and writers who were resurrected in the 1970s and 1980s, such as Mina Loy, Djuna Barnes, Mary Butts and H. D. The newer modernism of Rainey's anthology, and of this volume, includes both the old and the new. But this new modernism is unimaginable without the texts, and the assumed value, of those writers who have been modernists all along.

Both the literary value of modernist texts and the historical contradictions they embody need to be revisited and resurrected in new readings, if their modernism is not simply to wither away. But modernist texts required this active re-animation by readers from the first. It is for these reasons that this book has endeavoured to bring the excitement and possibilities of these texts alive through an attention to the formal innovations of modernist writing and the ongoing historical conflicts they express.

The historical possibilities of texts are still meaningful because they speak to contemporary preoccupations and debates. The instabilities of the capitalist system, for instance, continue to cause global political turmoil, and the financial crisis of 2008 has similarities with the Wall Street crash of 1929. Arguments about the status and value of literature in the context of the commercialisation of writing are ongoing. Literature is still defined by tensions between individualism and the promotional necessities of the group. Writers continue to grapple with the desire to write about particular geographical locations and to encompass global perspectives. There are ongoing questions about the moral and religious transgressions, as well as political possibilities, of literary writing. The historical conflicts of the early twentieth century, and the literary articulation of these conflicts, still resonate. Above all, however, modernist texts still live and excite because formally and thematically they speak to contemporary concerns. When one reads Stein's comment above about how an innovative writer becomes classical it is hard not to feel that she has revealed something about contemporary reading practices and readers. It is hard not to think that she saw us coming.

NOTES

1. Peter Brooker, Andrzej Gasiorek, Deborah Longworth and Andrew Thacker (eds), *The Oxford Handbook of Modernisms* (Oxford: Oxford University Press, 2010).
2. T. J. Clark, *Farewell to an Idea: Episodes from a History of Modernism* (New Haven: Yale University Press, 1999).
3. Gabriel Josipovici, *What Ever Happened to Modernism?* (New Haven: Yale University Press, 2010).
4. Peter Gay, *Modernism: The Lure of Heresy, From Baudelaire to Beckett and Beyond* (London: Vintage Books, 2007).
5. Chris Baldick, *The Modern Movement: The Oxford English Literary History, 1910–1940*, vol. 10 (Oxford: Oxford University Press, 2004), p. 3.
6. Alexandra Harris, *Romantic Moderns: English Writers, Artists and the Imagination from Virginia Woolf to John Piper* (New York: Thames and Hudson, 2010).
7. Peter Middleton and Nicky Marsh (eds), 'Introduction', in *Teaching Modernist Poetry* (Basingstoke: Palgrave Macmillan, 2010), p. 4.
8. T. S. Eliot, 'Tradition and the Individual Talent', in T. S. Eliot, *Selected Prose of T. S. Eliot*, ed. Frank Kermode (London: Faber and Faber, 1975), p. 38.
9. Gertrude Stein, 'Composition as Explanation', in Gertrude Stein, *Look At Me Now and Here I Am* (Harmondsworth: Penguin Books, 1984), p. 22.

Student resources

ELECTRONIC RESOURCES

General modernist websites

The Modernist Journals Project
http://www.modjourn.org
A joint project of Brown University and the University of Tulsa.
This site gives access to a wide range of modernist journals.

The Modernist Studies Association
http://msa.press.jhu.edu
This is the official association of the US Modernist Studies
Association, with its annual conference and in collaboration with
the journal *Modernism/modernity*.

British Association for Modernist Studies
http://www.bams.me.uk
This is a recently formed British centre for modernism studies, with
online information about conferences, publications and seminars.

The Academy of American Poets
www.poets.org
The site has extensive information about modernist poets
such as Mina Loy, H. D., Ezra pound and others. This is a

good site for contextual information such as manifestos and bibliographies.

National Poetry Foundation
www.poetryfoundation.org
This website has a comprehensive list of poetic texts and some helpful teaching material.

The Poetry Archive
www.poetryarchive.org/poetryarchive/home.do
This is an invaluable resource for recordings of modernist poets. It includes recordings of T. S. Eliot, Ezra Pound, W. H. Auden, Langston Hughes, Basil Bunting and other modernist poets.

GLOSSARY

Abstract art

A key term in modernist and avant-garde art, with significance for developments in poetry and prose. It generally denotes visual art which is non-figurative, or whose shapes are independent of the world conceived realistically. A number of early twentieth-century painters, including Matisse, Malevich, Braque and Picasso, explored abstract visual forms in the 1900s and 1910s.

Avant-garde

The term has a military origin ('advanced guard'). In the literary arts it denotes work that is innovative, experimental, iconoclastic, futuristic and revolutionary. It can be used to describe an isolated writing practice, but more generally indicates the innovative activities of an artistic group which often includes writers and visual artists.

Classicism

A term with a very long and extensive tradition in the history of aesthetics, but which was important to a number of formulations of modernist writing and art in the 1910s and 1920s. T. E. Hulme published an influential essay called 'Romanticism and Classicism', in which he argued that writers should turn away from Romantic themes and forms and embrace a new classical restraint in the arts.

Cubism

A new painting style in the visual arts initially associated with the early work of Georges Braque and Pablo Picasso (roughly 1907–11). The movement soon spread with artists such as Juan Gris extending earlier experiments with form. Guillaume Apollinaire famously discussed Cubism in *Les peintres cubists* (1913), where he described techniques in which objects are broken up and reassembled on the canvas, and the creation of multiple viewpoints.

Dadaism

An avant-garde group created in Zurich in 1915 and associated with Romanian-born French poet and artist Tristan Tzara. Its principles were iconoclastic, anti-establishment and anti-art. It was also pacifist and humorous in orientation, and promoted elegant and spontaneous aphorisms and physical gestures. Dada groups sprang up in different cities, including Barcelona, Paris and New York.

Fascism

A political system first associated with the Italian Fascist Party which seized power in 1922 under the leadership of Benito Mussolini. It involved a revolutionary nationalism led by a revolutionary élite, no constitutional restraints on the leader Mussolini's power, the eradication of other political parties, the abolishment of parliamentary elections and a totalitarian police state. Mussolini carefully manipulated the new mass media of the press, radio and cinema to create an image of fascism as the new political doctrine of the twentieth century.

Flâneur

A term used by Charles Baudelaire to describe a metropolitan individual who drifts around a city landscape giving himself up to the chance seductions of commodities and prostitutes. It was taken up by Walter Benjamin and made central to his essays on modernism and modernity in the 1920s and 1930s, and has subsequently become an important means with which to describe and understand the narrative techniques of a range of English-language modernists who depict the partial perspective of isolated individuals in the city.

Free indirect discourse

This is the name given to the narrative technique of presenting a character's voice partly mediated by the voice of the author. Gérard Genette influentially described this technique as involving the narrator taking on the speech of the character or when the character speaks through the voice of the narrator, and the two instances are then merged.

Free indirect style

This term is related to free indirect discourse. Some critics argue that free indirect discourse should refer to those instances where words have actually been spoken aloud and that free indirect style should be reserved for textual moments when a character's voice is probably the silent, inward one of thought.

Free verse

From the French term *vers libre*, first used as a term by the French poet Gustave Kahn in the late 1880s to denote verse which is not regular in metre, rhyme or length of lines. It is impossible to date the beginnings of free verse. Walt Whitman's poems in *Leaves of Grass* (1855), for instance, are non-metrical, oral-derived 'free verse' forms. It is true to say, however, that free verse becomes a dominant feature of Anglo-American poetry in the early to mid twentieth century.

Futurism

An iconoclastic avant-garde movement which attacked museums, tradition and sentimentality and celebrated modernity, speed, machines and dynamism. It was originally an Italian movement involving a group of writers and visual artists surrounding F. T. Marinetti, who published 'The Founding and Manifesto of Futurism' in 1909. The movement spread, with Russian Futurist groups emerging in 1913.

Gender

A term which rests on a distinction between biological sex and gender categories, in which masculinity and femininity are conceived as social constructs.

Liberal individualism

A theory of the individual central to liberal philosophy and politics. It involves creating the political and legal framework to limit the power of the state over the individual by protecting the individual's rights to own property, to free speech, liberty of religious worship, political participation and movement.

Imagism

The first English-language modernist group movement, spearheaded by Ezra Pound in 1914. Its principles of composition included free verse, clinical and sparse language, and making the image the basic unit of significance in poems.

Interior monologue

A prose style first developed by the French writer Édouard Dujardin in the 1890s, and adopted by a number of English-language modernists including Dorothy Richardson, James Joyce and Virginia Woolf. It is a narrative style which gives the impression of presenting thoughts as they occur to characters. Sometimes thoughts are presented as the involuntary response to external events or landscapes. Other techniques involve depicting memories as unstructured thoughts in which images and words are connected associatively rather than causally.

Intertextuality

A term first used in the 1960s by theorists to denote the techniques of quoting, half-quoting, ironising or otherwise referring to other texts. It can also refer to forms in which poems, stories or novels are shaped by other texts.

Liberal democracy

The political system that dominated Europe and America in the late nineteenth and early twentieth century. It generally involves some degree of suffrage, free and fair elections, a constitution which limits the authority of government, and an independent judiciary.

Mass culture

A term that synthesises the different forms of new media and cultural forms in the early twentieth century, such as an expanding mass-distribution newspaper network and readership, cheap mass-produced novels, the cinema and the radio, and implies that a capitalist logic of commercial exploitation holds them together.

Mass democracy

A term developed to describe the new political systems that emerged after the First World War in which the suffrage was extended to include most men and women. Mass democracies are extensions of earlier liberal democracies, and tend to have similar constitutional and judicial restraints. The terms 'mass democracy' and 'liberal democracy' are not mutually exclusive.

Modernisation

A term used to describe industrial, technological, commercial and employment developments. With regard to this guide, it denotes these fast-moving shifts in the late nineteenth and twentieth centuries.

Modernity

An epochal term which refers to shifts in philosophical, political and juridical ideas about subjectivity, the state and the world. It therefore denotes a range of socio-historical phenomena, including capitalist modes of organisation, bureaucracy, politics, judicial frameworks and philosophical beliefs.

Naturalism

A literary term connected to developments in fiction and drama in the late nineteenth century. In fiction it is most closely associated with the writing of Émile Zola who, in his *Les Rougon-Macquart* series of novels (published 1871–93), documented with dispassionate observation and meticulous detail the squalid environmental influences and instinctual nature of interrelated characters. Along with a number of late nineteenth-century writers such as Thomas Hardy and George Moore, the early texts of modernist writers such as D. H. Lawrence and James Joyce are naturalist in style.

Parataxis

The arrangement of clauses, propositions or phrases without linguistic or thematic connectives. This is an important principle of composition in many modernist poems.

Realism

One way of defining literary realism is to suggest that it aims to represent experiential reality through the accurate portrayal of details about character, time and place. Literary realism, however, is a shifting category, because the understanding of what constitutes reality, as well as the means by which a writer might capture this entity, vary according to time and place. Many modernist writers claimed that they were creating new kinds of fictional realism.

Vorticism

The first English-language avant-garde group, associated with Wyndham Lewis and Ezra Pound. The first Vorticist manifestos were published in the journal *Blast* in 1914, and included writers and visual artists. They attacked conventions, traditions and academic institutions, and celebrated the geometric, mechanical and non-representational features of art.

QUESTIONS FOR DISCUSSION

Chapter 1: Modernist networks, 1914–28: Futurists, Imagists, Vorticists, Dadaists

- To what extent was early modernist writing a product of group activities?
- Why were Imagism and Vorticism created by London writers?
- What was the relationship between Dada and war?
- Why did writers go to Paris in the 1920s?
- How would you describe the very different writing techniques of Gertrude Stein, Mina Loy, H. D., Pound, Joyce and Eliot?

Chapter 2: Modernism and geography

- Why has the figure of the *flâneur* been helpful in understanding the ways in which modernist fiction is written?
- Why are so many modernist texts located in cities?
- Is modernist writing different to realist fiction?
- What is the relationship between modernism and imperialism?

- What techniques do writers develop to capture the experience of exile?

Chapter 3: Sex, obscenity, censorship

- Why were so many modernist texts censored?
- Why did modernist writers want to explore sexuality and sexual relationships in writing?
- What techniques did writers develop to depict sex?
- Alongside sex, what other kinds of obscenity did modernist writers explore?
- In what ways was women's liberation important for modernist writing?
- What was the relationship between modernism and psychoanalysis?

Chapter 4: Modernism and mass culture

- How did new mass cultural forms energise modernist writing?
- Why were some modernist writers critical of mass culture?
- Does the modernist opposition between art and mass culture hold?
- What was the impact of cinema on modernist writing?
- Why were modernist writers hostile to journalism and how did this hostility affect the composition of poems and prose?

Chapter 5: Modernism and politics

- Why did modernist writers want to tie literature to politics?
- How did writers manipulate a political language?
- What were the political circumstances that encouraged writers to connect their work to politics?
- Why was there a reaction against political literature in the late 1930s?
- How did writers engage with the Second World War in their work?

GUIDE TO FURTHER READING

Primary texts

Artaud, Antonin, *The Theatre and Its Double*, trans. Victor Corti (London: Calder, [1938] 1993).

Auden, W. H., *The English Auden*, ed. Edward Mendelson (London: Faber and Faber, 1977).

Auden, W. H., *Selected Poems* (London: Faber and Faber, 1979).

Barnes, Djuna, *Ryder* (Normal: Dalkey Archive Press, [1928] 1990).

Barnes, Djuna, *Nightwood* (London: Faber and Faber, [1936] 1990).

Barnes, Djuna, *Ladies Almanack* (Manchester: Carcanet, [1928] 2006).

Butts, Mary, *Death of Felicity Taverner* (London: Wishart, 1932).

Butts, Mary, *The Journals of Mary Butts*, ed. Nathalie Blondel (New Haven: Yale University Press, 2002).

Eliot, T. S., *For Lancelot Andrewes* (Garden City: Doubleday Doran, 1929).

Eliot, T. S., *The Use of Poetry and the Use of Criticism* (London: Faber and Faber, 1933).

Eliot, T. S., *The Complete Poems and Plays* (London: Faber and Faber, 1969).

Eliot, T. S., *Selected Prose of T. S. Eliot*, ed. Frank Kermode (London: Faber and Faber, 1975).

Eliot, T. S., *Selected Essays*, 3rd edn (London: Faber and Faber, [1951] 1986).

Eliot, T. S., *Letters of T. S. Eliot, Volume 1: 1898–1922*, ed. Valerie Eliot (New York: Harcourt Brace Jovanovich, 1988).

Eliot, T. S., *The Letters of T. S. Eliot*, ed. Valerie Eliot and Hugh Haughton (London: Faber and Faber, 2009).

Ford, Ford Madox, *Parade's End* (Harmondsworth: Penguin Books, [1924–8] 1982).

Ford, Ford Madox, *The Soul of London* (London: Orion, [1905] 1998).

Forster, E. M., *A Passage To India* (Harmondsworth: Penguin Books, [1924] 1979).

Forster, E. M., *Howards End* (London: Penguin Books, [1910] 1989).

Forster, E. M., *Maurice* (London: Penguin Books, [1971] 2005).

Freud, Sigmund, *The Pelican Freud Library*, ed. Angela Richards, vol. 7 (Harmondsworth: Penguin Books, 1984).

Freud, Sigmund, *Civilization, Society and Religion: Group Psychology, Civilization and Its Discontents and Other Works*, trans. James Strachey (Harmondsworth: Penguin Books, 1985).

Gibbon, Lewis Grassic, *A Scots Quair* (London: Penguin Books, [1932–4] 1986).

Gibbon, Lewis Grassic, *Smeddum: A Lewis Grassic Gibbon Anthology*, ed. Valentina Bold (Edinburgh: Canongate, 2001).

H. D. [Hilda Doolittle], *Tribute To Freud* (Oxford: Carcanet, [1956] 1971).

H. D. [Hilda Doolittle], *Trilogy* (Manchester: Carcanet, [1944–6] 1973).

H. D. [Hilda Doolittle], *Bid Me To Live* (London: Virago, [1960] 1983).

H. D. [Hilda Doolittle], *Collected Poems, 1912–1944*, ed. Louis L. Martz (New York: New Directions, 1983).

Hulme, T. E., *Speculations*, ed. Herbert Read (London: Routledge and Kegan Paul, 1960).

Huxley, Aldous, *Brave New World* (London: Harper Collins, [1932] 1994).

Huxley, Aldous, *Point Counter Point* (London: Harper Collins, [1928] 1994).

Isherwood, Christopher, *Goodbye to Berlin* (St Albans: Panther Books, [1939] 1977).

Joyce, James, *The Letters of James Joyce*, ed. Richard Ellmann (London: Faber and Faber, 1966).

Joyce, James, *Finnegans Wake* (London: Faber and Faber, [1939] 1975).

Joyce, James, *Ulysses: The Corrected Text*, ed. Hans Walter Gabler with Wolfhard Steppe and Claus Melchior (London: Bodley Head, 1986).

Joyce, James, *A Portrait of the Artist as a Young Man* (Oxford: Oxford University Press, [1916] 2000).

Joyce, James, *Dubliners* (Harmondsworth: Penguin Books, [1914] 2000).

Joyce, James, *James Joyce: Occasional, Critical, and Political Writing*, ed. Kevin Barry (Oxford: Oxford University Press, 2000).

Lawrence, D. H., *Lady Chatterley's Lover* (Harmondsworth: Penguin Books, [1928] 1961).

Lawrence, D. H., *Women in Love* (Harmondsworth: Penguin Books, [1921] 1979).

Lawrence, D. H., *The Lost Girl* (Harmondsworth: Penguin Books, [1920] 1980).

Lawrence, D. H., *The Rainbow*, ed. John Worthen (Harmondsworth: Penguin Books, [1915] 1989).

Lawrence, D. H., *Kangaroo* (Cambridge: Cambridge University Press, [1923] 1994).

Lawrence, D. H., *Psychoanalysis and the Unconscious; and Fantasia of the Unconscious*, ed. Bruce Steele (Cambridge: Cambridge University Press, 2004).

Lewis, Wyndham, *The Apes of God* (Harmondsworth: Penguin Books, [1930] 1965).

Lewis, Wyndham, *The Roaring Queen*, ed. and intro. Walter Allen (London: Secker and Warburg, 1973).

Lewis, Wyndham, *The Revenge for Love* (Harmondsworth: Penguin Books, [1937] 1982).

Lewis, Wyndham, *Snooty Baronet* (Santa Barbara: Black Sparrow Press, [1932] 1984).

Lewis, Wyndham, *Tarr: The 1918 Version* (Santa Barbara: Black Sparrow Press, [1918] 1990).

Lewis, Wyndham, *Time and Western Man* (Santa Rosa: Black Sparrow Press, [1927] 1993).

Lewis, Wyndham, *Blast* (Santa Barbara: Black Sparrow Press, 2008).

Loy, Mina, *The Last Lunar Baedeker*, ed. Roger Conover (Manchester: Carcanet, 1982).

Loy, Mina, *The Lost Lunar Baedeker*, ed. Roger Conover (Manchester: Carcanet, 1996).

Miller, Henry, *Tropic of Cancer* (London: Harper Perennial, 2005).

Nietzsche, Friedrich, *Thus Spoke Zarathustra* (Harmondsworth: Penguin Books, 1969).

Orwell, George, *Inside the Whale and Other Essays* (Harmondsworth: Penguin Books, 2001).

Pound, Ezra, *Make It New* (London: Faber and Faber, 1934).

Pound, Ezra, *Literary Essays of Ezra Pound*, ed. T. S. Eliot (London: Faber and Faber, 1954).

Pound, Ezra, *Pound/Joyce*, ed. Forrest Read (London: Faber and Faber, 1967).

Pound, Ezra, *Selected Prose: 1909–1965* (London: Faber and Faber, 1973).

Ezra Pound, *Selected Poems: 1908–1969* (London: Faber and Faber, 1977).

Pound, Ezra, *The Cantos* (London: Faber and Faber, 1986).

Proust, Marcel, *Remembrance of Things Past*, vols 2–3, trans. C. K. Scott Moncrieff and Terence Kilmartin (Harmondsworth: Penguin Books, 1981, 1989).

Proust, Marcel, *Remembrance of Things Past*, vol. 1, trans. C. K. Scott Moncrieff and Terence Kilmartin (London: Vintage, 1992).

Rhys, Jean, *Good Morning, Midnight* (London: Penguin Books, [1939] 2000).

Rhys, Jean, *Voyage in the Dark* (London: Penguin Books, [1934] 2000).

Richardson, Dorothy, *Pilgrimage*, vols 1–4 (London: Virago, 1979).

Riding, Laura, *The World and Ourselves* (London: Chatto and Windus, 1938).

Riding, Laura and Robert Graves, *A Survey of Modernist Poetry* (New York: Haskell House Publishers, [1927] 1969).

[Riding, Laura] as Laura (Riding) Jackson, *The Poems of Laura Riding: A New Edition of the 1938 Collection* (Manchester: Carcanet, 1991).

[Riding, Laura] as Laura (Riding) Jackson, with Schuyler B. Jackson, *Rational Meaning: A New Foundation for the Definition of Words and Supplementary Essays* (Charlottesville: University of Virginia Press, 1997).

Silkin, Jon (ed.), *The Penguin Book of First World War Poetry* (Harmondsworth: Penguin Books, 1996).

Stein, Gertrude, *The Autobiography of Alice B. Toklas* (Harmondsworth: Penguin Books, [1933] 1966).

Stein, Gertrude, *Look at Me Now and Here I Am* (Harmondsworth: Penguin Books, 1984).

Stein, Gertrude, *Three Lives* (Harmondsworth: Penguin Books, [1909] 1990).

West, Nathanael, *Novels and Other Writings* (New York: Library of America, 1997).

West, Nathanael, *A Cool Million and The Dream Life of Balso Snell: Two Novels by Nathanael West* (New York: Farrar, Straus and Giroux, 2006).

Woolf, Virginia, *Collected Essays*, vol. 2 (London: Hogarth Press, 1966).

Woolf, Virginia, *The Diary of Virginia Woolf*, vols 1, 2 and 3, ed. Anne Oliver Bell, assisted by Andrew McNeillie (London: Hogarth Press, 1977, 1978, 1980).

Woolf, Virginia, *The Essays of Virginia Woolf*, ed. Andrew McNeillie, vols 1–3 (London: Hogarth Press, 1986–8).

Woolf, Virginia, *Between the Acts* (Harmondsworth: Penguin Books, [1941] 1992).

Woolf, Virginia, *The Years* (Oxford: Oxford University Press, 1992).

Woolf, Virginia, *A Room of One's Own and Three Guineas* (Harmondsworth: Penguin Books, 1993).

Woolf, Virginia, *To the Lighthouse* (Oxford: Oxford University Press, [1927] 2000).

Woolf, Virginia, *Moments of Being*, ed. Jeanne Schulkind, introduced and revised by Hermione Lee (London: Pimlico, 2002).

Woolf, Virginia, *Mrs Dalloway* (Oxford: Oxford University Press, [1925] 2008).

Woolf, Virginia, *Selected Essays*, ed. David Bradshaw (Oxford: Oxford University Press, 2008).

Anthologies

Anderson, Margaret (ed.), *Little Review Anthology* (New York: Hermitage House, 1953).

Dowson, Jane (ed.), *Women's Writing of the 1930s* (London: Routledge, 1995).

Jones, Peter (ed.), *Imagist Poetry* (Harmondsworth: Penguin Books, 1972).

Kolocotroni, Vassiliki, Jane A. Goldman and Olga Taxidou (eds), *Modernism: An Anthology of Sources and Documents* (Edinburgh: Edinburgh University Press, 1998).

Rainey, Lawrence (ed.), *Modernism: An Anthology* (Oxford: Blackwell Publishing, 2005).

Rothenberg, Jerome and Pierre Joris (eds), *Poems for the Millennium*, vol. 1 (Berkeley: University of California Press, 1995).

Scott, Bonnie Kime (ed.), *The Gender of Modernism: A Critical Anthology* (Bloomington: Indiana University Press, 1990).

Secondary criticism

Adorno, Theodor, Walter Benjamin, Ernst Bloch, Bertolt Brecht, Georg Lukács, *Aesthetics and Politics: Debates Between Theodor Adorno, Walter Benjamin, Ernst Bloch, Bertolt Brecht, Georg Lukács* (London: Verso, 1980).

Adorno, Theodor, *The Culture Industry* (London: Routledge, 1991).

Armstrong, Tim, *Modernism: A Cultural History* (Cambridge: Polity Press, 2005).

Attridge, Derek (ed.), *The Cambridge Companion to James Joyce* (Cambridge: Cambridge University Press, 1990).

Ayers, David, *Wyndham Lewis and Western Man* (Basingstoke: Macmillan, 1992).

Ayers, David, *Modernism: A Short Introduction* (Oxford: Blackwell, 2004).

Baldick, Chris, *The Modern Movement: The Oxford English Literary History, 1910–1940*, vol. 10 (Oxford: Oxford University Press, 2004).

Bell, Quentin, *Virginia Woolf: A Biography*, vol. 2 (London: Hogarth Press, 1972).

Benjamin, Walter, *One Way Street and Other Writings*, trans. Edmund Jephcott and Kingsley Shorter (London: Verso, 1985).

Benjamin, Walter, *The Arcades Project*, trans. Howard Eiland and Kevin McLaughlin (Cambridge: Harvard University Press, 1999).

Benstock, Shari, *Women of the Left Bank: Paris 1900–1940* (London: Virago, 1987).

Berman, Marshall, *All that is Solid Melts Into Air: The Experience of Modernity* (Harmondsworth: Penguin Books, 1982).

Bradbury, Malcolm and James McFarlane (eds), *Modernism: A Guide to European Literature, 1890–1930* (Harmondsworth: Penguin Books, 1976).

Bradshaw, David (ed.), *A Concise Companion to Modernism* (Oxford: Blackwell, 2003).

Brett, Dorothy, *Lawrence and Brett: A Friendship* (London: Martin Secker, 1933).

Brooker, Peter and Andrew Thacker (eds), *The Oxford Critical and Cultural History of Modernist Magazines: vol. 1, Britain and Ireland, 1880–1955* (Oxford: Oxford University Press, 2009).

Brooker, Peter, Andrzej Gasiorek, Deborah Longworth and Andrew Thacker (eds), *The Oxford Handbook of Modernisms* (Oxford: Oxford University Press, 2010).

Burke, Carolyn, *Becoming Modern: The Life of Mina Loy* (New York: Farrar, Straus and Giroux, 1996).

Bush, Ronald, *The Genesis of Ezra Pound's Cantos* (Princeton: Princeton University Press, 1976).

Clark, T. J., *Farewell to an Idea: Episodes from a History of Modernism* (New Haven: Yale University Press, 1999).

Craig, Cairns, *Yeats, Eliot, Pound and the Politics of Poetry: Richest to Richest* (London: Croom Helm, 1982).

Cullingford, Elizabeth, *Yeats, Ireland and Fascism* (London: Macmillan, 1981).

Dekoven, Marianne, *Rich and Strange: Gender, History, Modernism* (Princeton: Princeton University Press, 1991).

Donald, James, Anne Friedberg and Laura Marcus (eds), *Close Up, 1927–1933: Cinema and Modernism* (London: Cassell, 1998).

Ellmann, Maud, *The Poetics of Impersonality: T. S. Eliot and Ezra Pound* (Brighton: Harvester, 1987).

Ellmann, Maud, *The Nets of Modernism: Henry James, Virginia Woolf, James Joyce and Sigmund Freud* (Cambridge: Cambridge University Press, 2010).

Ellmann, Richard, *James Joyce* (Oxford: Oxford University Press, 1966).

Gardner, Helen, *The Art of T. S. Eliot* (London: Faber and Faber, 1949).

Gasiorek, Andrzej, *Wyndham Lewis and Modernism*, Writers and their Work, ed. Isobel Armstrong (Devon: Northcote House, 2004).

Gay, Peter, *Modernism: The Lure of Heresy, From Baudelaire to Beckett and Beyond* (London: Vintage Books, 2007).

Gilbert, Geoff, *Before Modernism Was: Modern History and the Constituencies of Writing, 1900–30* (Basingstoke: Palgrave, 2004).

Gilbert, Sandra and Susan Gubar, *No Man's Land: The Place of the Woman Writer in the Twentieth Century*, vols 1, 2 and 3 (New Haven: Yale University Press, 1988, 1989, 1994).

Goldman, Jane, *Modernism, 1900–1945: Image to Apocalypse* (Basingstoke: Palgrave Macmillan, 2004).

Harris, Alexandra, *Romantic Moderns: English Writers, Artists and the Imagination from Virginia Woolf to John Piper* (New York: Thames and Hudson, 2010).

Hough, Graham, *Image and Experience: Studies in a Literary Revolution* (London: Duckworth, 1960).

Hyland, Paul and Neil Semmels (eds), *Writing and Censorship in Britain* (London: Routledge, 1992).

Jameson, Fredric, *Fables of Aggression: Wyndham Lewis, the Modernist as Fascist* (London: University of California Press, 1979).

Josipovici, Gabriel, *What Ever Happened to Modernism?* (New Haven: Yale University Press, 2010).

Kenner, Hugh, *The Pound Era* (London: Faber and Faber, 1972).

Leavis, F. R., *New Bearings in English Poetry: A Study of the Contemporary Situation* (Harmondsworth: Penguin Books, 1932).

Levenson, Michael, *A Genealogy of Modernism: A Study of English Literary Doctrine, 1908–1922* (Cambridge: Cambridge University Press, 1984).

Levenson, Michael (ed.), *The Cambridge Companion to Modernism* (Cambridge: Cambridge University Press, 1999).

Linett, Maren Tova (ed.), *The Cambridge Companion to Modernist Women Writers* (Cambridge: Cambridge University Press, 2010).

Machin, Richard and Christopher Norris (eds), *Post-Structuralist*

Readings of English Poetry (Cambridge: Cambridge University Press, 1987).

Marcus, Laura, *The Tenth Muse: Writing about Cinema in the Modernist Period* (Oxford: Oxford University Press, 2007).

Mengham, Rod and John Kinsella (eds), *Vanishing Points: New Modernist Poems* (Cambridge: Salt Publishers, 2004).

Middleton, Peter and Nicky Marsh (eds), *Teaching Modernist Poetry* (Basingstoke: Palgrave Macmillan, 2010).

Miller, Tyrus, *Late Modernism: Politics, Fiction, and the Arts Between the World Wars* (Berkeley: University of California Press, 1999).

Morrison, Mark S., *The Public Face of Modernism: Little Magazines, Audiences, and Reception, 1905–1920* (Madison: University of Wisconsin Press, 2001).

Nicholls, Peter, *Ezra Pound: Politics, Economics and Writing: A Study of 'The Cantos'* (London: Macmillan, 1984).

Nicholls, Peter, *Modernisms: A Literary Guide* (Basingstoke: Macmillan, 1995).

North, Michael, *The Political Aesthetic of Yeats, Eliot and Pound* (Cambridge: Cambridge University Press, 1991).

North, Michael, *The Dialect of Modernism: Race, Language and Twentieth Century Literature* (Oxford: Oxford University Press, 1994).

North, Michael, *Reading 1022: A Return to the Scene of the Modern* (Oxford: Oxford University Press, 1999).

Parsons, Deborah, *Streetwalking the Metropolis: Women, the City, and Modernity* (Oxford: Oxford University Press, 2000).

Pease, Allison, *Modernism, Mass Culture, and the Aesthetics of Obscenity* (Cambridge: Cambridge University Press, 2000).

Perloff, Marjorie, *The Dance of the Intellect: Studies in the Poetry of the Pound Tradition* (Cambridge: Cambridge University Press, 1985).

Potter, Rachel, *Modernism and Democracy: Literary Culture, 1900–1930* (Oxford: Oxford University Press, 2006).

Potter, Rachel and Suzanne Hobson (eds), *The Salt Companion to Mina Loy* (Cambridge: Salt Publishers, 2010).

Rainey, Lawrence, *Institutions of Modernism: Literary Elites and Public Culture* (New Haven: Yale University Press, 1998).

Richards, I. A., *The Principles of Literary Criticism* (London: Routledge and Kegan Paul, 1924).

Rolph, C. H. (ed.), *The Trial of Lady Chatterley: Regina v. Penguin Books Ltd.* (London: Penguin Books, 1990).

Smith, Stan, *The Origins of Modernism: Eliot, Pound, Yeats and the Rhetorics of Renewal* (New York: Harvester Wheatsheaf, 1994).

Stonebridge, Lyndsey, *The Destructive Element: British Psychoanalysis and Modernism* (Basingstoke: Macmillan, 1998).

Surette, Leon, *Pound in Purgatory: From Economic Radicalism to Anti-Semitism* (Urbana: University of Illinois Press, 1999).

Thacker, Andrew, *Moving Through Modernity: Space and Geography in Modernism* (Manchester: Manchester University Press, 2003).

Tratner, Michael, *Modernism and Mass Politics: Joyce, Woolf, Eliot, Yeats* (Stanford: Stanford University Press, 1995).

Trilling, Lionel, *The Liberal Imagination: Essays on Literature and Society* (Harmondsworth: Penguin Books, 1970).

Trotter, David, *The English Novel in History, 1895–1920* (London: Routledge, 1993).

Trotter, David, *Paranoid Modernism: Literary Experiment, Psychosis, and the Professionalization of English Society* (Oxford: Oxford University Press, 2001).

Vanderham, Paul, *James Joyce and Censorship: The Trials of 'Ulysses'* (Basingstoke: Macmillan, 1998).

Williams, Raymond, *The Politics of Modernism: Against the New Conformists*, ed. Tony Pinkney (London: Verso, 1996).

Index

abstract art, 219
Adams, John, *Life and Works of John Adams*, 197
Adorno, Theodor, 3, 5, 146–7, 156
Aldington, Richard, 43, 49, 130
American Birth Control League, 124–5
American jazz *see* jazz and modernist writers
The Apes of God, Wyndham Lewis, 3, 39, 46
  cinematic imagery, 155–6, 166
  democracy, 187–8, 189–90
  fear of revolution, 186
  the General Strike, 185–9
  jazz images, 149
  political vacuum, 188–9
Apollinaire, Guillaume, *Les peintres cubists*, 220
Aragon, Louis, 198
Arensberg, Walter, 51, 53
art and the individual, 183
Artaud, Antonin, 148
Auden, W.H.
  Collected Works, 200
  failure of liberalism, 180, 193
  political views, 178, 200, 201
  'Spain 1937', 199, 200
  Spanish Civil War, 198, 199, 200
Authors Take Sides, Spanish Civil War, 198–9, 201
avant-garde, 181, 219
  groups, 181, 182, 183
  painting, 56

Ball, Hugo, 50
Barnacle, Nora, 22
Barnes, Djuna, 4, 7, 56, 67, 125, 131, 216
  censorship, 66, 72, 114, 120
Dada group, 51, 73
  explicit and experimental writing, 65, 66, 73–4, 137
  exploration of the obscene, 122–4
  the *flâneur*, 81
  Ladies Almanac, 66, 73–4, 137
  Nightwood, 6, 107, 122–4, 137, 205
  Ryder, 66, 73, 114
  Surrealism, 55
Barney, Natalie, 73, 137
  Académie des Femmes, 73
Bataille, Georges, 119
Baudelaire, Charles, 1, 60
  the *flâneur*, 80–1, 221
Beach, Sylvia, Shakespeare and Company, 38, 66
  publication of *Ulysses*, 65–6
Beckett, Samuel, 3, 211
  Murphy, 205
  Whoroscope, 120
Benjamin, Walter, 80, 182
  the *flâneur*, 80–1, 82, 221
Bennett, Arnold
  and modernist writers, 168
  and realism, 88, 89
Bird, William, 120
birth control, 124–5
Blake, William, 15, 96–7
Blast, 46, 47–9, 72, 103, 149, 151, 183, 225
Bloch, Ernst, 3
Boni, Albert, 10, 11
Bowen, Elizabeth
  Death of the Heart, 206
  The Heat of the Day, 202
  The Last September, 84
Bowling, Lawrence Edward, 26

Bradbury, Malcolm, 5
  Modernism: A Guide to European Literature, 4
Brâncuşi, Constantin, 56
Braque, 56, 219, 220
Brecht, Bertolt, 3
Breton, André, 6, 122
  Dadaism, 50
  Surrealist group, 55, 119
  'Surrealist Manifesto', 55
British General Strike, 9, 185–9
British Psycho-Analytic Society, 137–8
Brontë, Charlotte, 132
Browning, Robert, 46
Bryher, Winefred Ellerman, 43, 120, 137
  film and film-making, 153
Buñuel, Luis, Surrealist films, 153
Butts, Mary, 4, 7, 9, 120, 131, 138, 216
  on cinema, 10
  Death of Felicity Taverner, 11–12, 82

Camera Work, 52
The Cantos, Ezra Pound, 2, 3, 66, 67–9, 194, 195, 196–8
  'Adams Cantos', 197, 198
  history and myth, 67–8, 74
  language and historical crisis, 196
  layering of languages, 68–9
  Mussolini and fascism, 196–7, 198
  'Pisan Cantos', 197
  poetry and politics, 196–8, 202, 205
  reference to jazz, 150
  World War I, 67, 69, 71, 84
Carrington, Leonora, 55
censorship, 31, 38, 55, 66, 72, 75, 113–14, 120–1
  law and literature, 114–24
Certeau, Michel de, *The Practice of Everyday Life*, 81, 82, 90
cinema, 10, 152–67
  American Vitograph, 154
  avant-garde film and film-making, 152–3
  cultural impact of, 153
  development of, 152–3
  fantasy, illusion and wealth, 157–8
  film as metaphor for modern experience, 164–7
  'Hollywood', 154
  the Hollywood star system, 157, 160
  Lewis and American cinema, 153–7
  relationship to art, 154–5
  Surrealist films, 152–3
  Vitaphone, 152
cinema and H.D., 10, 158, 161–4
  art and the cinema, 161
  attributes of light, 162–3
  Close Up, 153, 161, 162

  distraction and identification, 163–4
  images of beauty, 161–2, 164, 167, 172
  'Projector' poems, 162–3
Clark, T.J., *Farewell to an Idea: Episodes from a History of Modernism*, 213
classicism, 219–20
Close Up, film journal, 153, 161
Cocteau, Jean, 56
Cohen, Bella, 130
Colmore, Gertrude, *Suffragette Sally*, 126
Conrad, Joseph
  'Preface' to *The Nigger of the 'Narcissus'*, 85, 87
  The Nigger of the 'Narcissus', 1
Contact Press, 38, 120
Courtney, W.L., 'The Soul of a Suffragette', 126
Cravan, Arthur, 51
The Criterion, 15, 67
crowds and crowd theory, 183–7
Cubism, 220
culture industry, 3, 5, 146–7, 156
cummings, e. e., 11, 56
Cunard, Nancy, 4
  the Hours Press, 120
  political views, 178
  Spanish Civil War, 198

Dadaism, 50, 51–4, 193, 220
Dadaists, 37, 181, 182
Dalí, Salvador, Surrealist films, 153
Dante, *Pergatorio*, 59
Darwin, Charles, 9
Davison, Donald, 169
de Certeau *see* Certeau, Michel de
de Mailla, *Histoire générale de la Chine*, 197
Defoe, Daniel, 96–7
democracy *see* liberal democracy
democratic liberalism *see* liberal democracy
Dixon, Ella Hepworth, 126
Doolittle, Hilda *see* H.D. (Hilda Doolittle)
Douglas, C.H., *Economic Democracy*, 193
Douglas, James, 72
Dublin and Joyce, 94–102
  A Portrait of the Artist as a Young Man, 98–9
  Dubliners, 95–6, 97–8
  geographical details, 95–6
  psychic aspects, 98–100
  Ulysses, 99–101
  variety of writing styles, 100–1
Duchamp, Marcel
  Dada group, 51, 53, 54
  'Fountain', 51
Dujardin, Édouard, *Les Lauriers sont coupés*, 24, 222
Dulac, Germaine, *La Coquille et le Clergyman*, 153

economic inequality/instability, 193–4
Egan, Jennifer, 211
The Egoist, 23, 40, 103
Eisenstein
    Battleship Potemkin, 153
    film theory, 152–3
    October, 153
    Strike, 153
Eliot, George, 132
Eliot, T.S., 3, 5, 6, 7, 39, 40, 56, 81
    background, 15
    censorship, 72
    criticism of liberalism, 4, 189
    editing *The Criterion*, 67
    free verse, 15–16
    modernist writing, 16, 19, 46, 49, 211, 215
    on poetry, 8, 16
    political views, 178, 189
    and Pound, 39–40, 46, 66
    preface to Loy's *Nightwood*, 122
    relationship to mass culture, 148, 150–1, 172
    religion and morality, 15, 189, 203–4
    response to World War II, 50, 203–4
    words and meaning, 19–20, 203–4
    WORKS
    Burnt Norton, 15
    The Dry Salvages, 15, 19, 204
    East Coker, 15, 19
    Four Quartets, 1, 3, 15, 19, 202, 203–4
    'Gerontion', 19
    The Idea of a Christian Society, 189
    Little Gidding, 15, 204
    'Preludes', 15
    Prufrock and Other Observations, 15
    'Rhapsody on a Windy Night', 15
    'The Function of Criticism', 8–9
    'The Metaphysical Poets', 19
    The Sacred Wood, 15
    The Use of Poetry and the Use of Criticism, 2, 16, 189
    'Tradition and the Individual Talent', 7, 168–9
    see also 'The Love Song of J. Alfred Prufrock', T.S. Eliot; *The Waste Land*, T.S. Eliot
Ellis, Havelock, 135–7
    Studies in the Psychology of Sex, 135
English Review, 38, 40
Epstein, Jacob, 46
exiled writing, 102–9

Faber and Faber, 15
Faber and Gwyer, 66
fascism, 220
    and Hollywood, 185
    Italian, 7, 9, 13, 54, 84, 177, 196, 220

    and modernism, 178–9
    in Spain, 199
feminism and modernism, 124–35
Finnegan's Wake, James Joyce, 1, 8, 11, 23, 66, 67, 69–72, 87
    'Anna Livia Plurabelle', 66, 67, 69, 70–1
    cinematic language, 101–2, 160
    contemporary references, 71–2
    geography of Dublin, 95, 101
    linguistic invention, 70–1, 74
    on psychoanalysis, 139–40
Fitzgerald, F. Scott, 65
the *flâneur*, 80–1, 82, 109, 221
Fletcher, John Gould, 43
Flint, F.S., 43
Ford, Ford Madox, 4, 39, 40, 49, 165
    journal editor, 38, 40, 69, 165
    political views, 178
    response to war, 54, 128
    women's freedom, 128
    writer and publisher, 40
    WORKS
    The Good Soldier, 48
    'Impressionism', 85
    Parade's End, 54, 128
    The Soul of London, 84–7, 109, 190
Ford, Henry, 11
Forster, E.M., 40
    A Passage To India, 13
    Howards End, 11
    Maurice, 136
    political views, 178
Foucault, Michel, 81
Frazer, James, 59
free indirect discourse, 28–9, 92, 221
free indirect style, 221
free verse, 15–16, 44, 221
The Freewoman (later *The New Freewoman* and *The Egoist*), 191
Freud, Anna, 137
Freud, Sigmund, 9, 12, 53, 55
    Group Psychology and the Analysis of the Ego, 184
    The Interpretation of Dreams, 136
    Three Essays on the Theory of Sexuality, 136
    and the unconscious, 137–41
Freytag-Loringhoven, Elsa von, 51
The Fugitive, 169
Fugitives group, 169
Futurism, 46, 222; *see also* Marinetti, F.T
Futurists, 37, 50, 181, 182

Gable, Clark, 157
Galsworthy, John, 88
Garbo, Greta, 161–2
Gardner, Helen, *The Art of T. S. Eliot*, 2
Gasiorek, Andrzej, 155

Gaudier-Brzeska, Henri, 46, 48, 49, 69
Gay, Peter, *Modernism: The Lure of Heresy, From Baudelaire to Beckett and Beyond*, 213
gender, 222
    and history, 128–31, 135
gender roles, women's liberation, 126–7
Genette, Gérard, 221
geography and modernism, 31, 75, 80–4
German Expressionism, 3, 37–8
Gibbon, Lewis Grassic
    A Scots Quair, 127
    essay on cinema, 158, 185
    modernist epic, 127, 128–9
    Sunset Song, 127
Gilbert, Sandra and Susan Gubar, *No Man's Land: The Place of the Woman Writer in the Twentieth Century*, 125
Gissing, George, 126
Goldsmith, Oliver, *Vicar of Wakefield*, 61, 71
Gramsci, Antonio, 146
Grand, Sarah, 126
Graves, Robert, 5, 140, 169
    A Survey of Modernist Poetry, 2, 169, 170
Gray, Cecil, 130
Green, Henry, *Party Going*, 205
Gubar, Susan, with Sandra Gilbert, *No Man's Land: The Place of the Woman Writer in the Twentieth Century*, 125

Haigh-Wood, Vivienne, 15
Hall, Radclyffe, 137
    The Well of Loneliness, 66, 72, 113, 137
Hallberg, Robert van, 5
Hamilton, Cecily, *Life Errant*, 126
Hamilton, Cuthbert, 46
Hamilton, Patrick, *Hangover Square*, 205–6
Hardy, Thomas, 224
    Jude the Obscure, 115, 126
Harrison, Jane, 59
H.D. (Hilda Doolittle), 13, 39
    the Blitz, 202
    film and film-making, 153
    free verse, 44
    and Freud, 138
    gender and history, 129–31, 132, 135
    Imagism, 43–5, 46
    and Lawrence, 130
    modernist poet, 4, 5, 7, 120, 125, 216
    personal affairs, 130, 137
    political views, 178
    and Pound, 43, 49
    response to World War II, 202, 203, 204–5
    WORKS
    Bid Me To Live, 42, 43, 129–30, 138, 163–4
    Borderline, 161
    'The Cinema and the Classics', 161

'The Flowering of the Rod', 204
Helen in Egypt, 1, 43
Her, 43
'Hermes of the Ways', 43, 44
'Mid-day', 44–5
'Oread', 44
'Projector' poems, 162–3
Red Roses for Bronze, 43
Sea Garden, 43
'Tribute to the Angels', 204
Tribute to Freud, 102, 138
Trilogy, 43, 202, 203, 204–5
'The Walls Do Not Fall', 14, 204
    see also cinema and H.D.
Hemingway, Ernest, 41, 56, 120
    For Whom the Bell Tolls, 199
    Spanish Civil War, 199
Hitler, rise to power, 9, 12, 13, 177–8, 199, 201
Hogarth Press, 58, 66, 67
Hollywood and fascism, 185
homosexuality, 135–7
    repressive attitudes to, 136
Hours Press, 120
Howe, Susan, 2
Huelsenbeck, Richard, 50
Hulme, T.E., 4, 19–20, 39, 42, 49, 69, 215
    'Romanticism and Classicism', 41, 220
Huxley, Aldous
    Brave New World, 82
    Point Counter Point, 121

Ibsen, Henrik, 1
Imagism, 4, 42–5, 222
Imagists, 37, 49
Impressionism, in writing, 85–6, 87
individual
    and art, 183
    and democracy, 190, 190–1, 192–3
interior monologue, 14, 24–30, 80, 82, 88, 128, 222–3; *see also* Joyce, James: interior monologue; Richardson, Dorothy; Woolf, Virginia
intertextuality, 223
Irish independence and nationalism, 9, 83–4
Isherwood, Christopher
    Goodbye Berlin, 157
    political views, 178
Italian fascists, 7, 9, 13, 54, 84, 177, 196, 220; *see also* Mussolini, Benito

Jackson, Schuyler B., 169
    Rational Meaning: A New Foundation for the Definition of Words, 169, 170
James, Henry, 24
Jameson, Frederic, 180
James, William, *The Principles of Psychology*, 24
jazz, and modernist writers, 148–51

Jews
  intellectuals in Europe, 200
  in Ireland, 84
  and Palestine, 83
  wandering, 107–9
John Lane, 11
Johnson, Brimley, *The Women Novelists*, 132
Jonathan Cape, 66
Josipovici, Gabriel, *What Ever Happened to Modernism*, 213, 214
journalism
  and modernist writers, 168–9
  and poetry, 169–70
Joyce, James, 22–3, 40, 67, 73
  and censorship, 22–3, 115–16, 119–20
  cinematic techniques, 101–2, 160
  cultural status of, 212
  and Eliot, 71
  experimentation, 8, 40, 95
  fictional realism, 40, 41, 96–7
  the *flâneur*, 81
  interior monologue, 14, 62, 99–100, 103, 109, 222: Leopold Bloom, 27–8, 89–90, 99–100; Molly Bloom, 23, 24, 25–7, 28, 29; Stephen Dedalus, 27, 28, 30, 99
  linguistic innovation, 148
  modernist writer, 3, 4, 7, 131, 211, 212, 215
  naturalism, 115–16, 224
  and obscenity, 113, 119–20
  political views, 178
  and Pound, 40, 49, 56, 71
  WORKS
  'A Painful Case', 95, 97–8
  A Portrait of the Artist as a Young Man, 3, 23, 40, 80, 98–9, 115–16
  Dubliners, 22, 23, 40, 80, 95–6, 113, 115
  Pomes Penyeach, 38
  'Realism and Idealism in English Literature', 96–7
  Stephen Hero, 22, 23
  'Two Gallants', 95–6
  'Work in Progress', 23, 69
  see also Dublin and Joyce; *Finnegan's Wake*, James Joyce; *Ulysses*, James Joyce
Joynson-Hicks, Sir William, 72

Kafka, Franz, 3, 211–12, 215
Kahane, Jack, 38
Kahn, Gustave, 221
Kennner, Hugh, 3–4
Keynes, John Maynard, 124
Kinsella, John, *Vanishing Points: New Modernist Poems*, 2
Klein, Melanie, 137
Kolocotroni, Goldman and Taxidou, *Modernism: An Anthology of Documents and Sources*, 212

Kreymborg, Alfred, 51
Kyd, Thomas, *The Spanish Tragedy*, 60

Larbaud, Valery, 25, 62
Larson, Nella, 4
law and literature, 114–24, 141
Lawrence, Frieda, 130
Lawrence, D.H., 39, 40, 67, 148
  on cinema, 10
  democracy and individual freedom, 190–1, 192–3
  free indirect discourse, 28–9
  and H.D., 130
  Imagism, 43, 46
  language of exile, 104–7
  and modernism, 7, 8, 38
  naturalism, 224
  and obscenity, 119–20
  politics and prejudice, 4, 178, 179
  response to war, 50, 54
  and women's liberation, 126–7
  WORKS
  Kangaroo, 54, 106–7, 190, 192
  Lady Chatterley's Lover 10, 66, 72–3, 82–3, obscene, 118–19, 120
  Psychoanalysis and the Unconscious, 140
  Sons and Lovers, 115
  The Lost Girl, 106
  The Rainbow 3, 113, 126–7, 190 banned, 118
  Women in Love, 3, 39, 104–6, 126–7, 191
Le Bon, Gustave
  charismatic leaders, 186
  The Crowd: A Study of the Popular Mind, 85, 184
Leavis, F.R., *New Bearings in English Poetry*, 2
lesbian relationships, 72, 73, 137
Levenson, Michael, *A Genealogy of Modernism: A Study of English Literary Doctrine, 1908–1922*, 4
Lewis, Wyndham, 4, 7, 38, 39, 40, 42, 49, 211
  American cinema, 153–7
  anti-Semitism, 178
  and censorship, 114, 120, 121
  cinematic imagery, 155–7, 166, 167
  depiction of Mussolini, 185
  evocation of Paris, 103–4
  on impact of Nietzsche, 191
  jazz, attitude to, 149
  language of revolution, 183
  on modernism, 49, 72
  politics and prejudices, 178, 179, 180, 205
  relationship to mass culture, 148–50, 151, 156, 172–3
  spatial/visual style, 102–4
  visual artist and writer, 46, 48
  Vorticism, 46–9, 225
  World War I, 49, 69

Lewis, Wyndham (*cont.*)
  WORKS
  Blast, 46, 47–9, 72, 103, 149, 151, 183, 225
  'Cantleman's Spring Mate', 114
  The Childermass, 46
  The Enemy of the Stars, 48
  Hitler, 178
  The Hitler Cult, 178
  Men Without Art, 47, 190
  The Revenge for Love, 10, 11, 46, 156–7
  The Roaring Queen, 168
  Snooty Baronet, 121
  Tarr, 3, 9, 46, 103–4, 149, 153–5, 191
  Time and Western Man, 47, 72, 120, 190
  see also *The Apes of God*, Wyndham Lewis
liberal democracy, 223
  and modernist writers, 4, 178–80, 190–3,
    202, 205
Linati, Carlo, 62
Linton, Eliza Lynn, *The Rebel of the Family*,
    126
Little Leather Library, 10, 168
The Little Review, New York, 23, 49, 89, 114,
    116
  moved to Paris, 120
Liveright, Horace, 11
London
  economic speculation, 84
  General Strike, 186, 187
  literary network, 39–49
  modern metropolis and power centre, 83,
    84–93
  The Soul of London, Ford Madox Ford, 84–7
'The Love Song of J. Alfred Prufrock', T.S.
    Eliot, 6, 14, 15–21
  contrasting juxtapositions, 17, 30
  critical responses to, 19
  failure, indecision and loss, 18–19
  free verse, 15–16, 44
  modernism of, 29, 30
  poetic fragmentation, 21, 30
  publication of, 40
  questions posed, 18
  significance of ephemera, 30
  time, examination of, 20–1
  words and meaning, 19, 20, 203–4
Lowell, Amy, 42, 46
Loy, Mina, 56, 73, 137, 138, 216
  and American jazz, 148
  art and politics, 183
  and censorship, 120, 121
  and cinema culture, 10, 157–8, 167
  critique of economic interests, 193
  cubistic form, 53, 54
  experience of love, 134
  exploration of female selfhood, 131, 132–5
  Futurism and Marinetti, 52, 53

gender roles, 133, 183
image of 'Pig Cupid', 52, 53, 133
Jewish wandering, 107–9
language of selfhood, 53, 138
modernist writer, 4, 5, 7, 38, 73, 125, 216
on modern poetry, 8, 148, 172
New York Dada group, 51, 52–4
political views, 178
significance of colour, 134–5
on Stein, 57
Surrealism, 55
temporal/cultural dissonances, 134
use of irony, 54, 135
  WORKS
  'Anglo-Mongrels and the Rose', 107–9
  'Aphorisms on Futurism', 52
  'Apology of Genius', 120
  'Café du Néant', 39
  'Feminist Manifesto', 132, 183
  'Hot Cross Bum', 140
  'International Psycho-Democracy', 193
  'Lion's Jaws', 53
  'Love Songs', 52–3, 68, 133
  'Mexican Desert', 148
  'Modern Poetry', 148, 172
  'O Hell', 1, 7, 121
  'Parturition', 52
  'Perlun', 157–8
  'Songs to Joannes', 132–3
  'the Beautiful', 121
  'Three Moments in Paris', 52
  'Virgins Plus Curtains Minus Dots', 52, 132
  'The Widow's Jazz', 148
Lukács, Georg, 3
Lytton, Constance, *Prisons and Prisoners*, 126

McAlmon, Robert, 38, 120
McCay, Claude, 4
MacDiarmid, Hugh, 178
  'A Drunk Man Looks at a Thistle', 185
McFarlane, James, 5
  Modernism: A Guide to European Literature, 4
Macpherson, Kenneth
  Borderline (film), 153
  Close Up, 153
Magnall, Richard, *Historical and Miscellaneous*
    Questions, 101
Mailla see de Mailla
Mann, Thomas, 3, 4
Mansfield, Katherine, 4, 131, 132, 135
Marcus, Laura, 160
Marinetti, F.T., 39, 81
  'Founding and Manifesto of Futurism', 1,
    11, 41–2, 46, 47, 222
  Futurism, 41–2, 46, 48, 50, 51, 53, 182
  Variety Theater Manifesto, 42
  Zang Tumb Tuuum, 42, 148

Marvell, Andrew, 18, 30
Marx, Karl, 9, 182
Marxism, 177, 181–2
mass culture, 10, 11, 223
   and modernism, 31, 75, 146–56, 172
mass democracy, 187, 223
mass media, 146
Matisse, 56, 219
Maude, Constance Elizabeth, *No Surrender*,
   126
Mengham, Rod, 2
   Vanishing Points: New Modernist Poems, 2
Mercury Press, 161
middle-class cultural power, 189
Millay, Edna St Vincent, 'The Ballad of the
   Harp-Weaver', 5, 6
Miller, Henry
   Surrealism, 55
   Tropic of Cancer, 38, 122, 200–2
   Tropic of Capricorn, 122
Mitchison, Naomi, 199
modern art, 47
modernisation, 224
modernism, 1–6
   cultural significance of, 213–14
   literary criticism and study, 212–14
   and the new media, 148–52
   permanent literary value, 215–17
   relationship to mass culture, 31, 75, 146–52,
      172
   twenty-first century relevance of, 216–17
   and the unconscious, 140–1
Modernism/modernity, 5
modernist
   journals, 38
   networks, 31, 37–9
Modernist Studies Association, 5
Modern Library, 11
Monet, 85
Moore, George, 115, 120, 224
Moore, Marianne, 4, 13, 38
Moore, Merril, 169
Morley, Catherine, *Modern American
   Literature*, 6
motor car, 11
Murger, Henri, *Scènes de la vie de bohème*, 104
Mussolini, Benito, Italian Fascist leader, 178,
   196, 200, 220
   march on Rome, 9, 13, 54, 177
   and modernist texts, 185

Nabokov, Vladimir, 211
National Fascist Party (Italy), 177, 196
nationalism and national identity, 13, 83–4
natural landscape, 82–3
naturalism, 224
Nerval, Gerard de, 'El Desdichado', 59

The New Age, 191
New Criticism, 169, 206
New Statesman, 199
'new woman' fiction, 125–6
New York Dada, 51
Nicholls, Peter, *Modernisms: A Literary Guide*,
   4–5, 197–8
Nietzsche, Friedrich, 9
   Beyond Good and Evil, 191
   The Birth of Tragedy, 191
   English translations, 191
   impact on modernist writers, 191–2
   On the Genealogy of Morals, 191
   The Case of Wagner, 191
   Thus Spoke Zarathustra, 191, 192
Nin, Anaïs, Surrealism, 55, 122
Norris, Margot, 101
North, Michael, 180, 188

Obelisk Press, 38
Obscene Publications Act, 114–15
obscenity, 72
   exploration of, 121–4
   the law, 114–15
   of literary texts, 66, 72–4, 113–24
Orwell, George
   Homage to Catalonia, 199
   'Inside the Whale', 200–2
   on literature and politics, 200–2
   political views, 178
   Spanish Civil War, 199
Others, New York journal, 38, 52, 133
Owen, Wilfred, 13–14, 196
The Oxford Handbook of Modernisms, 212

Pankhurst, Emmeline, *My Own Story*, 126
parataxis, 224
Paris, 54–66
   publishing, 56, 120
   Wyndham Lewis, 103–4
Penguin Books, 11
Perloff, Marjorie, 2
Picabia, Francis, 51
Picasso, 56, 219, 220
poetic fragmentation, 14, 21, 30, 80, 82, 89,
   128
Poetry American journal, 15, 40, 43
political polarisation of Europe, 178, 199
politics and literature, 200–2, 205–6
   Orwell essay, 200–2, 205, 206
politics of modernism, 178–98
   art and the individual, 183
   aspects of revolution, 183
   attitude to liberal democracy, 189–92
   avant-garde movements, 181–3
   crowd theory, 183–6
   economic inequality/instability, 193–4

politics of modernism (*cont.*)
  General Strike, 185–9
  historic crisis of liberalism, 179–80, 189
  Marxist ideology, 181–3
  Nietzsche, 191–2
  poetry and politics, 196–9
  politics-art relationship, 180–1
  Pound and politics, 194–8
  reality of democracy, 187–92
  response to political unrest, 183–4
  threat of revolution, 185–7
  urban and revolutionary crowds, 184–5
popular fiction, and modernist writers, 167–8
Pound, Ezra, 38, 67, 81, 215
  anti-semitism, 207
  and censorship, 120–1
  central to modernism, 3–4, 6, 7, 39, 40, 49,
    72, 211, 215
  critique of the economic system, 84, 194–5,
    196, 193.67
  and Eliot, 39–40, 46, 49, 69
  Imagism, 42–3, 46, 196, 222
  and jazz, 150
  and Joyce, 40, 41, 49, 64–5
  language, literature and the law, 195–6
  language and money, 194–5
  literary editor, 40
  middle-class cultural power, 189
  modern poetry, 46
  Mussolini, support for, 178, 196–8, 207
  in Paris, 55, 56, 73
  political views, 178, 179, 180, 194, 196–8
  publication, 65, 120
  relationship to mass culture, 148, 150, 151
  technological change, 11, 12
  vision of modernism, 49
  Vorticism, 46, 48, 225
  World War I, 54, 67, 69
  and Wyndham Lewis, 46, 49, 69
  WORKS
  A Draft of XVI Cantos, 66
  'A Few Don'ts by an Imagiste', 43, 45, 46
  A Lume Spento, 46
  Blast, 46, 47–9, 72, 103, 149, 151, 183, 225
  'Date Line', 195
  Des Imagistes, 42, 43, 49
  'Dubliners and Mr. James Joyce', 40
  essay on *Ulysses*, 195
  Exultations, 46
  'How to Read', 55, 195
  Hugh Selwyn Mauberley, 14, 54, 151, 168,
    191, 194, 195, 196, 197
  'In a Station of the Metro', 45
  Jefferson and/or Mussolini, 196
  'L'Homme Moyen Sensuel', 120–1
  Lustra, 113–14
  Personae, 46

'Preface to *Some Imagist Poets*', 43
'Salutation the Third', 168
Selected Poems, 66
'The Teacher's Mission', 195
  see also The Cantos, Ezra Pound
Proust, Marcel, 3, 11, 12, 26, 30, 131, 212,
    215
  In Search of Lost Time, 149
Prynne, J.H., 2, 211
psychoanalytic thinking, 138–41
publication of modernist texts, 38, 65–6,
    120
publishing industry, 167–8
Pynchon, Thomas, 211

Rainey, Lawrence, 5
  Institutions of Modernism, 65
  Modernism: An Anthology, 212, 216
Ransom, John Crowe, 169
Ray, Man, 51
  Return to Reason, 153
realism in literature, 87–8, 115
Rebel Art Centre, 46
Rhys, Jean, 4, 7, 40, 131, 165–6, 167, 173
  After Leaving Mr. Mackenzie, 165
  Good Morning, Midnight, 10, 165–6, 167,
    205
  The Left Bank, 165
  Quartet, 165
  surreal treatment of cinema, 165–6, 167
  Surrealism, 55
  Voyage in the Dark, 107, 165
  Wide Sargasso Sea, 165
Richards, Grant, 40
Richards, I.A., *The Principles of Literary
    Criticism*, 2
Richardson, Dorothy
  on cinema and film, 10, 153, 161
  feminine realism and femininity, 89–91,
    131
  the *flâneur*, 81
  forms of consciousness, 90
  fragmented reality, 89, 90
  free indirect discourse, 28
  interior monologue, 24–5, 89, 90, 91, 103,
    222
  and London, 87, 89–91
  psychic realism, 24–5, 88–91, 109
  urban experience, 91, 109
  WORKS
  'Continuous Performance', 161
  'Foreword' to *Pilgrimage*, 89, 90
  Interim, 88, 89
  Pilgrimage, 24, 25, 80, 88–9, 91, 92, 109
  Pointed Roofs, 88, 89, 90
  'Preface' to *The Prelude*, 138
  The Tunnel, 88, 89–91

Rich, Barbara, pseudonym of Laura Riding, *No Decency Left*, 170
Riding, Laura, 4, 5, 7, 13, 120, 148, 169–72
  and modernist writing, 170, 172
  poetry, ethics and journalism, 169–72
  political views, 178
  semantic precision, 169–70, 171
  women and a new moral Law, 199
  WORKS
  A Survey of Modernist Poetry, 2, 169, 170
  Collected Poems, 169, 170
  'Come, Words, Away', 171, 172
  'In Nineteen Twenty-Seven', 170
  Rational Meaning: A New Foundation for the Definition of Words, 169, 170
  Selected Poems: In Five Sets, 169
  The World and Ourselves, 199
  see also Rich, Barbara
Riviere, Joan, 137
Robeson, Paul, 153
Russell, Dora, 124
Russian Futurism, 222
Russian revolution, 54, 177, 200

Sackheim, Maxwell, 10
St Vincent Millay, Edna see Millay, Edna St Vincent
Sanger, Margaret, 124–5
Scherman, Harry, 10
Schreiner, Olive, *The Story of an African Farm*, 125–6
Scott, Bonnie Kime, *The Gender of Modernism*, 212
Sex Disqualification (Removal) Act, 124
sexuality and modernism, 75, 141
  café society, 38–9
  explicit writing, 55, 72–4, 121, 122
  exposure of repression, 118–19
  influence of scientific accounts, 135–7
  see also censorship; obscenity
Sharp, Evelyn, 'The Women at the Gate', 126
Simmel, Georg, *The Metropolis and Mental Life*, 85
Sinclair, May, 24–5
social networks, 38–9
Spanish Civil War, 9, 178, 198–202
  Authors Take Sides, 198–9
  call for writers' political commitment, 198–200
  response of writers and artists, 199–202
Spender, Stephen, 178, 198, 201
Stead, Christina, 199
Stein, Gertrude, 11, 13, 131
  and avant-garde painting, 56
  modernist writer, 4, 5, 7, 215–16
  in Paris, 56, 73

publication, 120
  writing style, 24, 56–8, 72, 87, 211
  WORKS
  Autobiography of Alice B. Toklas, 56, 137
  'Composition as Explanation', published lecture, 58, 215
  'Melanctha', 56–7
  Tender Buttons, 57–8
  The Making of Americans, 56
  Three Lives, 1, 56, 57, 58
Stern, Anatol, 148
Stevens, Wallace, 38, 51
Stopes, Marie, 124
Strachey, Alix and James, 137
'stream of consciousness', 24; see also interior monologue
Suffragette novels, 125, 126
Surrealist films, 152, 153
Surrealists, 37, 119, 181, 182
Svevo, Italo, 4

Tate, Allen, 169
technological change, 10, 11–12
Three Mountains Press, 120
Toomer, Jean, 4
Transatlantic Review, 40, 57, 69, 165
transition, 69
Trilling, Lionel, 179, 202, 206
Trotter, Wilfred, *Instincts of Herd in Peace and War*, 184
Troubridge, Una, 137
Tzara, Tristan, 50, 198, 220
  'Dada Manifesto', 50

Ulysses, James Joyce, 3, 14, 22, 23–8, 61–5, 72
  cinematic techniques, 160
  geography of Dublin, 80, 81–2, 99–101
  impact of, 65–6
  and journalism, 168
  Leopold Bloom, 27–8, 61, 65, 84, 89–90, 99–100, 109, 113, 167
  modernism of, 29–30, 58
  Molly Bloom, 23, 24, 25–7, 28, 29, 61
  multilingual, 62
  mythic parallels, 62–4
  nationalism and Irishness, 84
  naturalism, 115–16
  obscenity and censorship, 7, 38, 62, 66, 113, 117–18, 119–20
  publication, 38, 49, 65–6
  significance of ephemera, 29, 30
  Stephen Dedalus, 27, 28, 30, 61, 65, 99
  stylistic innovation, 6, 61, 62, 64–5
  see also Joyce, James: interior monologues
the unconscious, 137–41
urban experience, 80–3, 91
  an aerial perspective, 82, 83

van Hallberg, Robert *see* Hallberg, Robert van
Van Vechten, Carl, 51
Vidal, Peire, 46
Vizetelly, Henry, London publisher, 115
Vorticism, 4, 46–9, 50, 183
    literature and visual art, 47, 48
Vorticists, 37, 50, 72

Wadsworth, Edward, 46
Wall Street crash, 9, 193–4
war and modernism, 198–211
Warren, Robert Penn, 169
The Waste Land, T.S. Eliot, 19, 58–61, 68–9,
    204
    cinematic techniques, 160
    composition of, 40, 49
    critical opinion, 3, 4, 5
    impact of, 65
    international scope, 59
    and London, 80, 84
    modernist classic, 5, 15
    multilingual, 60
    myths and mythical figures, 60
    politics of, 179
    publication of, 65
    reference to jazz, 150–1
    as a response to war, 58–9
    revolution and the crowd, 183–4
    'The Fire Sermon', 60, 61
The Well of Loneliness, obscenity trial, 72
Wells, H.G., 88, 124
    Ann Veronica, 126
West, Nathaniel, *The Dream Life of Balso
    Snell*, 121–2
West, Rebecca, 72
    'Indissoluble Matrimony', 48
Whitman, Walt, 15
    Leaves of Grass, 221
Williams, Raymond, 180
Williams, William Carlos, 38, 51, 120, 211
women
    employment, 124
    and language, 131–5
    liberation, 126–7
    position of, 13
    suffrage movement, 125–6, 129
    urban experience, 91
    writers, 125, 212, 216
Women's Social and Political Union, 126
Wood, Thelma, 67
Woolf, Leonard, 58
Woolf, Virginia, 1, 13, 67
    on Arnold Bennett, 88, 89

censorship, 72
    on cinema, 10, 152, 153, 166–7
    cinematographic writing, 160–1
    cultural status of, 212
    experimental writing, 8
    the *flâneur*, 81
    free indirect discourse, 29, 92
    Hogarth Press, 58
    and homosexuality, 137
    interior monologue, 24, 28, 91–3, 103, 222
    on journalism, 168
    on modern fiction, 30, 168
    modernist writer, 7
    political views, 178
    and psychoanalysis, 139
    realism, 87–8, 89, 94
    response to war, 14, 54, 202–3
    urban wandering, 91–3, 109
    women and language, 131–2, 135
    WORKS
    A Room of One's Own, 125, 131–2
    Between the Acts, 1, 14, 83, 202–3
    'Character in Fiction', 88
    'Cinema', 152, 160
    'Modern Fiction', 88, 94, 168
    Mrs. Dalloway, 3, 54, 80, 91–3, 137
    Orlando, 66, 72, 73, 137
    'Street Haunting: A London Adventure',
       93
    'The Leaning Tower', 12
    The Years, 80, 129, 137, 203
    Three Guineas, 203
    'Time Passes', 160–1
    To the Lighthouse, 3, 6, 12, 93–4, 139, 160–1
Workers' Birth Control Group, 124
World War I, 9, 13–14, 49–50
World War II, responses to, 9, 202–5
    the Blitz, 202–3
    erosion of liberal values, 203
    psychic violations, 203, 204

Yeats, W.B., 4, 38, 40, 46, 71
    'Easter 1916', 83
    Irish nationalism and civil conflict, 83–4
    'Meditations in Time of Civil War', 84
    political views, 178, 179, 180
    'Sixteen Dead Men', 83
    The Tower, 3

Zola, Émile
    La Terre, 115
    Les Rougon-Macquart, 115, 224
    'Naturalism on the Stage', 115